Fraud Prevention and Detection

Warning Signs and the Red Flag System

Fraud Prevention and Detection

Warning Signs and the Red Flag System

Rodney T. Stamler
Hans J. Marschdorf
Mario Possamai

CRC Press
Taylor & Francis Group
Boca Raton London New York

CRC Press is an imprint of the
Taylor & Francis Group, an **informa** business

CRC Press
Taylor & Francis Group
6000 Broken Sound Parkway NW, Suite 300
Boca Raton, FL 33487-2742

First issued in paperback 2019

ISBN-13: 978-0-4665-5454-2 (hbk)
ISBN-13: 978-0-367-86732-4 (pbk)

Library of Congress Cataloging-in-Publication Data

Stamler, Rod.
    Fraud prevention and detection : warning signs and the red flag system / Rodney T. Stamler, Hans J. Marschdorf, Mario Possamai.
       pages cm
    Includes bibliographical references and index.
    ISBN 978-1-4665-5454-2 (hardback)
    1. Fraud--Prevention. 2. Fraud investigation. I. Marschdorf, Hans-Joachim, 1956- II. Possamai, Mario. III. Title.

HV6691.S673 2014
658.4'73--dc23
                                        2013040474

Visit the Taylor & Francis Web site at
http://www.taylorandfrancis.com

and the CRC Press Web site at
http://www.crcpress.com

CONTENTS

FOREWORD

Bob Lindquist, FCPA, CFE*

Over the past four decades, I have managed numerous cases around the world—cases involving a wide variety of domestic and international businesses and myriad fraud types.

Yet, there is a common thread running through virtually all of them: Red Flags. Before being discovered, just about every one of my cases had multiple indicators of fraud that, if addressed when first discovered, might have saved millions of dollars in losses and the untold pain that major frauds leave in their wake.

How to spot and take action on Red Flags in an effective manner is the subject of this book by Rod Stamler, Hans Marschdorf, and Mario Possamai.

It grew out of Rod's seminal work in the early 1990s, just after he retired from the Royal Canadian Mounted Police (RCMP) and joined my forensic practice. The Auditor General of Canada—roughly the Canadian equivalent of the US Government Accountability Office—had asked him to prepare a guidance document on how fraud can be detected much earlier in the fraud cycle.

As I write this, I am reminded of cases on which I worked with each of the three authors that had Red Flags at the core.

One that springs to mind involved a multinational computer manufacturer in the early 1990s. High-tech products can have a relatively short shelf life, which requires procedures to dismantle properly parts that are used, discontinued, or deemed to be surplus. Our client had chosen through the bid process to contract with various vendors to obtain this service with the agreement requiring the vendors to share their sale proceeds from recycled parts and not to sell parts scheduled for scrap. However, field investigators had found and confirmed the movement of the manufacturer's scrap in the "gray market" and our mandate was to determine if any person or group of persons within a certain division of the company was involved.

At the start of this matter, we met with the management in the division in question to advise of our investigation and to seek their cooperation.

---

* Robert T. Lindquist is the principal of Lindquist Forensics (www.lindquistforensics.com).

However, as we commenced, our primary subject of interest said he was too busy to be interviewed.

Now think about this: If he were honest he would have given me all the time I required. So I knew that his evasive behavior was a Red Flag, but now I had to establish the trail of evidence. Then, during an employee interview on the third day, a summary schedule of vendor bid prices was provided. A quick study of the document spoke "rigged bid." Several characteristics of a rigged bid were evident on this one piece of paper—an example of fraud knowledge or "Red Flags" at work.

Another case involved corruption and procurement fraud in the late 1990s in the construction of the international airport in the Republic of Trinidad and Tobago in the Caribbean. In one instance, 2 days before a contract was to be awarded, the requirements were changed and only two companies could meet the new requirements on time. It ended up being a winner pays loser scheme of procurement manipulation.

These cases had "Red Flags" written all over them. If these fraud indicators had been captured and acted upon earlier in the fraud cycle, our clients might have saved tens of millions of dollars in losses and prevented damage to their reputation.

There are many fraud books and articles aimed at accountants, auditors, and financial investigators—individuals whose professions have a fraud orientation. Increasingly, however, officers and directors in small, medium, and large companies; public agencies; nonprofits; charities; and foundations—individuals who usually do not have a fraud background—are being asked to take a leadership role in the prevention and detection of fraud. This book is intended to help the directing minds of public and private sector organizations—as well as their stakeholders—to know how to do so in an effective, efficient, and timely manner.

I believe that, in many cases of major corporate frauds, these disasters might have been averted—or at least their full impact diminished—if their boards had screened for Red Flags and taken action accordingly.

Readers of this book will acquire a general awareness of the nature, characteristics, and dynamics of fraud. They will also learn the process for determining whether a fraud has been committed. But, most importantly, they will learn how to find and take action on Red Flag indicators of fraud or suspicious transactions in financial statements, budgets, and contracts.

THE AUTHORS

Rodney T. Stamler is a former assistant commissioner of the Royal Canadian Mounted Police (RCMP), who originated the "Red Flag" fraud detection and prevention system at the heart of this book in the early 1990s during an engagement with the Auditor General of Canada. Rod, who holds a law degree, perfected that system as a partner in two international forensic firms in the 1990s and into the early 2000s. His major cases included chasing the hidden assets of the late Romanian dictator Nicolae Ceausescu in the early 1990s; investigating the $1 billion Bre-X mining scandal in Indonesia, the world's largest gold mining fraud; and investigating a massive, multinational procurement fraud at a Fortune 100 multibillion-dollar corporation. During his career in the RCMP Rod was known as an innovator who was instrumental in establishing the crime program. He served as a special advisor to the United Nations in the development of the international convention against laundering the proceeds of illicit drug trafficking. He was formerly a member of the board of directors and member of the audit committee for a multinational mining company. Rod is often called to provide advice and counsel on corporate governance matters.

Hans J. Marschdorf is a leading international forensic accountant who has conducted financial investigations for the past 23 years around the world, ranging from multinational corruption and procurement fraud investigations to money laundering investigations, investigations of elaborate Ponzi schemes, and frauds involving structured financial products. His experience includes a position as pan-European leader of a forensic services practice in a Big 4 professional services firm. Mr. Marschdorf, a dual citizen of Canada and Germany, now practices as a financial crime investigator from Greater Toronto, Ontario (www.marschdorf-forensics.com). He holds a PhD in business administration from the University of Cologne, Germany, and is admitted to practice accounting in the European Union and Switzerland. He holds the designation of certified fraud examiner in the United States and chartered director in Canada. Mr. Marschdorf has published a number of articles on aspects of fraud investigation and corruption, economic analysis of insolvency law, and international taxation.

He serves as chairman of the advisory board of the School of Governance Risk and Compliance of Steinbeis Hochschule, a Berlin business school, and is also a member of its faculty.

Mario Possamai is a senior fraud professional at a major Canadian financial institution and has managed complex fraud, asset recovery, and corruption investigations in North America, Europe, and Africa for more than two decades. A member of the Bre-X investigative team in Indonesia, Mario also provided forensic financial consulting services to the director of public prosecutions in a southern African country in the mid-1990s; was an expert witness for the Department of Justice in Canada on money laundering; and was senior advisor to Superior Court Justice Archie Campbell, who headed the judicial inquiry into the SARS outbreak in 2003. He is the author of a book on money laundering and for 10 years was a guest lecturer at the Financial Fraud Institute at the US Department of Homeland Security's Federal Law Enforcement Training Center in Glynco, Georgia.

1

An Introduction to the Red Flag System

A PERSISTENT THREAT

No entity is immune from fraud. Fraud indiscriminately affects all types of organizations regardless of sector, size, or geographical location. It does not distinguish between public or private entities, by what they do, by their environmental footprint, by their level of sustainability, by their public profile, or by the number of years they have been in existence. It is not softhearted: Nonprofits or charitable entities are potentially just as vulnerable to fraud as those focused on making profits. They may, in fact, be more vulnerable because they may not be able to afford more sophisticated controls or cannot afford to allocate sufficient resources to fraud prevention and detection.

Consider the following:

- A study by the Association of Certified Fraud Examiners (ACFE) estimated that a typical organization loses 5% of its revenue to fraud each year. The data for this study involved more than 1,300 cases in 100 countries.[*]
- A global survey by PriceWaterhouseCoopers (PwC) found that 34% of respondents had experienced a fraud in the previous 12 months. This survey involved 3,877 respondents around the world.[†]

---

[*] Association of Certified Fraud Examiners. 2012. Report to the nations on occupational fraud and abuse: 2012 Global fraud study, Austin, TX.
[†] PWC. 2011. Global economic crime survey, London: November 2011.

- The Kroll Global Fraud Report reported that six of ten companies surveyed had been affected by fraud in the previous year. This was based on a survey of nearly nine hundred senior executives worldwide.[*]

Fraud is costly in many ways:

- The median loss in the aforementioned ACFE study was $175,000 and more than one-fifth of the frauds analyzed involved losses of at least $1 million.[†]
- In the previously noted PwC study, one in ten suffered losses of more than $5 million.[‡]

But financial losses are just part of the adverse consequences of fraud. How a company deals with fraud says a lot about it and provides strong signals to stakeholders, employees, clients, vendors, shareholders, and regulators:

- How strong are its internal controls? Are they easily circumvented?
- Does it have a lackadaisical culture, where no one seems to care? Or is it a culture that does not tolerate fraud and other improprieties?

Recent research indicates that a significant proportion of a company's value (potentially over 60%) relates to intangible assets like reputation.[§] While its precise contribution to a company's worth is difficult to quantify, there is no doubt that reputation has significant economic value[¶] since reputational damage can adversely impact brand value and share price, including new financings.

---

[*] Kroll Advisory Solutions. 2012. Global fraud report 2012/2013, New York: October 2012.

[†] Association of Certified Fraud Examiners. 2012. Report to the nations on occupational fraud and abuse.

[‡] PWC, Global economic crime survey.

[§] Nick Rea and Adrian Davis. 2005. Intangible assets: What are they worth and how should that value be communicated? Published in *IP Value* 2005, Building and enforcing intellectual property value.

[¶] Dr. Baruch Levy of the Stern School of Business in New York defines the economic value of reputation as follows: "It is a seller's guarantee or commitment of contracted performance and product/service quality. Accordingly, the benefits to the owner of reputation are the premia paid by the counterparty (customers, employees, suppliers, investors) for the guarantee. The value of reputation, and its share in the market value of the company is the discounted value of the expected premia stream, net of the cost of maintaining reputation. Reputation is the outcome of a credible guarantee/commitment." Source: Baruch Levy. 2005. The art and science of valuing intangibles and managing reputation (or: The confession of a heartless economist), New York University, baruch-lev.com, September 2005.

A good reputation (and its contribution to an organization's value) can be quickly lost, sometimes overnight, if not properly managed. Significantly, reputation, as one author noted, "…is most at risk during a critical major event."[*]

An Oxford University study says companies that effectively manage critical incidents, like the public disclosure of a major fraud, gain market value, while the shares of ineffective ones can lose a lot of value. The study found that corporations lost an average of 15% in net stock value in the months following an ineffective response to a large-scale emergency. An effective response increased companies' total market value by about 22%.[†]

Reputation is especially important for nonprofits and charities that rely on government funding and individual or corporate donations:

- Donors may have second thoughts about giving to a charity that is vulnerable to fraud. They may have doubts about whether their donations are actually being used for their intended purpose.
- Trust in a community hospital may be eroded by a fraud, causing stakeholders to wonder whether there is sufficient oversight in other areas, like patient care and safety.
- Fraud against a school board can tarnish its reputation among parents, students, and teachers.
- Fraud committed against a religious institution can negatively impact its ability to carry out its charitable works and can cause rifts among its members and stakeholders.

Fraud can also dampen employee morale and create recruiting and retention problems. How would you feel if a fraud against your employer was splashed across the media? How would you answer related questions from neighbors, family, and friends?

Many lawsuits have been launched in recent years against directors and officers who failed to protect their companies sufficiently from fraud. Taking a proactive approach to fraud prevention and detection could help protect officers and directors from the consequences of having a major fraud erupt on their watch.

Moreover, if you are trying to attract strong candidates to your board or executive ranks, the fact that you have an effective, proactive system

---

[*] Bexon Brohman & Associates. 2007. Board oversight doesn't stop at the buck. January 24, 2007.

[†] Rory F. Knight and Deborah J. Pretty. 1996. The impact of catastrophes on shareholder value. Published in 1996 as part of the Oxford Executive Research Briefings, Templeton College, Oxford University.

for preventing fraud also can make your organization more attractive and enhance your recruitment efforts. Imagine that you are a strong candidate considering joining a company that has just become the victim of fraud. Would you not have second thoughts about such a move? The prospective candidate can take comfort that your organization is doing all it can to help directors and officers properly discharge their antifraud responsibilities and thus maintain their personal reputations.

Fraud can also cause major financial damage if committed by the corporation. Prominent examples relate to violations of bribery laws by large corporations and manipulations of procurement processes for the financial gain of such corporations. The list of enforcement actions by regulators in the United States, the UK, and Canada in bribery cases is impressive and includes violations by such large international corporations as Halliburton and KBR, Siemens, and DaimlerChrysler, to name just a few.[*]

The damage, again, is reputational, but the penalties and procedural costs can amount to several billion dollars. Former US Deputy Attorney General Paul McNulty in a keynote address famously stated: "If you think compliance is expensive, try noncompliance."[†]

THE RED FLAGS OF FRAUD

When it comes to fraud, there is no silver bullet—no single, magical solution. However, there are prudent measures that can help reduce the risk of fraud and increase the chances that it can either be prevented or detected much earlier.

Based on their more than 100 years of combined experience in the investigation and prevention of fraud in North America, Europe, and the Far East, the authors set out a structured approach—known as the Red Flag System—for the prevention, early detection, and appropriate investigation of fraud.

The Red Flag System is practical, effective, and empirically tested. It is based on the premise that to prevent fraud successfully or detect it as quickly as possible after it begins, an organization must have the capacity

---

[*] For a complete list of US enforcement actions from 1978 to 2012, see http://www.sec.gov/spotlight/fcpa/fcpa-cases.shtml (accessed July 23, 2013).

[†] Compliance Week Conference. 2009. http://www.compliancebuilding.com/2009/06/04/mcnulty-keynote-on-a-tale-of-two-sectors/ (accessed July 23, 2013).

to identify, analyze, and address possible indicators of fraud, known as "Red Flags," in a timely manner. "Red Flags" are like the first wisps of smoke in a forest. Detect them early enough and you can prevent a forest fire. Fail to move decisively and the whole forest may be in danger.

The Red Flag System can be especially beneficial for corporate officers and directors.

To understand the Red Flag System, keep in mind that frauds do not come out of the blue, and they do not happen overnight. They are not random one-off events. According to a study by the ACFE, the typical fraud lasts 18 months from the time it begins until it is discovered.[*] Some frauds stay undetected even longer.

For example, fake billing cases—in which payments are made for fictitious goods and services or invoices are inflated—may be undetected for 24 months.[†] Cases of ghost employees being added to the payroll take even longer to spot—as long as 36 months.[‡]

Consider what occurs over the life cycle of a fraud. The perpetrator may begin small but over time may perfect his or her skills so that larger frauds can be executed. A trusted bookkeeper, for example, may start by creating—and then paying—fake invoices to cover some overdue bills. The bookkeeper tells herself that this will never happen again. But little by little she gets hooked on the easy money. Over time, the bookkeeper also gets better at concealing her fraud. But somewhere along the way she would have created some Red Flags—indicators that something was amiss. If those Red Flags had been investigated, the fraud would have been stopped sooner.

Over the time frame of a fraud, there are usually Red Flags—indicators that something was amiss. And this aspect of fraud is precisely what is at the heart of the Red Flag System. Some examples include:

- A procurement fraud may have been heralded by the decision of a manager to get rid of established vendors in favor of smaller, less well-known suppliers. The manager might have claimed that this would save money and eliminate red tape. In fact, he was in collusion with a crime group that jacked up the cost of inputs. His scheme might have been halted if the decision to get rid of established vendors had been more deeply and rigorously investigated;

---

[*] Association of Certified Fraud Examiners. 2012. Report to the nations on occupational fraud and abuse.
[†] Ibid.
[‡] Ibid.

- A trusted bookkeeper dresses in the latest fashion and drives a luxury foreign sedan, telling everyone she had consistently done well at the local casino. In fact, she had created a dozen ghost employees and pocketed the proceeds. This scheme might have been cut short if someone had delved more deeply into how she had been able to afford this lifestyle;
- The chief financial officer (CFO) of a multinational mining firm recommended getting rid of a national auditing firm and hiring a small, two-person firm with an office in a suburban strip mall with no experience in the extractive sector. It was just a smart way to save money, the CFO told the board. In fact, the small audit firm conspired to help the CFO manipulate the accounts and perpetrate a financial statement fraud. A more aggressive scrutiny by officers and directors might have stopped this scheme in its tracks.

According to both fraud research and the coauthors' experience, the problem is that Red Flags often are either not captured or, if they are, they are not appropriately investigated in a timely manner.

Some of the research in this area has been done by the Big Four internationally operating accounting firms, PwC, KPMG, Ernst & Young, and Deloitte. A study by KPMG found that there had been signs of fraud in 45% of major fraud cases analyzed. However, in only one in four cases had the company investigated the Red Flags.* When KPMG looked at this issue again 4 years later, it found that 56% of the 348 major fraud cases analyzed were heralded by Red Flags. However, only 6% of Red Flags were acted upon.†

Why are fewer and fewer entities capturing and pursuing Red Flags?

In part this is because officers and directors are often under the mistaken view that laws, regulators, and law enforcement will protect them from fraud.

A key lesson can be drawn from major frauds. Whether the victim is a company, a public agency, a nonprofit, a foundation, or a charity, there was a higher likelihood that many frauds could have been prevented or detected earlier if Red Flags (i.e., the early warning signals that are the focus of this book) had been taken seriously.

But in the authors' extensive experience, officers, directors, and stakeholders also frequently do not know how to identify, analyze, and take action on "Red Flags." Their concentration is usually on building their

---

* Released in 2011, KPMG Analysis of Global Patterns of Fraud is based on an analysis of 348 actual fraud investigations in sixty-nine countries.
† Ibid.

business—not on how to safeguard it against fraud. They may have "blind spots" regarding employees in positions of trust who may be known to "cut corners" in the company's best interest.

To prevent and detect fraud effectively, entities must be able to identify, analyze, and take action on Red Flags in a timely manner. As noted before, ignoring these early warning signals of potential frauds or not investigating them appropriately risks allowing a fraud to take root or, in a worst-case scenario, to persist unseen.

The adverse effects on the bottom line, on an entity's ethical framework, and on officers'/directors' personal liability can be considerable.

To be sure, the Red Flag System is not a magic bullet. It is not a guarantee that you, your company, your foundation, or your charity or other public and private entity will not be a victim of fraud. But it will provide you with the tools to address the fraud challenge more effectively and be in a better position to detect a fraud earlier in the fraud cycle.

DEFENSE IN DEPTH

The Red Flag System is not a stand-alone defense against fraud. Rather, its effectiveness requires an integrated fraud prevention and detection strategy. It is a bit like the alarm system in a building. You cannot just install an alarm system and hope that it is enough to keep out intruders. You need trained staff to monitor the system and appropriately investigate alarms, including differentiating between false alarms and incidents that warrant investigation. You need appropriate entry and exit systems so that only employees can enter the building and access areas relevant to their jobs and responsibilities.

Ultimately, you need what security experts call "defense in depth":

> The concept of defense-in-depth…involves concentric rings of protection that utilize the physical structure of a location to block or impede the progress of burglars towards their targets, as well as making it more difficult for them to exit with stolen property. Layers of security should serve to initially deter intruders. Where this fails, delays at each stage should allow sufficient time for a detection system to alert an appropriate guardian who can intercept the intruder.[*]

[*] Tim Prenzler, PhD. 2009. Preventing burglary in commercial and institutional settings. ASIS Foundation, Arlington, VA.

Similarly, with the Red Flag System, to function effectively, the system needs to be anchored within policies, procedures, and systems that comprise an effective fraud defense in depth. These include:

- A strong ethical culture, including setting the right tone at the top—the lack of ethical behavior by an organization's leaders can percolate down throughout an organization, creating an environment where employees are more likely to engage in fraudulent activities
- Effective internal controls[*] that reduce a fraudster's ability to perpetrate his or her schemes, and avoid early detection and investigation
- The presence of detection systems, including fraud analytics and audits, to foster an environment in which a potential fraudster is aware that his or her chances of detection are significant
- Employee education in fraud detection and prevention
- Hotlines for employees to report unusual activities safely without fear of retribution

Conversely, it is important to ask yourself the following questions:

- Does my entity have a strong ethical culture?
- Does it have strong and effective internal controls, whose presence is validated by outside auditors?
- Are there effective detection systems?
- Are employees educated in fraud prevention and detection?
- Are there hotlines for employees to report unusual activities?

If you answer "no" to one or more of these questions, your organization may have a heightened vulnerability to fraud.

By having an effective fraud defense in-depth program, Red Flags can be effectively captured, analyzed, and action taken in a timely manner. However, it is important to note that, on their own, internal controls and the other elements of a fraud defense in-depth program are not enough and can even create a false sense of security without a dynamic proactive approach like the Red Flag System.

---

[*] "Internal controls are put in place to keep the company on course toward profitability goals and achievement of its mission, and to minimize surprises along the way. They enable management to deal with rapidly changing economic and competitive environments, shifting customer demands and priorities, and restructuring for future growth. Internal controls promote efficiency, reduce risk of asset loss, and help ensure the reliability of financial statements and compliance with laws and regulations." Source: The Committee of Sponsoring Organizations (of the Treadway Commission); see http://www.coso.org/publications/executive_summary_integrated_framework.htm

An organization's internal controls, for example, may appear sound and comprehensive, but they may not be oriented to the prevention and early detection of fraud.

A case in point involved the giant French bank Société Générale, which discovered a $7.2 billion fraud. It appears that Société Générale's internal controls were, in themselves, effective, identifying nearly one hundred operational anomalies, or Red Flags, over a 2-year period. The problem appears to have been that no one took notice. No one followed up by rigorously analyzing these anomalies in a timely manner—a fundamental feature of the Red Flag System.

As the *Wall Street Journal* reported: "Société Générale SA's $7.2 billion loss on a series of fraudulent trades is just the latest example of a breakdown in internal controls that are supposed to protect financial firms from disaster."[*]

CAN YOU RELY ON REGULATORS OR LAW ENFORCEMENT?

Perhaps at greatest risk of fraud are organizations that believe law enforcement and regulators can protect them. Consider the following quote: "The things he was able to do in carrying out his swindle would never again be possible, and in that sense he may also be said to have been the last of a free-wheeling breed."[†]

This could have been written about the masterminds behind the Enron,[‡] Bernie Madoff, Tyco International,[§] and WorldCom[¶] scandals. In fact, it referred to Ivar Kreuger, a notorious 1930s Swedish financier who was dubbed "the world's greatest swindler."

---

[*] *Wall Street Journal*. Once again, the risk protection fails, January 25, 2008.

[†] *The Economist*. The match king, December 19, 2007.

[‡] Based in Houston, Enron Corporation had been one of the world's top energy traders until revelations in 2001 of institutionalized, systematic accounting fraud. It filed for bankruptcy protection in late 2001.

[§] Incorporated in Bermuda, Tyco International was a rapidly expanding conglomerate that fell victim to accounting scandals in 2002. In 2005, its former chief executive and his top lieutenant were convicted of fraud. In 2007, the company agreed to pay almost $3 billion to defrauded investors, the largest ever such payment.

[¶] Based in Clinton, Mississippi, WorldCom was a telecommunications giant that filed for bankruptcy protection in 2002 following the disclosure that fraudulent accounting methods had been used to conceal declining earnings.

His securities—issued in small denominations and paying annual dividends of more than 20%—had been the most widely held in the world. Unfortunately, the dividends came from capital, not profits. This created "a giant pyramid scheme, which was hidden from the investing public by Kreuger's insistence that financial statements not be audited."* When the scheme crashed in 1932, the resulting bankruptcy was the largest on record and helped lead to the passage of the landmark US securities acts in 1933 and 1934.[†]

Big financial scandals like Kreuger's or those involving Madoff, Enron, Tyco International, and WorldCom are nothing new. They have been around for a long time and we have not seen the last of them.

As occurred in the early 1930s, after the dot.com bubble at the start of the twenty-first century and after the global meltdown in 2008, major frauds invariably cause lawmakers to try to close the loopholes the scandals exposed. Modern history is full of such legislative hand-wringing.

Unfortunately, the new regulatory regimes are more suited to fighting the last war instead of the next one. They may address the fraud still fresh in everyone's mind, but will not necessarily stop other types of fraud.

It is similarly not prudent to believe that law enforcement will protect you and your entity from fraud. To be sure, there are many cases where law enforcement is able to stop a fraud in progress. But while there are some successes, they are usually in frauds that have reached a critical point. An example was the epidemic of mortgage fraud and Ponzi schemes that came to light after the 2008 financial crisis.

As Michael J. Byrne, chief counsel of the Pennsylvania Securities Commission, has noted:

> These schemes collapse because ultimately they lose their credibility and thus their ability to recruit the new investors necessary to maintain performance of the outstanding promises. With regard to Madoff, Warren Buffett's aphorism is instructive, "When the tide goes out you learn who is not wearing a bathing suit." In other words, you learn who does not have the funds necessary to perform their outstanding promises. The turmoil in the market resulting from the [2008] financial

---

* Dale L. Flesher and Tonya K. Flesher. 1986. Ivar Kreuger's contribution to US financial reporting. *Accounting Review* LXI (3), July 1986.
† "These two acts required companies to publish audited financial statements before selling securities to the public and established the Securities and Exchange Commission to oversee corporate financial reporting." Source: Paul M. Clikeman. 2003. The greatest frauds of the (last) century. Robins School of Business, University of Richmond, Virginia, May 2003.

meltdown caused an unprecedented number of Madoff's investors to decide to leave the stock market for safer havens. Madoff could not raise the funds necessary to cover the increasing demands for redemptions.*

Law enforcement is more typically reactive than proactive. It usually responds to complaints. It has neither the resources nor the mandate to act as a guardian angel to detect and prevent fraud.

The bottom line: History shows that you cannot rely solely on laws, regulators, or law enforcement to prevent fraud because white-collar criminals invariably find a way around those barriers. It almost goes without saying: When it comes to compliance violations, your goose is already cooked when law enforcement knocks on your door. This places the officer or director of a company or a nonprofit in a difficult position:

- On the one hand, he or she has a fiduciary duty[†] to safeguard the organization's assets and reputation from fraud.
- On the other, the officer or director takes on this huge responsibility even though he or she usually is not trained in fraud prevention and detection or was not primarily hired for this purpose.

In most instances, fraud prevention and detection were likely the last thing on the officer's or director's mind when he or she accepted this position.

So what can you do to protect yourself and your organization against fraud?

Based on our decades-long experience, we have come to the conclusion that prudent corporate officers or directors would implement the Red Flag System for the prevention and early detection of fraud. It is practical, effective, and empirically tested. It is based on the premise that to prevent fraud successfully or to detect it as quickly as possible after it has begun, an organization must have the capacity to identify, analyze, and address possible indicators of fraud, known as "Red Flags," in a timely manner.

Red Flag fraud detection requires skills and expertise that are outside the normal duties and practices of those who manage and run organizations. Under normal circumstances, most people in an organization, from the chairman of the board to the members of the Audit Committee to the internal auditors and the external auditors, have not been selected because of their ability to detect fraud.

---

* http://www.legis.state.pa.us/cfdocs/legis/TR/transcripts/2009_0157_0001_TSTMNY.pdf (accessed July 23, 2013).

† "The duties of a fiduciary include loyalty and reasonable care of the assets within custody. All of the fiduciary's actions are performed for the advantage of the beneficiary." Source: *West's Encyclopedia of American Law.* Copyright 1998 by The Gale Group, Inc.

Unlike police organizations, regulatory agencies, and accounting firms, which have specially trained fraud investigators or forensic accountants, most people are hired or invited to join an organization as director or hired as an officer to further its objectives.

The Red Flag System helps directors and officers to discharge their responsibility to prevent and detect fraud, even though they are not fraud investigative specialists.

Red Flag fraud detection also requires a thought process outside the usual practices of financial review and audit. Financial auditing relies on generally accepted auditing standards to express an opinion on financial statements based on the audit. It is not primarily intended to detect the Red Flags of fraud.

Rather, a financial audit is based upon a structured step-by-step approach whose objective is to find material errors and irregularities in either the financial statements or in the appropriate handling of revenues, investments, and assets. Financial auditing is not designed to detect all errors, irregularities, and fraud since it is based on sampling techniques that are driven by the accounting concept of materiality.* Finally, such audits are always subject to budget or fee restrictions.

A fraud investigation is not a checkbox exercise. Often its progress and direction depend on professional judgment applied to findings as they develop. The findings usually arise from the analysis and further investigation of one or more Red Flags that initially suggested the potential for fraud.

ABOUT THIS BOOK

This book sets out a no-nonsense approach known as the Red Flag System for the prevention and early detection of fraud. It reflects the coauthors' more than 100 years of combined experience in the investigation and prevention of fraud in North America, Europe, and the Far East. The authors have included cases, laws, and regulations from a number of different

---

* "Accounting information is considered material if its deletion or misstatement would alter or affect the judgment of any reasonable individual relying on the information. Materiality, therefore, guides accountants in determining which accounting information should be disclosed." Source: Kenneth J. Fowler. 1993. Quantitative guidelines: Guidance based on professional pronouncements. *CPA Journal*, March 1993.

countries and jurisdictions, in order to give the reader a more international perspective in dealing with corporate fraud and corruption.

Many people can benefit from this book. It will help officers and directors fulfill their fraud prevention and detection responsibilities and duties. While they have a fiduciary duty to safeguard their organization against fraud, officers and directors may not be trained or experienced in fraud prevention and detection. At any rate, this is not likely why they were hired or appointed in the first place, though there is an expectation that they can help safeguard their entity from fraud. This book will help them to discharge their responsibilities, even though they are not fraud investigative specialists.

But it will also be useful to others as well, including:

- Shareholders so that they can better monitor the companies in which they have investments
- Managers and supervisors who want to improve their business units' and departments' fraud prevention and detection capabilities
- Union leaders and members interested in keeping an eye on the antifraud effectiveness of their employers
- Journalists who cover business and financial matters
- Regulators
- Stakeholders in charities, foundations, and other entities in the not-for-profit sector

Readers of this book will:

- Acquire a general awareness of the nature, characteristics, and dynamics of fraud
- Understand the process for determining whether a fraud has been committed
- Develop an understanding of enterprise risk management approaches for fraud risk management, compliance risk management, and managing the risk of fraudulent financial reporting, including an understanding of the limitations inherent in these approaches
- Learn how to find Red Flag indicators of fraud or suspicious transactions in financial statements, budgets, and contracts
- Know how to ensure that, once a Red Flag has been identified, appropriate action is taken

Moreover, this book is designed to:

- Increase the general awareness of the possibility of fraud that may be committed by management and employees or by third parties who are carrying on business with an organization
- Describe the changing role and responsibility of directors and committee members who have the responsibility to examine and approve financial statements, budgets, and contracts
- Help to understand how to look for and identify fraud by identifying Red Flags as an indicator
- Increase awareness of how to conduct the examination required to detect and scrutinize Red Flags
- Outline how to examine individuals that are presenting financial documents for approval
- Describe how to report when a Red Flag has been identified
- Outline how to coordinate the various internal and external systems that may be utilized to investigate Red Flags
- Review the roles of lawyers, auditors, forensic accountants, public officials, and other experts that may become involved in the Red Flag investigation
- Ensure that as a member of a board of directors or a board committee you will not be included as a party or conspirator to a civil or criminal charge that may result because of negligence on the part of the board, the committee, or certain of its members

2

Fraud 101
A Primer

INTRODUCTION

The next two chapters of the book are intended to introduce the reader to the nature and characteristics of fraud. This chapter is a primer—what we like to call Fraud 101—that introduces the basic elements of fraud from both a criminal and civil perspective.

WHAT IS FRAUD?

The current meaning of a word is often at odds with its historical roots. This is not the case with the word "fraud." Its earliest use is in the Middle Ages and is traced back to a Latin word (*fraudem*) for deceit and injury.[*]

True to its etymological origins, fraud is a consensual and deceptive activity and not easily detected until after a loss has occurred. As will be demonstrated throughout this book, detecting fraud in the early stages requires an aggressive screening process, which we call screening for Red Flags.

Fraud embraces all the different ways human ingenuity can devise to convince people to act against their own best interest or the best interest of the organization they represent. Fraud includes the commission of any

---

[*] Online Etymology Dictionary. Source location: Douglas Harper, historian. http://dictionary.reference.com/browse/fraud (accessed July 23, 2013).

act of deceit, deception, or the submission of false information or material that is designed to obtain some advantage or benefit. In other words, fraud is any form of artifice, contrivance, guile, treachery, concealment, or disguise intended to induce another to part with money, property, or other legal rights, unjustly or unfairly. Fraud is a criminal offense in most jurisdictions of the world and it is also a civil wrong.

There are many different acts that constitute criminal or civil fraud. The most common fraud involves obtaining a benefit by deception. This may include such acts as forgery, false pretense, and impersonation, as well as that which is less well known by the general public, theft by conversion.*

Other acts, such as bribery, money laundering, mail fraud, secret commissions, and other similar acts, are often committed to facilitate fraud. Many of these acts are dealt with in more detail in the chapters that follow.

It is important to keep in mind that fraud can be the solitary act of an individual, like the bookkeeper in the Chapter 1 example, or fraud can be perpetrated by a group of people. Conspiracy to defraud is an extension of the substantive offense of fraud. This means that an agreement between two or more persons to commit an act to defraud someone is a criminal act in itself.

THE ELEMENTS OF FRAUD

Fraud has a number of clear and distinct elements:

1. There must be at least two parties to a fraud—namely, the fraudster and the party who was defrauded (otherwise known as the victim).
2. The fraudster must make or facilitate a false representation, either knowingly or unknowingly.
3. There must be intent by the fraudster that the false representation be acted upon by the victim.
4. The victim must have the legal right to rely on the representation.
5. There must be either actual injury or a risk of injury to the victim as a result of the reliance.

---

* Conversion: In criminal and tort law, the intentional deprivation of another of the benefit and use of his property, without his authorization or lawful justification, by possessing or disposing of the property as if it were one's own or by an act (such as damaging or destroying it) that interferes with or is inconsistent with the owner's right to sue and possess the property. *Webster's New World Law Dictionary.* Copyright 2010 by Wiley Publishing, Inc., Hoboken, New Jersey.

In summary, fraud is characterized by acts of deceit, trickery, conceal-ment, or breach of confidence that are knowingly or unknowingly used to gain some unfair or dishonest advantage. This is not a legal definition, but it is a useful guide to identify a fraudulent act.

Fraud includes the commission of any act of deceit, deception, or the submission of false information or material that is designed to obtain some advantage or benefit. In other words, fraud is any form of artifice, contrivance, guile, treachery, concealment, or disguise intended to induce another to part with money, property, or other legal rights, unjustly or unfairly.

There is a variety of specific schemes that have been identified by name. For example, there is financial statement fraud, in which a company may fraudulently misrepresent its financial health. Or there is procure-ment fraud, in which there is fraud in a company's purchase of goods and services. The names simply identify the type of business transaction or process that is involved in the fraudulent scheme. All the elements of the fraud remain basically the same in every case.

CRIMINAL FRAUD AND CIVIL FRAUD

Before proceeding further and examining the difference between crimi-nal and civil fraud, it is useful first to differentiate between criminal and civil legal environments.

- Criminal law involves legal regulations made by legislative bodies and modified through judicial rulings and precedents. Infringements of criminal laws are investigated by law enforce-ment and prosecuted by a government representative.
- Civil law, on the other hand, involves legal actions by private indi-viduals and entities to protect their rights and seek remedies for private wrongs.

What Is Criminal Fraud?

Criminal fraud involves fraudulent actions that are prosecuted in the pub-lic interest by state/provincial or federal authorities. Criminal fraud, to the average person, is deception practiced on another for personal economic, social, or political gain. It commonly takes the form of lying, cheating, or the wrongful conversion of property.

Criminal courts give fraud a more precise definition as a false representation that has been made

- Knowingly
- Without belief in its truth
- Recklessly or carelessly whether it is true or false

Some criminal courts have held that fraud is synonymous with cheating, the willful telling of an untruth, and the gaining of an unfair or unjust advantage over another. Fraud in the criminal sense must have the element of intentional dishonesty.

What Is Civil Fraud?

A civil fraud may have all the elements of a criminal fraud, except that it does not require the element of the intention to deceive at the outset.

Civil fraud involving a contract may constitute a breach of contract in which a loss occurred or some damage resulted because of deception. Whether a particular act can be pursued as a criminal prosecution depends in part on the intention of the individuals perpetrating the fraudulent act. This element of the offense is referred to as *mens rea,* or guilty mind.

Example Case

"A" enters into a contract to buy an automobile from "B," with the promise that there will be immediate delivery of the vehicle, with the payment to be made 30 days after the delivery. After the 30-day period, A fails to pay the amount promised.

Now the question is whether A has committed a criminal offense or A has simply breached the terms of the contract with B, in which case A would be liable for civil damages.

The answer depends entirely on whether A intended to make the payment at the outset of the contract. If A had no intention of making the payment when he promised to pay in 30 days, then a criminal offense of fraud has been committed.

On the other hand, if A intended to make the payment, but for some unforeseen reason he elected not to make it, then he simply breached the contract and could only be pursued in a civil action for damages. Even if A committed a criminal offense, he may also be sued in a civil action for fraud in respect of this contract.

CONSPIRACY

Research has found that many frauds involve a conspiracy. A study by the Association of Certified Fraud Examiners, for example, found that 42% of the cases it examined for a global fraud study involved multiple perpetrators.[*]

A separate study by KMPG found an increase in conspiracies in fraud. In a study it undertook in 2007, about one-third of fraudsters engaged in a conspiracy. By 2011, this proportion had grown to 61%.[†]

Consequently, it is useful to understand the conspiracy provision, which is found in the criminal law of many jurisdictions and usually attaches to all criminal offenses. Essentially, conspiracy is an agreement among two or more people to plan to carry out a criminal act at some time in the future. It is not necessary that the substantive criminal act be actually committed. The offense is complete once an agreement among the perpetrators is reached.

Conspiracy usually extends the jurisdiction of the offense to those areas where the co-conspirators were situated and to those jurisdictions where the fraud occurred or was intended to occur when the agreement was made. This means that the crime may extend from one jurisdiction to another or even from one country to other countries.

With an agreement to defraud, when one person in one place communicates, by various means, with other persons, all parties can be included in the unlawful act. The communication does not have to be face to face, but can include communication by mail, e-mail, telephone, or other electronic means.

Many jurisdictions do not have conspiracy as part of their criminal law. What if a person who is situated in a country where conspiracy laws exist conspires with a person who is situated in a country where there is no criminal conspiracy? In this case, both persons may be liable under the criminal law in the jurisdiction that has conspiracy law.

---

[*] Association of Certified Fraud Examiners. 2012. Report to the nations on occupational fraud and abuse: 2012 Global fraud study, Austin, TX.

[†] Released in 2011, KPMG Analysis of Global Patterns of Fraud is based on an analysis of 348 actual fraud investigations in sixty-nine countries.

CONCLUSION

This chapter has introduced the reader to what constitutes fraud—both from a civil and a criminal perspective. This sets the stage for an examination of the dynamics and root causes of fraud. The term "fraud" used in this chapter is a general term and includes many other specific acts dealing with fraudulent behavior, such as false pretenses, stock market manipulation, uttering a forged document, bid fixing, and so on.

3

The Dynamics and Root Causes of Fraud

INTRODUCTION

Now that the reader understands the basic elements of fraud, we move on to an essential component of the Red Flag System: the dynamics and root causes of fraud.

WHO COMMITS FRAUD?

There is a great deal of research on who commits fraud. Studies have found the following characteristics of the typical fraudster:

- Roughly two-thirds of fraud cases are committee by males.[*]
- About half of all fraudsters are between the ages of thirty-one and forty-five.[†]
- More than half of fraudsters have a college degree or higher.[‡]
- More than one-third of fraudsters work in a finance function.[§]

---

[*] Association of Certified Fraud Examiners. 2012. Report to the nations on occupational fraud and abuse: 2012 Global fraud study, Austin, TX.

[†] Ibid.

[‡] Ibid.

[§] Released in 2011, KPMG Analysis of Global Patterns of Fraud is based on an analysis of 348 actual fraud investigations in sixty-nine countries.

- About 35% of fraudsters were in senior management and 18% were at the board level.[*]
- About half of fraudsters were at their organization for 6 years or more; 22% of them had been there for more than 10 years.[†]

THE FRAUD TRIANGLE AND THE FRAUD DIAMOND

There are two widely used models for understanding what motivates fraudsters and the related environmental conditions that facilitate fraud. One is the "fraud triangle." It was developed in the 1950s and 1960s by the late American criminologist Donald Cressey. The second is the "fraud diamond," an enhancement of Cressey's model that was developed in the 2000s by two American accounting experts, David Wolfe and Dana Hermanson. We will present both models because they are in many ways complementary.

The Fraud Triangle

Interested in finding out why otherwise trusted employees turned to fraud, Cressey interviewed about two hundred fraudsters and concluded that trusted persons become trust violators when three conditions are present:

1. They see themselves as having a serious financial problem that no one else can resolve.
2. They conclude that they can secretly resolve this problem by violating the trust placed on them.
3. They are able to rationalize their behavior in such a manner that they still believe they are "trusted persons with their conceptions of themselves as users of the entrusted funds or property."[‡]

From his empirical evidence, Cressey developed the Fraud Triangle. It comprises the three factors he believed must be present whenever an ordinary person commits fraud:

- Pressure: Incentives arising from addictions to alcohol, gambling, or drugs, or from desiring a lifestyle that is not commensurate with earning ability and financial means.

---

[*] Ibid.
[†] Ibid.
[‡] Donald Cressey. 1973. Other people's money, 30. Montclair, NJ: Patterson Smith.

- Rationalization: Means of justifying fraudulent behavior. An employee may justify committing a fraud against an employer because of the perception that he or she is underpaid and/or underappreciated.
- Opportunity: Absence of sufficiently strong controls and/or oversight that provide an individual with the ability to commit a fraud. This is the only element of the Fraud Triangle that an entity can affect.

The Fraud Diamond

In reviewing the fraud triangle, American accounting experts Wolfe and Hermanson concluded that it was missing an important fourth element. They called it "capability" and said it comprised the fraudster's personal traits and abilities that play a pivotal role in whether fraud may actually occur even with the presence of the other three elements."[*]

According to Wolfe and Hermanson, many frauds, especially the most egregious ones, occurred because the right person with the right capabilities was in the position to commit them. In their words:

> Opportunity opens the doorway to fraud, and incentive and rationalization can draw the person toward it. But the person must have the capability to recognize the open doorway as an opportunity and to take advantage of it by walking through, not just once, but time and time again.[†]

THE UNDERLYING DYNAMICS OF FRAUD

Fraud is almost always committed when greedy people have the opportunity to acquire personal benefits by deceiving others. Opportunity occurs in the corporate setting when there is a lack of governance. With this lack of governance from the top, greedy managers have the opportunity to maximize their personal benefits through fraudulent activity. This type of activity produces a culture of greed within the entire organization.

---

[*] Literature refers to these four aspects as the fraud diamond; David T. Wolfe and Dana R. Hermanson. 2004. The fraud diamond: Considering the four elements of fraud. CPA Journal Online, http://www.nysscpa.org/cpajournal/2004/1204/essentials/p38.htm (accessed July 23, 2013).

[†] Ibid.

In general terms, as Wolfe and Hermanson have postulated, fraud is committed when four conditions are present[*]:

- When an individual is motivated to commit fraud
- The opportunities to commit fraud without detection are maximized
- When an individual is in a position to rationalize her actions
- When an individual has the capability to commit the fraud

The Fraudster's Motivation

In this book, the motivation to commit a fraud refers to the mental disposition of individuals most likely to commit fraud. Although the motive for a criminal act is not a necessary element to establish the crime, understanding the motive will help to construct the theory of the case, an important exercise to solving most fraud cases. It will also help to establish systems, processes, and procedures to prevent fraud.

As a general rule, motives can be categorized into four main areas:

- Economic
- Egocentric
- Idealistic
- Psychotic

Economic motivation is the most common motive for fraud. Individuals want or need money they cannot obtain legitimately. Often, individuals who commit fraud admit that they had unbearable financial problems. Normal sources of funds, they will claim, were unavailable.

Individuals with **egocentric motives** desire more prestige, greater recognition, or higher status. They believe these can be obtained through the commission of the fraudulent act. Individuals in this category are often motivated by their emotions, which can include jealousy, spite, revenge, anger, hatred, and pride. They usually believe that they are superior to others and that they can commit fraud without being detected.

Individuals that are **idealistically motivated** feel that their cause or values are morally superior to those of the victim. They often believe that they have been exploited, abused, or discriminated against.

Those with **psychotic motives** are compulsive fraud artists. They commit fraud for reasons other than need, greed, personal satisfaction, or ideologies.

---

[*] Ibid.

The Fraudster's Rationalization

The four categories of fraud motivations described in the previous section provide perpetrators with a basis for justifying and rationalizing their acts. Many employees accused of fraud will use one or more of the following justifications:

- I am underpaid and deserve what I have taken.
- Others (in the organization) are doing it.
- The organization is so big that no one will miss what I have taken.
- I only wanted to make the department look good.
- I needed the money on a temporary basis and I intended to repay it.

Many contractors or third parties accused of fraud will use one or more of the following justifications:

- I am saving the organization (victim) money.
- Other contractors are doing the same thing.
- The benefits that I gave to the employees of the victim organization did not influence them.
- The special gifts we provided to the employees of the victim organization were only intended to promote our company.
- I am losing money on this contract.
- I lost money on my last contract.

ENVIRONMENTAL INDICATORS

Research into the causes of fraud—together with our real-life experience—has shown that the environment in an organization can either promote or deter fraud. This section outlines environmental indicators of vulnerabilities to different types of fraud.

Environmental indicators of a vulnerability to management fraud include:

- Authority is centralized and exercised only by top management.
- Strong and authoritarian management controls exist but are not monitored for compliance.
- Management override of internal controls is not monitored.
- Management's orientation is low in trust and is power driven.
- Planning is centralized and short range.

- The department suffers from a "we–they" syndrome: management versus nonmanagement personnel or middle management versus top management.
- The top management is insensitive, feared, insecure, impulsive, tight-fisted, bombastic, and highly emotional.
- There is evidence of spite, hate, hostility, or jealousy among management groups.

Environmental indicators of a vulnerability to employee fraud include:

- Supervision and monitoring of employee performance and behavior is minimal or nonexistent.
- Feedback on employee performance is critical and negative.
- There are no rules and sanctions against theft, fraud, embezzlement, and bribery.
- Personnel policies are ignored.
- The reward system for employees is punitive and selectively administered.
- Salaries and fringe benefits are not equitable or competitive with other similar positions in the organization.
- Pressures for peak performance are so great that people are burning out or becoming disgruntled.
- There are high turnover, burnout grievances, and absenteeism among employees.

Environmental indicators of a vulnerability to fraud by a contractor or outside vendor include:

- The culture is such that no value is placed on integrity.
- Non-arm's-length transactions are not monitored.
- Competitors are assumed to be less than ethical.
- The firm and the industry have a history of regulatory noncompliance.
- Litigation and complaints are pending against the firm by regulatory authorities, vendors, customers, creditors, and competitors.
- Complaints from customers, shareholders, or employees are ignored.
- The contractor has financial difficulties caused by loss of business or poor management.

CONCLUSION

The past two chapters have introduced the reader to what constitutes fraud—both from a civil and a criminal perspective—and to the dynamics and root causes of fraud. This sets the stage for the next section of this book—how the Red Flag System functions with regard to the most prominent types of frauds.

4

The Red Flag System

INTRODUCTION

Now that the reader has an understanding of the elements of fraud, as well as its dynamics and root causes, this chapter introduces the key elements of the Red Flag System, its underlying concepts, and its core process.

WHAT IS A RED FLAG?

A fraud does not happen in a vacuum, or overnight. Long before a fraud is discovered, there are often Red Flags that something may be amiss and should be investigated. Red Flags focus the spotlight on anomalies in business activities and in human conduct. These anomalies provide sufficient reason to conclude that a heightened risk of fraud exists and justify further inquiry.

Here are examples of two common Red Flags:

- Vendors that have no physical address or whose address matches an address linked to an employee could be a sign that an employee is engaged in procurement fraud.
- A manager who is secretive and/or evasive regarding key financial data and who steers auditors away from operations that generate Red Flags could be a sign that he or she is "cooking the books" and is actively trying to avoid detection.

Developed by Australian criminologists Peter Grabosky and Grace Duffield,[*] a useful way to organize Red Flags is by grouping them by one of the following three source categories:

- Behavioral
- Statistical
- Organizational

The classic behavioral Red Flag is someone who lives beyond his or her legitimate means—a lowly bookkeeper, for example, who lives in a mansion and drives a Ferrari. There may be an innocent explanation. Perhaps the bookkeeper's family won the lottery and kept the news quiet or a wealthy relative left them a large bequest. But such an imbalance in a trusted employee between lifestyle and known legitimate income warrants further scrutiny. Indeed, a study by the Association of Certified Fraud Examiners (ACFE) found that about 37% of fraudsters were living beyond their means.[†]

This kind of analysis is often undertaken in criminal investigations of drug dealers and was famously used to convict Al Capone in 1931 of tax evasion.[‡]

Statistical Red Flags involve the following kinds of anomalies in financial reports:

- Negative cash flows that have plagued the company all year suddenly, and unexpectedly, turn significantly positive in the final quarter. This could be an indicator of financial statement fraud.
- There is an unusual increase in inventory but no concomitant increase in sales. This could be a sign that asset valuations are being fraudulently inflated to manipulate profits.

Organizational Red Flags involve activities that are not consistent with an ethical corporate culture. An example is management override of internal controls, which has been called "the Achilles heel of fraud

---

[*] Peter Grabosky and Grace Duffield. 2011. Red flags of fraud. Trends and Issues in Crime and Criminal Justice, no. 200. Australian Institute of Criminology, March 2011

[†] Association of Certified Fraud Examiners. 2012. Report to the nations on occupational fraud and abuse: 2012 global fraud study, Austin, TX.

[‡] http://www.bus.lsu.edu/accounting/faculty/lcrumbley/AlCapone.pdf (accessed July 23, 2013).

prevention."* (The authors have found this is often done in the name of "increased efficiency.")

The American Institute of Certified Public Accountants has stated that all entities—regardless of whether they are publicly held, private, not for profit, or governmental—face the risk that management will override controls. This is for the simple reason that management has the primary responsibility for designing, implementing, and maintaining internal controls.[†]

The American Institute further stated that senior management may engage in fraudulent financial reporting when two factors are present: the opportunity to override internal controls combined with powerful incentives to meet accounting objectives.[‡] It concluded: "Thus, otherwise effective internal controls cannot be relied upon to prevent, detect, or deter fraudulent financial reporting perpetrated by senior management."[§]

A few words of caution, however, are warranted.

First, a Red Flag is not evidence that an illegal act has occurred or will occur, but it indicates that the potential for fraud is sufficiently high to warrant further scrutiny. Second, Red Flags are not always indicators of fraud. They may simply reflect errors or omissions due to such factors as incompetence, lack of experience, lack of training, etc. In many cases, the earlier the Red Flag is identified while a fraudulent scheme is unfolding, the harder it may be to distinguish from the normal course of mistakes or omissions.

Recall that frauds do not come out of the blue and are not random one-off events. According to a study by the ACFE, the typical fraud lasted 18 months from the time it began until it was discovered.[¶]

It is important to be able to recognize the difference between an error and an indicator of fraud. If the results of an investigation into a Red Flag are negative, it is vital to document the inquiries undertaken to reach that conclusion. Those inquiries may become very material if additional Red Flags are thrown up involving the same individual or scheme. The initial Red Flags may simply have occurred at an early, incomplete stage in the

---

* Management override of internal controls: The Achilles' heel of fraud prevention, http://www.aicpa.org/ForThePublic/AuditCommitteeEffectiveness/DownloadableDocuments/achilles_heel.pdf (accessed July 23, 2013).
† Ibid.
‡ Ibid.
§ Ibid.
¶ Association of Certified Fraud Examiners. 2012. Report to the nations on occupational fraud and abuse: 2012 Global fraud study.

evolution of the fraud, when there was insufficient information to make a firm determination.

THE RED FLAGS OF FRAUD

The Red Flag System is a disciplined, structured process for discerning, discovering, and documenting allegations of fraud, theft, embezzlement, and corruption so that they can be addressed in an efficient and timely manner as early as possible in the fraud cycle. The system involves looking beyond and behind actual or proposed financial transactions to determine whether there are any Red Flags that indicate the possibility of problems.

Once a Red Flag is detected, the process is like solving a jigsaw puzzle but with two major differences: You do not know what the picture is supposed to look like, and only one or two of the pieces of the puzzle may be initially provided. When looking for Red Flags, you are looking for oddities or events outside the normal course of business and/or human relations. Finding them requires experience, judgment, and intuition.

Because a Red Flag is a signal that something is different from what is expected as to time, place, personality, or amount, the difference does not necessarily have to be large or significant. An accumulation of small differences is often the very essence of a sophisticated large fraud. A simple example is the case of a bank employee who arranges for a fraction of one cent to be deducted from all accounts and transactions and deposited into his or her personal bank account. This unnoticeable fraction of a penny turns into millions of dollars for the personal benefit of the bank employee.

Some transactions require more scrutiny than others. Special attention needs to be paid to procurement contracts with a greater fraud risk to identify elements that are questionable or "just do not feel right." Red Flag detection is more of an art than a science, requiring innovative, creative thinking and a well-honed sixth sense.

While financial audits often rely on general standardized checklists, they are not always effective in identifying Red Flags. For one thing, checklists and computer programs cannot be all inclusive because there are so many ways to commit fraud. For another, checklists and computer programs are often based on commonly detected frauds and fraud schemes. Savvy fraudsters can always tweak their methodology to "fly under the radar" of such lists and computer programs.

THE FOUR PHASES OF THE RED FLAG SYSTEM

There are basically four phases in the Red Flag detection process:

- Phase 1—screening for Red Flags
- Phase 2—scrutinizing Red Flags
- Phase 3—in-depth examination
- Phase 4—formal reporting/referral

Phase 1—Screening for Red Flags

The screening phase involves looking for Red Flag indicators that fraud may have occurred. This can be done manually or as a result of computerized analytical tools that can detect Red Flags by scanning transactions.

The authors believe that the most important screening opportunity occurs at the level of the entity's board of directors. In their experience, many frauds could have been prevented or detected far earlier if directors had probed deeper and prudently and aggressively asked the right questions. For directors, the screening process is a manual one and typically begins when a director is presented with documents related to the budget, financial statements, corporate acquisitions, contract opportunities, and money transfers. These are opportunities for directors to look for unusual or questionable indications that may be the first indication of fraud. Later in this book, we will outline specific Red Flags that are indications of fraud and other related unlawful activity.

For the informed director, looking for these indicators is not a complicated procedure as long as he or she can focus on the key issues and ask the right questions. Screening for Red Flags is like looking for a gold nugget in a pan full of gravel: You have to know what a gold nugget looks like and be able to distinguish it from all the other rocks in the pan.

In addition to the manual screening, recent years have seen the emergence of fraud analytical software that uses complex algorithms and social network analytical tools to identify Red Flags. These tools are expensive and may be beyond the capabilities of small- and medium-sized entities. But they are worth noting nonetheless because their benefits are significant, including:

- Providing a holistic cross-enterprise view of transactions and relationships
- Uncovering previously unknown relationships between insiders and outside fraudulent agents

33

- Generating a holistic view of fraud, disclosing, for example, that a formerly trusted insider may have been involved in a number of fraudulent activities across a number of business units

For example, a manufacturer may want to scan the transactions in its supply chain, as well as its own supply chain employees, for Red Flags. Such a scan may find indications that a vendor and an employee share the same address or that a vendor is operating out of a virtual office.

As a side benefit, such software can also be used to detect Red Flags that customers are becoming less credit worthy and thus their accounts need closer monitoring.

Phase 2—Scrutinizing for Red Flags

The scrutinizing phase involves a preliminary review of Red Flags identified during the screening stage to validate the suspicion that fraud or a related unlawful act has occurred. Best practices on how to scrutinize a Red Flag are detailed in Chapter 17.

Phase 3—In-Depth Examination

In this phase, an in-depth examination is performed to obtain evidence and information that will support the initiation of a formal investigation or the referral of the matter for administrative, judicial, or other remedial action. This may involve internal and external legal, auditing, and investigative resources. In some instances, directors may decide to turn over the investigation to an independent outside party, often a law firm or a forensic accounting firm.

There are many reasons for doing this. The issues may be too complex for internal auditors or investigators. The issues may be so troubling that—to maintain the entity's reputation and that of its board—they are best dealt with by someone who is fully independent, has no prior relationship with the entity, and can follow the facts wherever they may lead. Independent outside investigators are likely the best course of action, for example, if the case involves a senior manager who has overridden internal controls.

Best practices for this phase will be further discussed in Chapter 17, "Screening, Scrutinizing, and Investigating Red Flags."

Phase 4—Formal Reporting/Referral

In this phase, the results of the in-depth examination are referred for administrative, judicial, or other external remedial action. Internally, they may generate changes to policies, procedures, controls, and systems to ensure there is no recurrence.

CONCLUSION

The Red Flag System is not a panacea. It cannot, on its own, inoculate an organization from fraud. Rather, it works best as an integral part of a program that also eliminates the root causes of fraud and organizational factors that promote it. It is most effective in an organization that is already working to eliminate the structural elements that can make it more vulnerable to fraud.

If frauds do not emerge in a vacuum, then neither can the Red Flag System be successfully implemented in one. It works optimally in an organization that has good governance and whose directors appropriately discharge their fiduciary duties.

5

Financial Statement Fraud

INTRODUCTION

Now that the reader has been introduced to the concepts underpinning the Red Flag System, we turn to examining its actual application in one of the highest profile types of fraud: financial statement fraud, also known in some circles as accounting fraud.

WHAT IS FINANCIAL STATEMENT FRAUD?

There is a common thread linking the major fraud scandals among publicly traded companies in the United States in the late 1990s and early 2000s: financial statement fraud. Enron, WorldCom, and Health South were all brought down by efforts to fraudulently misrepresent the health of the company by manipulating financial statements. This had far-reaching negative consequences—for shareholders, creditors, and the thousands of employees who lost not only their jobs but also their retirement savings.

It also resulted in the enactment of the Sarbanes–Oxley Act in 2002, which has two key provisions:

- A requirement that senior management certify the accuracy of the reported financial statement (Section 302)
- A requirement for the establishment of internal controls and reporting methods on their adequacy (Section 404)

These provisions underline the fact that financial statement fraud targets individuals and entities that rely on financial statements, including shareholders and creditors. It usually involves one or more of the following:

- Overstating assets or revenues
- Understating liabilities or expenses
- Deliberately omitting or misrepresenting material information used to prepare financial statements
- Intentionally circumventing the proper application of accounting principles when recording material events, transactions, and/or accounts

Research suggests that companies experiencing financial statement fraud face a greater risk of negative outcomes, including higher rates of bankruptcy, stock market delisting, or major asset divestments than those experienced by comparable firms not affected by fraud.[*] Often the impact is felt quickly. One study found that news coverage of an alleged financial statement fraud resulted in an average 16.7% abnormal stock price drop in the 2 days after the news became public.[†]

SCOPE AND EXTENT OF FINANCIAL STATEMENT FRAUD

For a sense of the extent and scope of financial statement fraud, we turn to two landmark studies conducted by the influential Committee of Sponsoring Organizations of the Treadway Commission (COSO). Established in 1985, COSO has been an influential voice in the development of frameworks and guidance on enterprise risk management, internal control, and fraud deterrence.

The studies examined cases of fraudulent financial reporting by public US companies during two 10-year periods: 1987–1997 and 1998–2007. COSO found that the problem appeared to persist after the high-water mark of the Enron/WorldCom cases that came to light at the start of the 2000s:

- There were 347 alleged cases of fraudulent financial reporting by public companies from 1998 to 2007. That is up from 294 cases in the earlier COSO study covering the 1987–1997 period.

---

[*] Committee of Sponsoring Organizations of the Treadway Commission. 2010. Fraudulent financial reporting 1998–2007. An analysis of US public companies, Durham, NC.
[†] Ibid.

- Because the 1998–2007 period had so many large cases like Enron and WorldCom, the total of fraudulent financial reporting soared in 1998–2007 to nearly $120 billion, or about $400 million per case. This compares to a mean of $25 million per sample fraud in COSO's 1999 study.
- While the largest frauds of the early 2000s skewed the 1998–2007 total, the median fraud of $12.05 million in the 1998–2007 period was nearly three times larger than the median fraud of $4.1 million in the 1987–1997 period.
- The companies cited in the 1998–2007 cases had median assets and revenues just under $100 million. By comparison, those in the earlier study had median assets and revenues under $16 million.[*]

A 2012 study by the Association of Certified Fraud Examiners (ACFE) shed some further light on financial statement fraud. In the cases it reviewed, the frequency of instances of financial fraud was relatively small—accounting for about 8% of cases. However, those cases had, by far, the largest median loss: $1 million. And it found that financial statement frauds last on average 24 months.[†]

Most financial statement fraud methods analyzed by COSO involved the overstatement of either revenues or assets. Over half the frauds were committed by overstating revenues through fictitious invoices or premature recognition of revenue. Many of these fraudulent revenue transactions were recorded near the fiscal year end. About half the frauds involved the overstatement of assets by

- Understating the bad debt allowance for receivables
- Overstating the value of inventory, property, plant and equipment, and other tangible assets
- Recording fictitious assets

Financial fraud schemes, which became widely known through the failures of large corporations like Enron, can also occur in smaller entities.

It is particularly important to note that, in this day and age, the use of tax haven shell companies to create or enable financial statement fraud schemes has become widely available. Such structures are openly advertised in mainstream business magazines. Creating a shell company in a

---

[*] Ibid.
[†] Association of Certified Fraud Examiners. 2012. Report to the nations on occupational fraud and abuse: 2012 Global fraud study, Austin, TX.

tax haven can cost as little as $3,000 with yearly administrative costs of as little as $2,000.

Consider the scandal over slush funds by the German multinational Siemens AG. A former senior manager of Siemens has admitted in court to setting up an elaborate system at the request of his superiors to help Europe's biggest technology group win overseas contracts through bribes.*

The case demonstrates how both simple and complex schemes can be used to create large secret pools of money in tax haven entities. At the simple end were phony consultancy contracts. On the more sophisticated side were schemes that channeled Siemens products through tax haven companies. Profits were artificially inflated and, with each transaction, a portion of the profits was left behind in the tax haven companies. To disperse the funds, fees may be paid to lawyers, accountants, and consultants by the tax haven entity.

WHAT ARE FINANCIAL STATEMENTS?

Before proceeding further, it is worth briefly reviewing what financial statements are. Prepared by management, they typically comprise several statements that summarize an organization's accounting data for a financial year and indicate its financial condition. The most prominent statements are the following:

- The *balance sheet* presents the organization's financial health at a single moment in time as measured by its assets, which include cash, inventories, and amounts owed by customers; and its liabilities, which include loans and debts owed to trade creditors.
- The *income statement* summarizes an organization's revenues and expenses during a particular time period as a way of measuring its financial performance.
- The *retained earnings statement* summarizes changes in an organization's retained earnings (i.e., net income that is retained instead of being distributed to shareholders) over a particular time period.
- The *cash flow statement* summarizes an organization's sources of cash and how it has used that cash during a particular time period.

---

* *The Guardian,* Siemens boss admits setting up slush funds, May 2, 2008.

When examining these statements, it is also important to review the attached notes. They detail how accounting principles are applied to the financial statements and also contain additional information to help understand an organization's financial position.

In addition to financial statements, public corporations also have to disclose a very useful document as part of their annual reports: Management Discussion and Analysis (MD&A). An MD&A is particularly helpful because, unlike a financial statement with its rows and columns of numbers, it is a narrative discussion and analysis by management regarding the health of an organization and its future prospects.[*]

An MD&A should provide an overview of the previous year's operations and an outlook on the upcoming year, outlining goals and approaches to new projects, products, and markets. It should provide a narrative explanation of a company's financial statements that enables investors to see the company through the eyes of management. An MD&A has to be consistent with financial statements and should identify reasons for material changes in financial statement items. It should also provide information about the quality of a company's earnings and cash flow so that investors can ascertain the likelihood that the past is indicative of future performance.

WHAT ARE THE MOST FREQUENT TYPES OF FINANCIAL REPORTING FRAUD?

Most often, financial reporting fraud involves overstating or understating an organization's net assets[†] or earnings.[‡] Overstatements generally occur in the following business scenarios:

- In preparation for major divestiture activities
- In preparation of joint venture arrangements as a defense mechanism to deter hostile takeovers
- To improve credit rating and to obtain favorable financing conditions
- To demonstrate compliance with financing/loan agreements

---

[*] "The purpose of MD&A is, as regulators have determined, to provide a narrative explanation, through the eyes of management, of how a company has performed in the past and its future prospects." Source: Canadian Institute of Chartered Accountants. 2004. Executive summary, guidance on management's discussion and analysis, May 2004.

[†] The value of an entity's assets less liabilities.

[‡] Also known as profit.

- To postpone insolvency proceedings
- To increase bonus entitlements for management
- To stave off situational pressures created by unrealistic budgets or sudden changes in the market

Understatements generally occur in the following business scenarios:

- To reduce an organization's tax burden
- In buyouts of minority shareholders
- As clean-up strategies upon change of senior management, in what is often called "big bath accounting"
- To make it easier to get financial assistance in government contracts since they typically make funds more easily available to entities with lower financial capabilities

In some instances, fraudsters will use a combination of overstatement and understatement, depending on the circumstances of their scheme.

WHAT IS THE MOTIVATION FOR FINANCIAL REPORTING FRAUD?

In essence, financial reporting fraud is not necessarily committed to reap immediate personal gain. Management often sees it as a means to benefit the whole organization. Nevertheless, there may also be a personal gain aspect because it can be argued that management's survival in a given situation—let alone its remuneration—is often so closely linked to the organization's performance that an organization's success translates directly into personal benefit.

HOW IS FINANCIAL REPORTING FRAUD USUALLY PERPETRATED?

Introduction

The methods used to perpetrate financial statement fraud can be classified into three categories:

- Manipulation of net assets—that is, of assets less liabilities
- Manipulation of earnings
- False or inadequate disclosure

How Are Net Assets Typically Manipulated?

Balance sheets provide information about the net asset position of an entity and the composition of its assets, liabilities, and equity. Manipulation of net assets—total of all the assets less the liabilities owed to outsiders—can occur in any balance sheet items, but especially with regard to the following:

- *Fixed assets* that can be defined as assets such as land, buildings, and machines that are continually used in the business
- *Inventories* that comprise raw materials, work in progress, and finished products ready for sale
- *Accounts receivables,* which are debts owed by customers
- *Cash* that is in banks
- *Liabilities and accrued liabilities,* which are liabilities recorded in an organization's financial records before they are paid or even invoiced by the vendor.

How Are Fixed Assets Typically Manipulated?

Under accounting rules, the value of fixed assets is recorded in financial statements at their initial, or historical, cost—that is, what they cost when first acquired less accumulated depreciation. Depreciation involves the wearing out over time of machinery, buildings, vehicles, etc. Fictitious third-party transactions or forged invoices—usually involving a manipulated valuation report to justify the higher cost—can inflate the initial or historical cost of the fixed asset above its true market value. A variation is the "asset flip": The price is bumped up through fictitious sales or sequential sale-and-lease-back agreements among related parties whose relationships are not disclosed. One notorious technique was at the center of the WorldCom scandal. Expenses were recorded in financial statements as assets, leading to a fraudulent misreporting of its financial performance.

The WorldCom case was extraordinary not only because of the extent of the fraud, but also because of the relative simplicity of the accounting maneuvers used. WorldCom, a long-distance phone service provider, had entered into long-term contracts to lease line capacity required to deliver its services. When the market for long-distance services contracted in the late 1990s, WorldCom was sitting on quasi-fixed expenses at a time when revenues were falling.

An important measuring standard for the performance of long-distance service providers was their expense/revenue ratios. Prior to the market correction, WorldCom's expense/revenue ratio was approximately 42%. WorldCom was determined to maintain this 42% ratio and, in order to do that, needed to slash its expenses. As that was impossible due to its long-term commitments, WorldCom's leadership decided to record the cost for line expenses as capital expenditure, fixed assets. This not only violated generally accepted accounting standards, but was also counter-intuitive. Line capacity can only be used during the period for which it is leased and cannot be carried forward. Thus, there was no asset to be used in the future.

This was done in a rather simple manner, by entering the necessary accounting entries in the general ledger of WorldCom's headquarters. This was done primarily because many CFOs of subsidiaries resisted the push from headquarters to make those entries.

Auditors should have easily discovered this, but they did not. When the auditors asked for access to the general ledgers for audit purposes, that access was denied. The auditors not only should have insisted on getting access, but also should have reported access limitations to the board of directors. Neither took place, so the catastrophe took its course.

As illustrated later, manipulation of how fixed assets are recorded in financial statements can create many other opportunities for fraud.

Fixed assets manufactured by an entity can be recorded at an inflated cost if management decides to raise the costs recorded in financial statements above the actual manufacturing cost. Under accounting regulations, the cost of repairing and maintaining fixed assets must be expensed during the financial year. But the fixed asset's historical cost can be over-stated by adding repair and maintenance expenses.

Fixed assets that are being leased can also provide fertile ground for fraud. Such leases should be recorded in financial statements as both an asset and a corresponding liability. But if the lease is recorded as an asset without the corresponding leasing liability, then the net asset position will be overstated.

The Enron scandal highlighted the use of sophisticated manipulation of accounting regulations to hide debts and overvalued assets behind the smoke screen of the so-called "asset-light strategy." Enron's executives took the position that, unlike traditional energy businesses, it did not need to own power plants, pipelines, or other types of energy transmission systems. It believed that "this business was best dealt with through contracts with private partners."[*]

---

[*] *Australian Financial Review.* 2002. Enron's Australian cousins, February 28, 2002.

Enron overstated net assets in its financial statements by transferring assets whose value was below their initial cost and the assets' corresponding liability to a type of accounting structure known as a "special purpose entity." This provided two benefits to Enron:

- It was able to record gains on transactions with the "special purpose entity" in its financial statements.
- The debts and overvalued assets transferred to special-purpose entities were not included in Enron's balance sheet. Accounting rules allowed a "special-purpose entity" to be used if it was independent from the company that created it.

In the case of Enron, however, the company and the many "special-purpose entities" it created were closely linked.

But these relationships were carefully concealed, as was outlined in a 2002 report by a court-appointed examiner, who suggested that many of the deals were shams. Partnerships, he found, were established to obtain financing. Typically, Enron would sell an asset to the partnership, but would retain control of it and would pay interest to the partnership. The examiner said:

> Most of the time, the assets were difficult to sell or did not have sufficient cash flow to cover the partnership's purchase price.
>
> Enron intended the transfers of assets to be sales for financial reporting purposes. On the other hand, the economic consequences to Enron of these transactions were substantially similar to loans.*

Often, the "special purpose entities" were owned by trustees acting on behalf of Enron through undisclosed trust agreements. By using this type of entity, Enron was able to overstate its net assets in its financial statements.

Those who perpetrated a huge fraud at Global Crossing used the so-called "round-tripping" technique—a series of circular transactions often found in frauds in the energy and telecommunications sectors to manipulate their fixed assets. With executive offices in California, Global Crossing accumulated $12.4 billion in debt building a worldwide fiber optic network before collapsing in 2002.

In this kind of fraud, network capacity to transmit either a form of energy or data is sold from one co-conspiring market participant to another—and then repurchased at an inflated price. To manipulate the

---

* *New York Times,* Enron examiner raises more questions, September 22, 2002.

financial statements, the sale of the fixed asset is recorded as if it were a regular sale. Then, to complete the "round-tripping," the repurchase is recorded as a fixed asset with an inflated value.

Depreciation, where the initial cost is expensed over future years, also can be fraudulently manipulated. One technique is to depreciate an asset over a longer period than its true life span. Another is to avoid writing-down the initial cost of the fixed asset where its true value is less than the cost.

How Is Inventory Typically Manipulated?

The value of inventories can be misrepresented by

- Manipulating the physical inventory counts
- Overstating or understating the cost applied to determine the value of counted inventories

Physical inventory counts can be manipulated through forging of count sheets and through manipulation of counting, measuring, or weighing equipment or the movement of inventory to and from other secret locations. More sophisticated methods include:

- Counting of inventory on consignment as being actually owned by the entity
- Borrowing the inventories of co-conspirators
- Including so-called "bill and hold" items, which were already booked in the financial records as having been sold, as inventory

The unit costs can be manipulated by overallocating or underallocating in the financial statements the cost for work in progress (i.e., partially manufactured goods) or by avoiding inventory write-downs in accordance with the "lower of cost or market" (LCM) accounting test. The LCM rule is used when items in inventory decrease in value because they are less expensive in the marketplace. An example would be if a company held an inventory of cell phones whose technology was made outdated by newer models.

Sophisticated methods include manipulating:

- The percentage of completion documentation in large manufacturing and construction projects
- The split of long-term construction projects into individual project components when applying the completed contract method of valuation, which can also lead to fraudulent recording of both the sale of a project and its inclusion as work in progress

How Are Accounts Receivable Typically Manipulated?

Accounts receivables can be manipulated through the recording of non-existent receivables in the financial statements or by valuing receivables at amounts greater than their true value. While fictitious receivables can result from fictitious sales (to be addressed later in this chapter), they can also involve recording and overvaluing volume bonuses and commissions from suppliers. This method was employed at a fraud involving subsidiaries of Dutch grocery giant Royal Ahold NV. In 2004, it settled Securities and Exchange Commission charges that subsidiaries fraudulently inflated earnings by nearly $830 million between 2000 and 2002.

The intentional failure to write off or reduce accounts receivables may involve:

- Manipulating documentation about the credit worthiness of customers
- Dividing a large receivable with one customer into numerous smaller receivables with several customers
- Manipulating the aging of receivables
- Using a circular flow of funds to make the receivable appear paid
- Factoring receivables—that is, raising cash by selling its accounts receivables at a discount to nonconsolidated entities similarly to the "asset light strategy" for fixed assets

How Is "Cash in the Bank" Typically Manipulated?

Cash in the bank can be overstated by successively increasing fictitious bank balances in subsidiary accounts. This typically involves fictitious balances at foreign banks and requires the creation of forged bank confirmation letters. Another method of manipulating cash at banks involves holding funds in accounts owned by trustees. The primary purpose is not to misrepresent financial information, but rather to build up slush funds to be used for corrupt payments or remuneration to managers.

Both methods were employed by Italian food processing giant Parmalat and uncovered when it filed for bankruptcy protection in 2003. With annual sales at its peak of $9.2 billion, Parmalat employed 35,000 people in 30 countries, including the United States.

How Are Liabilities and Accrued Liabilities Typically Manipulated?

According to the ACFE's *Fraud Examiner's Manual,** the preferred method of concealing liabilities or accrued liabilities is simply to fail to record them.

One concealment method is to incur liabilities through nonconsolidated entities—that is, through subsidiaries or related parties whose financial results are not included in the statements of the parent entity. Such liabilities become, in effect, liabilities of the parent organization. This scheme was employed by Adelphia Communications, the fifth largest cable television company in the United States, before it declared bankruptcy in June 2002. In 2004, a federal jury found Adelphia's founder John J. Rigas and his son, Timothy, the former chief financial officer, guilty of conspiring to loot the cable television company of millions of dollars.

According to the Securities and Exchange Commission:

> Between mid-1999 and the end of 2001, John J. Rigas, Timothy J. Rigas, Michael J. Rigas, James P. Rigas, and James R. Brown, with the assistance of Michael C. Mulcahey, caused Adelphia to fraudulently exclude from the Company's annual and quarterly consolidated financial statements over $2.3 billion in bank debt by deliberately shifting those liabilities onto the books of Adelphia's off-balance sheet, unconsolidated affiliates. Failure to record this debt violated GAAP requirements and laid the foundation for a series of misrepresentations about those liabilities by Adelphia and the defendants, including the creation of: (1) sham transactions backed by fictitious documents to give the false appearance that Adelphia had actually repaid debts when, in truth, it had simply shifted them to unconsolidated Rigas-controlled entities, and (2) misleading financial statements by giving the false impression through the use of footnotes that liabilities listed in the Company's financials included all outstanding bank debt.†

Accrued liabilities are expenses recorded in an organization's financial records before they are paid or an invoice received by the vendor. Examples include warranty costs, product recall costs, costs for guarantees of third-party debt, accrued pension costs, etc. When financial statements are prepared, estimates of these liabilities are recorded, which provides scope for manipulation.

---

* Association of Certified Fraud Examiners. 2007. *Fraud examiners' manual* (Canadian ed.).
† The Securities and Exchange Commission. 2002. SEC charges Adelphia and Rigas family with massive financial fraud. http://www.sec.gov/news/press/2002-110.htm (accessed July 23, 2013).

How Are Sales Typically Manipulated?

The manipulation of sales has serious consequences. It not only affects profitability, but also deceives stakeholders about an organization's success in its core business activity. Sales can be manipulated through the recording of fictitious revenues, premature revenue recognition, round-tripping, sales swapping, and recording of nonrecurring items such as the sale of fixed assets as a normal sale.

Fictitious sales involve recording transactions that did not occur. This may involve the creation of an invoice to a domestic shell company or to a co-conspiring friendly organization. The latter often goes hand in hand with round-tripping or sales swapping.

A less sophisticated method involves forging sales invoices for actual transactions by altering the quantity and/or prices of goods or services sold. In more sophisticated schemes, the invoice is addressed to a shell company in a tax haven.

Premature revenue recognition occurs when conditional sales are recorded in a financial year as if all conditions were met. It can also involve recording undelivered orders or deliveries on consignment as sales.

As noted earlier, round-tripping is in itself a form of sales manipulation. It involves the sale of capacity to co-conspiring friendly organizations and the renting of third-party capacity, thereby generating inflated sales and inflated expenses for capacities. This serves to cover up under-utilization of capacity. A variation of this scheme involves the capitalization of the repurchased capacities as fixed assets.

Round-tripping became widely known when it was uncovered in the scandals at Enron, Global Crossing, and QWest Communications International.*

Sales swapping involves inflated invoicing for goods or services to co-conspiring friendly organizations and the acceptance of equivalent amounts of purchases from these co-conspiring entities. This method was employed by AOL Time Warner in its dealings with various counterparties. The recording of nonrecurring items as sales was another method employed when the company was awarded damages in a lawsuit and induced the losing party to purchase advertising space and time in lieu of payment of damages.

---

* In February 2002, it was revealed that Qwest, the telephone service provider for 14 mostly Western states, inflated revenue using network capacity "swaps" and improper accounting for long-term deals. Qwest admitted that an internal review found that it incorrectly accounted for $1.16 billion in sales.

This enabled AOL Time Warner to record the payments as normal sales as opposed to an extraordinary (nonrecurring) sale.

How Are Expenses Typically Manipulated?

Manipulation of expenses mostly occurs in the form of untimely recording of expenses. Essentially, the recording of the expense is postponed until the next financial year. This gives the organization time to resolve some issues, such as short-term budgetary pressures or weakness in sales. As described in the chapter on fixed asset manipulation, expenses can also be manipulated by recording them as assets, especially fixed assets.

How Are Notes to Financial Statements Typically Manipulated?

Notes to financial statements provide:

- Information about accounting policies
- Details on some items in the financial statements
- Additional information on commitments and potential business risks

While each part of a note can be subject to manipulation, the area most prone to false representation is information on commitments and potential business risks. This might include:

- The nondisclosure or understatement of the amount of future lease commitments and guarantees for third party liabilities
- Risks resulting from off-balance sheet items such as trading in derivatives

How Are Management Discussion and Analysis Reports Typically Manipulated?

Management discussion and analysis (MD&A) reports may be prone to incomplete or false information, but it is difficult to prove that such information was intentionally false because of the reports' soft nature. False information in MD&A can, for example, portray a potential customer's interest or intent as being a completed sale. Or, it might involve the inclusion of fictitious orders from foreign shell companies as part of the order books. There can also be omissions of negative developments, such as

- The loss of key customers
- The cancellations of joint venture arrangements
- The loss of key suppliers
- Setbacks in technological developments that render the organiza-tion's manufacturing processes inferior to its competitors or make substantial investments necessary in the near future

The description of business risks can be too vague and might focus on less relevant risks than the key business risks.

Nondisclosure of looming product liability risks is specifically prob-lematic in pharmaceutical or other health care industries, where indica-tions of health risks can lead to product discontinuation and exposure to substantial damage claims from customers.

MD&A reports also need to provide a near-term outlook. Management might omit information about worsening scenarios, such as the expecta-tion of loss of market share due to new or stronger competitors.

Organizations operating in industries exposed to increased low-cost competition from Eastern Europe or Asia may need to keep a close watch on their own position relative to potential new market players.

Industry sectors relying heavily on research and development, such as the pharmaceutical industry, might tend to overstate the success poten-tial of new products and understate risks such as the odds of timely gov-ernment approval. Mining and energy companies, for their part, might provide an overly optimistic assessment of exploratory test results.

CONCLUSION

This chapter has outlined the many techniques that can be used to manip-ulate financial statement fraud. This sets the stage for the next chapter—a discussion on the Red Flags to financial statement fraud.

6

Red Flags for Financial Statement Fraud

INTRODUCTION

Now that the reader understands how financial statement fraud can be perpetrated, this chapter sets out Red Flags for its detection.

TYPES OF FINANCIAL STATEMENT FRAUD RED FLAGS

Red Flags for financial statement fraud can be behavioral, situational, organizational, financial, or transactional in nature:

- Behavioral Red Flags refer to conspicuous behavior of senior management and/or individuals with significant roles in the financial process.
- Situational Red Flags refer to developments in markets, technological developments, changes in performance over time, or expectations by stakeholders. These developments increase the risk of manipulative actions by individuals with significant roles in the financial process.
- Organizational Red Flags refer to the quality of the control environment over the financial process.
- Financial and Transactional Red Flags are indicators based on financial statements or accounting data.

Behavioral Red Flags

Analyses of financial statement fraud cases have shown that dominant and aggressive management styles were the most common behavioral pattern. Dominant management styles generally imply oppressive behavior by superiors, which can create a culture of fear. Dominant behavior often coincides with a lack of respect for

- Oversight institutions
- Regulatory authorities
- Laws and regulations in effect in countries other than the company's home country

Of course, a dominant management style does not necessarily mean that the vast majority of dominant managers tend to be fraudsters. But it does mean that a higher level of vigilance may be warranted when a number of Red Flags occur in an institution with this type of management behavior.

Additional behavioral Red Flags include high levels of conflict in senior management and high rates of fluctuation or dominance of an organization by one individual or a small group of individuals.

Another behavioral Red Flag is the intense participation of nonfinancial management in the selection of accounting principles or other significant accounting issues.

Situational Red Flags

Situational Red Flags relate to conditions specific to an organization or to its industry. Red Flags pertaining to organization-specific conditions include:

- Dependence on small numbers of products, suppliers, customers, or business transactions (bulk risks)
- Risk of hostile takeovers
- Rapid business expansion
- Liquidity shortage due to rapid expansion
- Rapid increase of corporate acquisitions
- Conflict between shareholders or groups of shareholders with CEO or members of senior management having strong relations to one group of shareholders

Industry-specific Red Flags include:

- Operating in highly competitive markets
- Operating in industrial sectors with short product life cycles, often due to susceptibility to technological changes
- Profitability inconsistent with industry sector (i.e., profitability substantially above or below industry standards
- Operating in markets with a high degree of saturation and shrinking margins
- Increasing number of bankruptcies within the industry sector

Organizational Red Flags

Organizational Red Flags are warning signs resulting from deficiencies of governance structures and internal controls over the financial process.

Weaknesses in internal control systems are strongly correlated with the occurrence of financial statement frauds. Red Flags for weak internal controls often involve their lack of integration in the organization or their performance. External and internal auditors are crucial to the success of an organization because they have the highest level of insight over internal controls. Such Red Flags include:

- Internal audit staff not reporting to the board of directors or its audit committee
- Any indications that management is trying to control or inhibit communications from internal audit staff to the board of directors
- A reduction of or increased turnover in internal audit staff
- Internal audit not meeting the audit schedule or not adequately covering significant risk areas
- A significant decrease in the audit budget
- Unexplained or unexpected changes in external auditor or significant changes in the audit program
- Internal or external auditors relying heavily on the other's conclusions
- Audit reports not addressing identified internal control weaknesses
- Significant deficiencies in internal controls noted in audit reports that have not been corrected
- A qualified, adverse, or disclaimer opinion from an external auditor
- The inability of management to provide timely and accurate financial, operational, and regulatory reports

Financial Red Flags

Financial Red Flags result from financial ratio analysis or the observation of phenomena that have been found to be correlated to financial fraud schemes. Such Red Flags include:

- Recurring negative cash flows from operations while reporting positive earnings or even earnings growth
- Unusual growth in the number-of-days sales in accounts receivables
- Unusual surge in sales by a minority of units within the organization or surge in sales by corporate headquarters
- Unusual growth and profitability, especially compared to that of other companies in the same industry—not only is rapid growth a Red Flag for fraud in itself, it also coincides regularly with weaknesses in internal control systems if growth achieved through acquisition and integration of internal controls tends to lag behind
- Unusual increase in gross margin or gross margins in excess of industry peers
- Unusual decline in the number-of-days purchases in accounts payables
- Significant declines in customer demand and increasing business failures in the industry
- Assets based on significant estimates that involve subjective judgments or uncertainties that are difficult to corroborate
- Declining allowances for bad debts or excess or obsolete inventories
- Unusual change in the relationship between fixed assets and depreciation
- Increases in fixed assets, while the industry is reducing its capital intensity

Transactional Red Flags

Transactional Red Flags relate to anomalies in certain types of transactions that can indicate the use of structures to perpetrate financial statement fraud schemes:

- Significant levels of transactions with entities in tax haven countries
- Subsidiaries in tax haven jurisdictions
- Significant level of transactions with organizations not subject to audit requirements
- Significant sales volume with entities whose substance and ownership is not known

- Existence of legal entities without perceived relationship to core business activities
- Accumulation of significant transactions close to period end
- Existence of significant numbers of transactions whose reasons and structures are difficult to comprehend or justify

EMPIRICAL EVIDENCE: RED FLAGS IN FINANCIAL STATEMENT FRAUD CASES

Over time, a number of empirical studies of financial statement fraud cases have provided indications about typical Red Flags, which were observed in actual cases.[*]

Most cases of financial statement fraud show a high degree of dominance in top management by one individual or a small group of individuals. This typically leads to blocking and overriding of controls by other members of senior management.

There often are weaknesses in control.

Stakeholders' expectations, when too ambitious, can cause management attempts to satisfy such overly ambitious expectations. This can be particularly damaging when stakeholder expectations are expressed in metric criteria, based on specific financial statement ratios.

It was observed that in more than a third of the surveyed cases, the profitability of companies with manipulated financial statements was inconsistent with the standard in their sectors. Companies with manipulated financial statements also had a disproportionately higher level of bankruptcies than others in their industry sector. On the other side if this spectrum, rapid growth that is inconsistent with industry standards falls into the same general category.

Large numbers of complex transactions also appear to be conducive to financial statement frauds. Complex transactions absorb a lot of time and can also be intimidating to auditors. Pride can lead auditors not to attempt to audit the transactions in detail as they might have to admit that

[*] James Loebbecke, Martha Eining, and James Wiilingham. 1989. Auditors' experience with material irregularities: Frequency, nature and detectability. *Auditing: A Journal of Practice and Theory* 8:1–28; Committee of Sponsoring Organizations of the Treadway Commission. 2010. Fraudulent financial reporting 1998–2007. An analysis of US public companies, Durham, NC; Committee of Sponsoring Organizations of the Treadway Commission. 1999. Fraudulent financial reporting 1987–1997, an analysis of US public companies, Durham, NC; The Committee of Sponsoring Organizations of the Treadway Commission (COSO): Fraudulent financial reporting: 1998–2007.

they do not understand them. Auditing complex financial products falls into this category.

When a company has to rely heavily on estimates for balances of otherwise insignificant accounts, this, too, lends itself to manipulations. Balances based on percentage of completion considerations, in particular in the construction industry, are typical examples for this. In particular, when paired with strong dependence of a company's financial performance on individual transactions, this showed increased risks of manipulation.

Other noteworthy examples of empirically observed Red Flags are cash flow shortages and rapidly changing industries.

PREVENTION VERSUS DETECTION

When it comes to financial statement fraud, there are two overarching categories of Red Flags:

- Those that are preventive
- Those that can minimize and mitigate the potential damage of fraud

Behavioral, situational, and organizational Red Flags are preventive in nature. Financial and transactional Red Flags, on the other hand, are helpful for detecting fraud and minimizing potential damage if prevention fails.

The drawback of financial and transactional Red Flags is that they may be uncovered just when a corporation is about to disclose financial information. This would put a board of directors in a tough spot because it takes time to investigate the Red Flags. This, in itself, is highly problematic because delayed disclosure regularly leads to a drop in share prices.

If, on the other hand, suspected false financial information is disclosed, the board of directors and, in particular, the audit committee can be held liable. If disclosure is postponed, and an in-depth investigation does not produce hard evidence of false financial information, the board might be held liable for causing a drop in share prices due to hesitant behavior.

In essence, it is highly desirable that all preventive measures be taken so that a board of directors avoids facing such decisions.

PREVENTING FINANCIAL STATEMENT FRAUD

A COSO study published in 2010 contains important insights into the deficient control environment of companies that experienced financial statement fraud.* Top senior executives were frequently involved. In 72% of the cases, the chief executive officer (CEO) and, in 65% of cases, the chief financial officer (CFO) were associated with the financial statement fraud. In 89% of the cases, the CEO and/or the CFO was associated with the financial statement fraud. Other individuals observed as being involved included controllers, chief operating officers, other senior vice presidents, and board members.

The role of the audit committee was also addressed in the COSO study and it had changed substantially over the previous decade. A study for the period 1987–1997 showed that

- Most audit committees of the surveyed perpetrators of financial statement fraud only met about once a year.
- Some companies had no audit committee.
- When there was an audit committee, most committee members did not appear to be certified in accounting or have current or prior work experience in key accounting or finance positions.

A more recent study covering the period 1998–2007 provides a different picture. Companies exposed to financial statement frauds had audit committees just as often as companies not exposed to financial statement frauds. The average audit committee had three members for both groups and, on average, audit committees met four times in a financial year.

The previous study for 1987–1997 also came to the conclusion that boards of directors were dominated by insiders and "gray" directors with significant equity ownership and apparently little experience or additional education to serve as directors of other companies. A gray director is defined as an individual who is considered an outsider but has a relationship to the company or its management. Collectively, the directors and officers owned nearly one-third of the companies' stock. Changes in requirements for stock exchange listings led to findings of a different kind—namely, that governance characteristics are only slightly different between nonfraud companies and companies caught in financial statement frauds.

At first sight, the studies and the evolution of their respective findings provide a picture of progress. But they also show a troubling conclusion upon more detailed reflection. Many of the governance changes

---

* The Committee of Sponsoring Organizations of the Treadway Commission (COSO): Fraudulent financial reporting: 1998–2007, http://www.coso.org/documents/COSOFRAUDSTUDY2010_001.pdf (accessed June 21, 2013).

considered to be important to curb fraud were implemented during the period of the most recent study. Yet, financial statement fraud not only still occurred, but also caused more damage than ever: "The size of the cumulative misstatement or misappropriation in the current study was substantially larger than the cumulative misstatement or misappropriation summarized in COSO's 1999 study."[*]

Financial statement fraud is typically perpetrated with the goal of enhancing the economic appearance of a company by covering high levels of debts or lost assets. There also may be benefits resulting directly from the fraud by selling stock and receiving performance bonuses. Management also benefits indirectly from financial statement fraud when it is used to inflate the selling price of a company. The COSO study supports this finding.

The Association of Certified Fraud Examiners sets out detailed advice and counsel regarding the prevention of financial statement fraud. It is based on Donald Cressey's research, outlined in Chapter 3.

According to Dr. Donald R. Cressey's "Fraud Triangle," people commit fraud when they are under financial or social pressure, have an opportunity to gain funds undetected, and can rationalize their actions. Any attempt to prevent financial statement fraud should focus on these three factors.

Reduce the Situational Pressures That Encourage Statement Fraud

The core situational pressure involves the earnings expectations. To avoid it, the expectation should not be set at an unachievable level. In a world of proxies, earnings goal setting is often left to what could be described as swarm intelligence—namely, expectations by analysts. It might therefore not be accessible to modification. What can, however, be changed are direct expectations by shareholders. Carefully evaluated and set goals can keep the pressures up without making it impossible to achieve the goals by legal means.

Accounting personnel should not be exposed to external pressures in the preparation of financial statements. This is more of an organizational precaution, which lends itself to monitoring by the board of directors. Establishing clear and uniform accounting procedures with no exception clauses can contribute to the avoidance of unreasonable pressures.

---

[*] Ibid.

When there are operational obstacles blocking effective financial performance, such as working capital restraints, excess production volume, or inventory restraints, that may be beyond control of management held accountable for the financial performance, such blockages should be removed or the goals should be adjusted for the existence of such constraints.

Reduce the Opportunity to Commit Financial Statement Fraud

Reducing the opportunity to manipulate financial results starts with maintaining accurate and complete internal accounting records, an organizational measure. This should go hand in hand with establishing a physical security system to secure company assets, including finished goods, cash, capital equipment, tools, and other valuable items.

Separation of duties by dividing important functions between employees has been a time-proven tool and is part of any core control activity over the integrity of financial information.

Business transactions and interpersonal relationships of suppliers, buyers, purchasing agents, sales representatives, and others who interface in the transactions between financial units need to be monitored carefully and should be subject to employees providing written confirmations of their independence.

Strong supervisory and leadership relationships as well as team values should be encouraged within groups to ensure enforcement of accounting procedures.

Reduce Rationalization of Fraud—Strengthen Employee Personal Integrity

Leading by example is a management principle so fundamental that it should not need to be mentioned. Yet, it is often ignored—in particular when there is dishonesty in business dealings. Dishonest acts by management, even if they are directed at targets outside the organization, can create a dishonest environment and a perception of acceptability that can be used to rationalize other illicit business activities by employees or external contacts.

In addition to leadership by example, honest and dishonest behavior should be formally defined in company policies. The question of how to handle controversial areas in accounting procedures must be dealt with in organizational policies and procedures. Communicating clearly that manipulation of financial statements is not tolerated and that viola-tions will lead to civil and criminal action can help reduce the possibility to rationalize.

CONCLUSION

The past two chapters have examined financial statement fraud and the Red Flags most frequently associated with it. We will now turn to examin-ing another high-risk area of fraud: Procurement.

7

Procurement Fraud

INTRODUCTION

After examining how financial statement fraud is perpetrated and the Red Flags most frequently associated with it, we now turn to examining a high-risk area: procurement. This chapter introduces the reader to the nuts and bolts of the procurement process, including its vulnerabilities and controls.

OVERVIEW OF PROCUREMENT FRAUD

The procurement process is how all entities—regardless of whether they are publicly held, private, not for profit, or governmental—acquire the goods and services they need to maintain their operational requirements. In some cases, procurement contracts will be the main source of income for a corporation; for others, they will be an incidental process to support their main operational activity. While this process tends to be on the less glamorous side of most businesses, it does have a significant impact on the profitability of an organization. In addition, it is also high risk and susceptible to fraud and corruption. Procurement in this respect can extend from the purchase of office supplies to the construction of a complex office building.

Procurement contracts have among the highest incidences of fraud, including bid-rigging and corruption, over any other type of transaction within an organization. A 2011 survey in the UK by the Chartered

Institute of Purchasing and Supply found that 10% of respondents had suffered at least one procurement fraud in the previous year.[*]

A study by the Association of Certified Fraud Examiners found that billing schemes—that is, any scheme in which a person deceptively causes his or her employer to issue a fraudulent payment—were involved in one in four cases reviewed.[†]

Fraudulent procurement contracts are usually detected after they have been committed. However, many of these improper or fraudulent activities could be prevented if officers and directors had been more vigilant in detecting Red Flags in the process of preparing and examining the budgets and financial statements.

Directors and audit committee members are encouraged to adopt the Red Flag approach outlined in this chapter to begin the process of fraud detection.

TYPES OF CONTRACTS

To understand the nature and characteristics of procurement fraud, it is useful to begin by examining the procurement function. It is essential to understand the inner workings of procurement to detect Red Flags of possible fraudulent activities:

- **Construction contracts** are for the construction, repair, renovation, or restoration of any work and include, for example, the erection of a building or structure, demolition of a building or structure, road or highway construction, airport construction, hydrodam construction, paving, and excavating or clearing land.
- **Goods contracts** are agreements for the purchase of articles, commodities, equipment, goods, materials, or supplies. Goods contracts would include, for example, the following: purchase of office supplies; purchase of furniture, computers, and software; purchase of automobiles and other transportation vehicles; purchase of construction equipment, such as tractors,

---

[*] Finance & Management, "Tightening the chain on fraud," September 2012. http://www.cips.org/Documents/Knowledge/fraud_in_the_supply%20chain_.pdf (accessed July 23, 2013).

[†] Association of Certified Fraud Examiners. 2012. Report to the nations on occupational fraud and abuse: 2012 Global fraud study, Austin, TX.

bulldozers, and other building material; and purchase of movable buildings.

- **Services contracts** are agreements to provide either consulting or nonconsulting services, but they do not include employment contracts. Services contracts include consulting services contracts for the provision of advice, studies, or investigations and usually provide for the submission of a report, findings, and/or recommendations.
- **Professional services contracts** are for services provided by individuals who are qualified professionals, such as lawyers, accountants, and scientific or technical people like engineers or environmental experts.
- **Nonconsulting contracts** are for services other than for the provision of advice, findings, or recommendations. These would include plumbers, electricians, and other trade experts who install, repair, or carry out a particular task.
- **Real estate contracts** are contracts for the purchase of nonmovable buildings and land.
- **Leases or rental contracts** are agreements to provide leasehold interest in real property, such as lands or buildings, including tenancy agreements to lease a house or apartment or to obtain lodging. They would also include agreements to rent or lease any equipment or movable property such as an automobile or vessel.
- **Marine construction and ship building contracts** include the construction of docks, wharfs, oil rigs, ships, and marine vessels. This would include dredging river- and lakebeds for improved ship navigation.

Competitive and Noncompetitive Contracts

All contracts awarded by corporations or government are either competitive or noncompetitive:

- A competitive contract is one where two or more valid bids are sought and received. Either the lowest bid or the bid providing best value will be accepted. The two parties subsequently enter into a contract.
- A noncompetitive contract is one for which bids were not solicited or, if bids were solicited, the conditions of a competitive contract were not met.

Many government regulations require that all contracts be awarded through the competitive process. The public often believes that non-competitive contracts are more vulnerable to fraud and collusion than are competitive contracts. In this chapter we will show that both types of contacts are equally vulnerable to fraud and bribery.

METHODS FOR PRICING PROCUREMENT CONTRACTS

There are three main pricing methods for contracts:

1. *Fixed fee or firm fee:* In these types of contracts, the total fee is a fixed lump sum or an amount made up of fixed unit prices. In such cases, both parties agree on the price to be paid before the contract is awarded, and no deviations are allowed regardless of the number of units used in the contracting process.
2. *Fixed cost per unit:* A fixed price per unit is specified as the total payable for each individually specified unit. The total amount of the contract is then determined by multiplying the units supplied by the fixed price. Units will refer to such components as labor hours, material supplied, and another item that is specifically identified.
3. *Cost plus:* A contractor receives actual costs incurred plus an agreed fixed fee (or a percentage of cost), which could represent the contractor's profit. A cost-plus contract may also include a set fee or cost for the service portion of the contract and an additional amount for the actual cost of specified goods the contractor has to install or deliver. The goods are often available from one particular manufacturer or supplier.

PROCUREMENT METHODS

While there are many different types of procurement methods for goods and services, the following are the most common:

- Local purchase orders
- Standing offers
- Specific contracts

Local purchase orders are the most frequent types of procurement purchases and tend to be for low-value goods and services. These purchases are usually approved by lower level managers and are made by the material management staff through a local purchase order (LPO). The dollar value limits for LPOs are usually outlined in directives and policy.

Standing offers are agreements with suppliers to provide goods and services on demand, according to set terms and conditions. This type of contract could include legal services and emergency services such as trade professionals including plumbers and electricians.

Specific contracts include most other situations that do not fit into either of the preceding categories. For example, a party may require a special item, good, or piece of real estate that is only available from one supplier or seller. In this situation, seller and purchaser negotiate the specific terms of the contract.

STAGES OF PROCUREMENT CONTRACTS

There are three stages in most procurement contracts:

1. Requirements definition
2. Bidding and/or selection
3. Contract performance and evaluation

Requirements Definition Stage

This the most important phase in the contracting process because it sets out in great detail the contract's specifications. It will also reflect the budget and the time line for the delivery of the goods and services being acquired and the penalties for failure to meet the contract requirements. The subphases of this stage include:

- Identifying the requirements
- Specifying the requirements
- Assessing alternatives to meet the requirements
- Preparing users' requests to assess the specifications
- Examining the procurement planning process

The procurement process can be manipulated to favor a particular supplier, contractor, or product at this stage because the specifications detail is what is required from the contractor. Under such circumstances, a competitive bid may be useless, because the process has been rigged to ensure that only one party will be able to meet the requirements or specifications of the proposed procurement successfully.

Key Control Features for the Requirements Definition Stage

The following are essential controls to prevent fraud at the requirements definition stage:

- Ensure that the needs are appropriately defined and clearly linked to the objectives of the proposed procurements.
- Ensure that there is a detailed statement of the specifications, including such things as compliance with relevant standards and requirements regarding performance, quality, time line, and cost.
- Ensure that a detailed schedule is developed for the cost-effective management of the procurement process.
- Ensure that alternatives to meeting the requirements are identified and assessed, including with regard to cost, viability, and time lines.
- Ensure that the request to proceed with the procurement is properly documented and authorized.

Bidding and/or Selection Stage

The lead role in the bidding and/or selection stage is usually played by staff at a central purchasing and procurement function. Their responsibilities include identifying sources of supply, developing and issuing a request for proposals, analyzing responses, selecting contractors, defining the terms of the contract, and ensuring proper authorizations for the acquisition of the contractor's services.

If line management has conducted the requirements definition phase with one supplier in mind, the bidding and selection process becomes mainly a technical formality rather than an analytical "value-added" step.

The following are subphases of the bidding and selection process, based on the specifications prepared by management:

- Preparation of specifications
- Preparation of tender documents
- Decision on distribution of tenders (by invitation or public)
- Preselection and evaluation of contractors
- Tender solicitation
- Receipt of bids
- Bid evaluation
- Contract approval and award

Key Control Features in the Bidding and/or Selection Stage
The following are essential controls to prevent fraud at the bidding and/or selection stage:

- When it is cost effective to do so, all qualified firms should have an opportunity to compete for contracts.
- Possible relationships between management and bidders should be scrutinized.
- In an "invitation only" bidding process, each invitee must be closely examined for possible relationships, and thus possible collusion, between the company and the winning bidder.
- Specifications should directly meet the actual needs specified by the company.
- Critical information not included in the tender documents, including budgets, should be held on a highly confidential basis.
- Unusual or unnecessary conditions in the tender documents must be closely scrutinized.
- The distribution of bid submissions must be handled in a highly controlled environment and all information must be maintained on a need-to-know basis.
- Any decision to cancel the bidding process and for new tenders requires additional scrutiny and control.

Contract Performance and Evaluation Stage

This stage of the procurement process ensures that the contract meets the time, cost, and performance criteria specified in the contract or the requirements definition.

Material management staff will usually have the responsibility for contract evaluation. They should ensure that financial controls, such as signing authorities and separation of duties, are enforced. When required, they receive progress reports on the financial status of the contract and ensure that line management receives technical reports. They also resolve contract disputes and ensure that any necessary contract amendments receive appropriate scrutiny. Individual contracts should be monitored to ensure that the contract met all policy and procedural requirements as specified.

In the case of service contracts, line managers have an integral role to play. They are responsible for the day-to-day management of the contract and the certifications that services have been received.

The following are subphases of the contract performance and evaluation stage:

- Contract monitoring
- Contractor and technical evaluation
- Progress reports
- Financial controls
- Dispute resolution
- Contract amendments and add-ons

Key Control Features in the Performance and Evaluation Stage

The following are essential controls to prevent fraud at the contract performance and evaluation stage:

- Contracts should be administered in accordance with appropriate policies and procedures and in a manner that is consistent with accepted financial controls.
- Pursuant to a set schedule, the contractor should provide progress reports on the financial and technical status of the contract.
- Bid protests and contract disputes should be appropriately addressed and resolved in a timely manner by an independent person or unit.
- Contracts should not be amended or altered unless it can be documented that the amendments are in the best interest of your organization.
- Contract performance should be monitored and evaluated to ensure that the contract meets the identified requirements.

CONCLUSION

This chapter has introduced the reader to the "nuts and bolts" of the procurement process, including its vulnerabilities and controls. It sets the stage for an understanding of how procurement fraud is perpetrated and its attendant Red Flags.

8

Procurement Fraud
Methods and Red Flags

INTRODUCTION

This chapter introduces the reader to how procurement fraud is perpetrated and its attendant Red Flags.

PROCUREMENT FRAUD AND ITS RED FLAGS

Red Flags that indicate procurement fraud may exist at any stage of the contracting process. Whether at the budget, award, or performance stage, Red Flags that indicate and establish fraudulent activity may have criminal, civil, contractual, and/or administrative ramifications on everyone involved.

Company directors will most likely rely on management and auditors to detect the Red Flags. However, by understanding the nature of the contracting process as well as being able to identify when managers and employees may be a party to a procurement fraud, they will be able to develop tools to tackle this very difficult and complex issue.

What makes such cases so difficult and complex is the depth of employee involvement. In many cases, employees or management have solicited or accepted personal benefits and been corruptly influenced by the contractor. In other cases, they may even have a financial interest in the ownership of the contractor's organization. There have been situations where employees or managers of the organization have secretly owned and even controlled the contracting company.

These kinds of insider relationships can be extremely difficult to detect, unless Red Flags are identified and fully investigated.

It is a commonly held belief that contracts that are put out for competitive competition through the bidding/tendering process will provide the best value for the expenditures incurred and will be free of fraud and collusion. It is also widely believed that contracts that are solely sourced are more susceptible to fraud, collusion, and bribery. Fraud investigations over the years have shown that this common belief is not necessarily true. Sole-source contracting is a legitimate method of procurement and can produce better results than a tendered contract, especially when collusive bidding is involved.

Many factors come into play when company insiders or public officials become party to fraud and bribery. We will deal with bribery and corruption of both public and nonpublic officials in greater detail in the next chapter.

Whether the contract is solely sourced or put through the process of competitive bidding is no guarantee that one process will be more susceptible to fraud than the other. Many contractors have not only provided benefits to company insiders and public officials to elevate them into favored positions when preparing and presenting bids, but have also teamed up with their competitors in collusive agreements to eliminate competition.

In this section we will identify some of the schemes that have been used and outline the Red Flags that may be present to indicate certain types of fraud, collusion, and corruption.

PROCUREMENT MANIPULATION SCHEMES

Collusive Bidding or Bid Rigging

Collusive bidding, or bid fixing, is a fraudulent activity that involves an agreement between two or more parties involved in a procurement contract to arrange secretly for one supplier to win the contract. The arrangements are made to make it appear that a competitive and honest process of awarding a contract has taken place. It may on occasion be carried out without the knowledge or the assistance of the employees or officers of the party calling for the contract by tender. However, often these schemes are combined with bribery and corruption of employees and officers to ensure that the appropriate selection process is followed during the invitation to bid.

Groups of prospective contractors enter into an agreement or arrangement to eliminate or limit competition. For example, a group of contractors agrees in private that one of them will bid lower on a particular contract, while the others will submit complementary high bids. These agreements are usually ongoing and may often be governed by territorial limits or by rotation.

In particular, Red Flags indicating collusive bidding will include the following variations:

- Bid suppression
- Bid rotation
- Complementary bidding
- Subcontracting
- Contract splitting
- Contract bundling

Red Flags of Collusive Bidding or Bid Rigging

Bid suppression occurs when contractors in a region are successful in keeping outside contractors from bidding on contracts. This may be done through bribing employees to limit or restrict advertising the project and the request for tenders. It can also be done by arranging for a short time period between advertising date and the closing date.

Bid rotation will commonly show successive bidding by the conspirators on contracts. The lowest bidder on one contract may become the high bidder on the next contract tender call. Collusive bidders may follow territorial strengths to decide who will bid low and who will bid high in which territory. In this situation, the same contractor will always have the low bid in a specific territory.

Complementary bids will contain a higher price and the bid will not necessarily comply with the specifications. The details in this type of tender will not have much detail. The bidder will include a bulk material such as nonrelevant brochures and other nonessential documents to bulk up the submission.

Other schemes that are identified by Red Flags include:

- One or more of the unsuccessful bidders become subcontractors after the contract is awarded. Contractors who would normally bid alone become subcontractors or joint venture partners.
- Bid prices are reduced when a new contractor becomes involved in the bidding process.
- Bid prices are separated by an equal percentage difference.

- Losing bidders cannot be located, have no telephone or e-mail contact information, and address information is vague or misleading. All this indicates that a fictitious company may have submitted a complementary bid.
- Winning bidder rents equipment from the losing bidders.
- There is public or private information that an industry or sector is controlled by organized crime.
- There are forged bid and performance bonds.
- False financial statements are submitted to prove capability to perform the contract.

Red Flags Indicating Corruption and Bribery in the Collusive Bidding Process

- Advertising for tenders is done on a restricted basis. Ads are placed in limited locations to which only some contractors have access.
- There is a short time period between tender call and bid closing date. Only favored contractors are able to bid, having been provided with the contract specifications at an earlier date.
- The invitation to bid is sent only to certain contractors and other qualified contractors are not invited.
- Bids are opened in private or opened early before the bid closing date, indicating that bid prices may have been released to the favored bidder.
- The lowest and potentially the successful bid contains information that closely resembles confidential information on price and favored methods of performing the project work.
- Specifications are tailored. Restrictive specifications fit the capability of a specific contractor:
  - Specifications call for bid bonds or performance bonds that only one bonding company can issue. An insider of that company is also involved in the bribery and collusive bidding scheme and will release information on the bid prices to the favored contractor.
  - Other requirements in the specifications will direct bidders to one location to release bid information with the same results as the bid bond issue.
  - Requirements are that only one supplier/manufacturer may supply the required items or goods. Each bidder will be required to seek pricing from that one supplier. The supplier/manufacturer

may decrease prices to a favored bidder and increase the price to the other bidders.

- There is a requirement for an excessive amount of bid and performance bonds, for the sole purpose of limiting the number of contractors that would be able to acquire the bonds.
- There is a requirement for excessive net worth of contractors relating to contract performance capability.
- Change orders are implemented after the tender has been awarded. They provide that additional funds are paid to the successful contractor. These additional funds will make up for a low bid that was previously arranged and promised.

- Conflict of interest and corporate ownership are suggested:
    - Employee or manager is related to the owner of a favored bidder.
    - Employee or manager has a secret financial interest in the company that is a favored bidder.
    - Employee or manager secretly owns company that is a favored bidder.
    - Employees have been offered future employment with successful bidder.
    - Employee is a member of same club, group, or church as favored bidder.
    - Employee is intimidated or pressured into providing confidential information.

Example of Schemes to Defraud through Collusive Bidding and Bid Rigging: A Dredging Industry Case

A federal government agency advertised that it would receive sealed bids from qualified bidders for a contract to dredge portions of the St. Lawrence River bordering Canada and the United States.

The river is used by ocean-going vessels to transport goods up the St. Lawrence River to the Great Lakes as far west and north as Lake Superior. The river has numerous locks to allow big ship navigation. From time to time because of the action of the water in the river, portions of the navigable channels become heavily silted. This means that the larger ships will run aground unless the silt is removed. This removal of silt is called dredging.

From time to time, this government agency, responsible for navigation on the river, called for tenders to dredge certain areas of the shipping channels on the river. Historically, five major contractors were capable of performing this work.

Capability to complete the contract was determined by the type of equipment each company owned or controlled. Large dredges are unique pieces of equipment that are expensive to manufacture and costly to use and maintain, particularly when the equipment would only be used over a short period of time during the spring, summer, and fall seasons. Government agencies that control the navigation regularly offer major dredging contracts on the river, lakes, and harbors in this area, which is collectively known as the St. Lawrence Seaway.

These five contractors had been involved in the initial construction of the seaway when the channels were deepened and widened and the locks built. Even though there was enough work for all the contractors during this construction phase, they decided at that time to split up the territory, where each one would end up with a specific territory along the river. Any tendered contracts for work in one area would be offered to all five; however, by an ongoing collusive agreement, the favored contractor would be allowed to bid low and the others would submit complementary bids.

Each of the complementary bidders would receive a percentage of the contract price, which would then be added to the low bidder's tender price. The successful bidder would then pay the agreed amounts to the other companies for their complementary bids. These payments were made through the submission of false invoices. Every marine construction contract was arranged in this manner during the construction phase.

Following the completion of the seaway, the same companies entered into a similar type of arrangement when bidding on any dredging or marine construction work. Over 55 dredging contracts were the subject of collusive bidding. Bribes were paid to public officials whenever necessary in order to maintain control of this collusive bidding scheme. The use of false invoices became the favored method of paying bribes to public officials as well as paying the other companies for complementary bids.

One enterprising harbor commissioner became aware of the bid-fixing scheme that had been in operation along the seaway. When a large marine construction and dredging project was being planned in his harbor, he decided that he wanted a piece of the action. He made contact with one of the companies and negotiated a bribe payment in return for information on how much the budget would bear on the upcoming work.

The favored contractor received the information and negotiated the amount of the bribe with the harbor commissioner. It was agreed that payment would be made through the upcoming purchase of a ship that was in the process of being transferred from a third company to the favored contractor's company. Since the price of the ship had already been negotiated between the parties, it was agreed that the sale would be made to a front man for the commissioner. This person was a retired banker and a close friend of the commissioner.

The ship was sold to him by the third party and then resold to the favored contractor by the banker for an amount that included both the original purchase price and the bribe payment. Both the purchase and sale transactions occurred simultaneously, so the banker did not have to provide the initial purchase payment, but simply received the amount of the bribe payment from this transaction.

The banker then received the funds and, through his connections at his former bank, had the funds transferred to a secret foreign bank account, where the funds were converted to cash and placed in a safety deposit box, under the control of the harbor commissioner. The retired banker received a fee for his services.

Both the retired banker and the harbor commissioner were subsequently prosecuted for bribery and both sentenced to prison terms. The retired banker remained loyal to his friend the harbor commissioner throughout the trial and sentencing process.

The harbor commission accepted the low bid by the favored contractor. This occurred prior to the arrest and conviction of the harbor commissioner. This contractor was able to obtain the total amount budgeted for this project.

The contractor paid the other bidders for their accommodation bid by receiving false invoices for the rental of equipment. One invoice on a dredging project was for the rental of a dredge that was owned by the complementary bidder. A monthly fee was paid for the dredge, which was allegedly working on the dredging site all summer.

In fact, the dredge never left its home harbor during that period. Other false equipment rental invoices were paid in much the same way. More than 16 officials and corporations were prosecuted and most convicted following a judge and jury trial that lasted more than 1 year. Fines and prison terms were issued in this case.[*]

Example of Schemes to Defraud through Collusive Bidding and Bid Rigging: A Construction Case

This case involved a major construction project in a small country in the Americas. The contracting party was an agency of government. The multimillion dollar project consisted of clearing land, building roads and paved areas, and the construction of a large building.

---

[*] *R. v. McNamara et al.* (No.1) (1981), 56 CCC (2nd) 193 (Ont. CA).

This project was split into more than 15 separate contracts. Most of the contracts were tendered and bids were requested from short-listed contractors. A few contracts were offered on a sole-source basis. Several high-ranking government officials became personally involved in directing and overseeing various parts of the contract, even though the project was not part of their portfolio. One company became the favored contractor.

The president and chief executive officer of this company happened to be a close personal friend of the high-ranking public officials. He was also closely connected to a major bonding company in the country. In fact, one of the executives of the bonding company was a silent partner/investor in the favored construction company. The company had never undertaken any project of the size and magnitude being offered in this project. It had very few full-time employees and did not have the equipment that would be required in any of the contracts forming part of this project. In addition, the company did not have the financial capability to undertake any of the contracts being offered.

During the course of preparing the specifications, the tendering process, and the performance of the various contracts, there were numerous Red Flags that indicated collusive bidding, bid-fixing, bribery, and fraud.

The specifications set out a requirement that all bidders had to provide bid bonds and performance bonds that exceeded the usual level. The bonds could only be obtained from a domestic bonding company that restricted the choice to only one domestic company. The specifications also provided for an unusually high company financial capability. These two items were so restrictive that it eliminated a number of potential bidders.

The favorite contractor was able to falsify the company financial statements to make it appear that the company's financial position was within the requirements called for in the specifications. In addition, the company had no difficulty obtaining the necessary bid or performance bonds. A number of competent and capable contractors did not enter the bidding process because of the financial and bonding requirements in the specifications.

All the bids by the various companies tendering on the contracts were required to be submitted to the one domestic bonding company that had a financial relationship with the favorite contractor. The bid information and price were provided to the favorite contractor, which was able to adjust its bid to be lower than all the others.

In one contract that was offered by tender, several bids were received. Because of some unusual circumstances, it was not clear which of the bidders had the lowest bid. The tender was scrapped and retendered so that the favorite contractor could be certain that its bid was, in fact, the lowest.

The favorite contractor was successful in bidding lower than any other bidder in every contract. Numerous change orders were made after the contract was awarded, which significantly increased the initial cost estimates.

The favorite contractor was able to manipulate the contract work with the concurrence of the public officials. This allowed the company to increase profits by maximizing income and minimizing the quality of the work performed.

The favored contractor set up a fictitious invoice scheme that moved funds from this project to secret offshore bank accounts. These funds were used to benefit the public officials and the bonding company executive.

Contract Splitting

A project that would normally be put out for tenders is split up into various contracts in order to bypass policy or regulations and allows employees or managers fraudulently to sole-source the contracts to a favorite contractor. This scheme is used when employees and managers cannot control the bidding process to benefit a favorite contractor.

Many of the Red Flags that are listed under the "Collusive Bidding" section will apply to this type of scheme. But there are some additional Red Flags that apply more particularly to contract splitting:

- Numerous contracts for smaller amounts are issued for the same project, which was budgeted as one project.
- There are questionable relationships between employees and favorite contractors and suppliers.
- Contracts that were previously bundled into one contract are split into several smaller ones.
- Goods that were ordered in certain quantities are split into smaller quantities from different suppliers.

Contract Splitting—Case Example

A public official was planning to leave his government position and enter the private sector. He was offered a high-ranking position with a company that periodically bid on procurement contracts that the public official supervised. A major construction project was being planned in his department that would normally have been tendered in one contract. Under government policy for this size of contract, the entire tendering process would have to be supervised by an outside committee.

In order to control the bidding process, the public official split the project into five contracts. Under the existing policy, each contract could now be totally controlled by the public official. Needless to say, all of the five contracts were awarded through a tendered bidding process to his favorite contractor.

Contract Bundling

This is the opposite of contract splitting. In this scheme, contracts that were normally separate are bundled together so that, instead of going to sole-source contractors, they are put forward as a tendered contract. In this situation, an employee or manager has more control to award the contract to a favorite contractor through the bidding process.

Again, many of the Red Flags listed in this chapter will apply to this scheme. But there are some additional Red Flags that are particular to contract bundling:

- Employees have control over the collusive bidding process, indicating a conflicted relationship with contractors involved in the bidding system.
- The goods or services that are involved in the one contract are not related.
- Smaller contractors, who would normally bid, are unable to do so because of the larger bundled contract.

Contract Bundling—Case Example

A senior official of a public company was responsible for planning and awarding contracts for the construction of shopping plazas. All the contracts related to one shopping plaza were historically offered by tender and were broken into various segments. One contract would be for land preparation. This involved clearing trees and preparing the area for the upcoming construction work. The next contract would be for preparing and paving the parking lot. The final contract was for the construction of the building.

One major shopping plaza was planned for a region that was historically controlled by an organized crime group. This crime group was also involved in the construction business. The crime group wanted the entire contract and approached the company official and lobbied for the three contracts to be bundled into one.

For reasons that are unknown, the senior official complied with the request and only one contract was prepared for tender. Three contractors submitted bids; however, the contact was awarded to the organized crime group's construction company.

Red Flags That Identify Billing Schemes Suggesting Corruption, Fraud, and Theft in the Procurement Process

Over the years many different schemes have been developed to provide benefits to contractors and to corrupt employees by using the procurement process to conceal the payment of personal benefits and to provide profits to contractors who are involved in the collusive contracting schemes. They include:

- Organized crime's control of an industrial sector or territory
- Comingling contracts
- Duplicate contract payments
- Defective pricing
- False invoices

Control by Organized Crime of an Industry or Territory

We know that organized crime groups control many illegal activities in North America and around the world. They certainly have control over illicit drug production and trafficking, prostitution, and smuggling of licit and illicit products. While involved in many traditional criminal activities, occasionally in some jurisdictions they also control normal business and commercial activity. There are jurisdictions where organized criminals have taken control of highway and bridge construction.[*] In other jurisdictions, they have taken over all commercial activity in waterfront and harbor areas[†] or the waste disposal business.[‡]

Corporations wishing to participate in procurement contracts in areas or jurisdictions controlled by organized crime must employ the same tactics to avoid getting ensnared in corrupt schemes as those recommended for high-risk countries where corruption is part of the local culture.

---

[*] Justice France Charbonneau, the head of the public inquiry into allegations of corruption in Quebec's construction industry.

[†] North Jersey and New York seaport industry. New Jersey Senate Hearings, 2012.

[‡] Federal prosecutors indicted twenty-nine people in an alleged organized-crime conspiracy to control commercial-waste disposal businesses in New York and New Jersey using intimidation, extortion, and violence. *US v. Franco*, 13-cr-015, *US v. Giustra*, 13-CR-014, *US v. Lopez*, 13-cr-015, US District Court, Southern District of New York (Manhattan), 2013.

The problems, procedures, and Red Flags are described in detail in Chapter 9.

Control by Organized Crime of an Industry or Territory—Example

One major organized group owned and controlled all the companies that installed drywall used in the construction of houses and other buildings. Every construction project that required the installation of drywall was completely controlled by this particular group. They received kick-back payments from major construction companies and used differential pricing tactics to control which company would be awarded building contracts.

Comingling Contracts
A contractor bills for the same work in more than one component of the contract. For example, demolition costs are billed four times in separate contracts for construction of the foundation, walls, ceiling, and floors.

Duplicate Contract Payments
The contractor submits two copies of the same invoice for payment or submits more than one original invoice for the same goods or services. In one case example, a contractor found that a public agency had a poor record-keeping system. He accidently submitted a second invoice for services that had already been performed. Realizing that the agency did not notice the duplicate payment, he continued the practice of sending a second invoice as a matter of course. The fraudulent practice was discovered when an internal auditor examined the contract payments.

Defective Pricing
The contractor submits invoices that have been inflated. Some contracts will pay the contractor for some goods that must be provided with the service. The contractor has been awarded the contract and there is an agreed price for the service. However, the contractor may bill for the actual costs for the goods that must be supplied. This type of contract is referred to as a cost-plus contract. When a contractor inflates the price of goods, defective pricing occurs; this practice is a fraudulent practice.

False Invoices
The contractor submits invoices for goods that have not been delivered. In all contracts parties will submit invoices for payment. These invoices

will become part of the contract file. Invoices become a key document that may reveal evidence of fraud. Red Flags relating to false invoices include:

- Time and date on the invoice not commensurate with services rendered and goods delivered
- Frequency of invoices—too many or too few
- Incorrect locations described on the invoice, such as delivery addresses or receiving information
- Anomalous amount on invoices—too high, too low, too consistent, too alike, too different
- Name of supplier or contractor on the invoice—for example, a vague corporate name
- Address of supplier or contractor—either not shown on invoice, fictitious, a mailbox, a virtual office, an office address is that of the home of an employee or relative
- Telephone numbers not shown on invoice or appear to be a cell phone number
- Website generic looking and not consistent with supplier qualified to deliver goods and services or no website
- E-mail address—using Yahoo, Gmail, or other similar e-mail addresses, as opposed to a corporate address

False Representations

The contractor makes misrepresentations of various kinds and for various purposes. False representations are often made about the quality of the products to be supplied by the contractor. Another common false representation will usually concern the contractor's ability to perform the services required in the manner outlined in the specifications.

False Representations—Case Example

Contract specifications issued on a public works contract required that all of the contractors submit details concerning their financial status along with a list of required equipment. One of the bids was from a previously unknown contractor and it contained a financial statement that was completely false. The financial statement contained a certification from a known independent audit firm, which was forged. The equipment list contained equipment that the contractor did not own or possess.

Front-End Loading or Advance Payment Fraud

The contractor inflates costs of the initial contract work so that when the percentage of completion billing method is applied, the contractor receives inflated cash flows relative to the actual work completed. The costs of the later contract work are in fact understated with the anticipation that change orders will be approved to make up for the understatement.

Information Theft

Employees release unauthorized procurement information to third parties. For example, a potential contractor receives information concerning the bids received from competing contractors so that a lower or winning bid can be submitted. Security breaches involving unauthorized computer system access or physical breaking and entry into offices have also been used to gain bid information.

In some cases disgruntled former employees will willingly provide information to competitors and give them confidential information to gain access to protected internal information. Many contractors will engage the services of undercover agents and spies to gain valuable confidential information that will be useful in gaining advantage over the competition.

Information Theft—Case Examples

In a case where a contractor wanted to obtain confidential and protected information from a competitor, it engaged the services of a computer hacker to penetrate the competitor's computer system. The hacker was able to gain access to confidential bidding information that provided method and pricing. With this information the contractor was able to submit the lowest bid and was successful in being awarded the contract.

In another case, a contractor competing in a tendering process used the services of a local organized crime group to secure vital information from a public agency that was preparing an invitation to tender on a major building project.

A key employee involved in a major international procurement contract traveled to a distant location for a tender/bid meeting. After checking into a local hotel, his computer and documents were stolen. The purpose of the theft was obviously to gain information that would assist a competitor.

Local Purchase Order or Split Purchases

The contractor has been engaged to provide goods or services whose costs exceed the amount allowed by policy. The total order is then split into smaller amounts so that the purchase remains within the authority of a particular employee. For example, ten purchase orders are issued over a 2-year period for a total of $100,000. The employee issuing the orders has an authorization limit of $10,000. The purchase should have been covered by a single contract and authorized by a higher authority.

Phantom Contractor

An invoice from a nonexistent company is submitted for payment. This can be done by an employee who then authorizes the payment. Or, it is submitted by an outsider with the expectation that the payment will be automatically authorized. An example would be invoices for look-alike items that are ordered or used on a regular basis. Some examples include local advertising, office supplies, or delivery charges. The amount on the invoice is usually relatively small, but the amounts can be significant because invoices are submitted on a regular basis.

Phantom Contractor—Case Example

A scheme that has been used many times in many jurisdictions involves the submission of forged invoices that resemble the invoices of regular known companies. In this scam, a look-alike invoice is sent out to a company that is known to do regular business with a particular supplier.

In this one case, it involved advertising in a business directory. Every detail in the legitimate invoice was copied, except the address or account where the remittance was to be made. This system worked because the scammers knew that the companies involved would pay by bank check and simply mail the payment to the address listed on the invoice. In many cases the company receiving the phony invoice would discover the false invoice or believe that it had already been paid and simply discard it. However, in most cases the payments were sent out to the benefit of the scammer.*

---

* *May 18, 2010—St. Paul, MN*—The Better Business Bureau of Minnesota and North Dakota (BBB) is warning businesses that Yellow Pages billing scams are making the rounds, and urges all companies to keep a close eye on the invoices they receive—they may have been sent by scammers! What these scammers are counting on is people being too busy to notice they are being tricked into paying a debt they do not owe.

Product Substitution

This refers to goods or services supplied under an existing contract that do not conform to the contract specifications. Some contractors have been accused of using poor-quality building material, such as cement. This scheme often surfaces when bridges, highway overpasses, and tunnels fail.

Product Substitution—Case Example

In the city of Montreal, Canada, road construction contractors have been accused of using inferior products in the construction of the various highway overpasses that have been built over the years. A number of overpasses have failed and cement and steel rods that were used have caused the structures to fail and make them unsafe for future use.

Progress Payment Fraud

The contractor submits invoices for progress payments based on falsified information. In such cases, invoices often include charges for costs that were not incurred.

Purchases for Personal Use

Employees may purchase items intended for their personal use or may make excess purchases of items that are otherwise legitimately acquired.

Time Limitations and Restricted Advertising

Response times for the submission of proposals are so restrictive that only bidders with inside knowledge will have the opportunity to prepare and submit bids. Invitations to bid or to submit proposals are advertised in such a way that many potential bidders or suppliers will not receive the information. This will favor the favorite bidder or supplier who has inside information on the upcoming contract or project.

Time Limitations and Restricted Advertising—Case Example

A paving contract tender offer was being prepared by a public agency. The specifications called for the standard requirements and a number of paving contractors in the area were capable of performing the work.

A prequalification process was called, which meant that all interested parties had to make a very basic submission on capability to be short listed for the tender. The details of the prequalification requirement were advertised in a trade journal that most of the contractors in the area would not receive.

In addition, the time frame only provided 1 week to respond and attend. Only three out of a possible ten contractors attended the meeting and were qualified. It was later proven that the three contractors were involved in a territorial collusive bidding scheme.

Unnecessary Purchases

As illustrated in Table 8.1, each of the three procurement stages has its own particular fraud vulnerabilities.

Table 8.1 Procurement Fraud Matrix

	Requirements Definition Stage	Bidding and Selection Stage	Performance and Evaluation Stage
Bribery	2	1	3
Change order	3	2	1
Comingling	3	2	1
Collusive bidding	2	1	3
Price fixing	2	1	3
Conflict of interest	2	1	3
Duplicate contracts	3	2	1
Defective pricing	3	2	1
False invoices	3	2	1
False representations	3	1	2
Front-end loading/advance payments	3	2	1
Information theft	2	1	3
Local purchase order and split payment fraud	2	1	3
Phantom contractor	2	1	3
Product substitution	3	2	1
Progress payment fraud	3	2	1
Purchases for personal use	2	1	3

continued

Table 8.1 (continued)   Procurement Fraud Matrix

	Requirements Definition Stage	Bidding and Selection Stage	Performance and Evaluation Stage
Tailored specifications	2	1	3
Time limitations	2	1	3
Unnecessary purchases	1	2	3

Notes: 1 = occurs most often at this stage; 2 = sometimes occurs at this stage; 3 = rarely occurs at this stage.

Bids are solicited for goods or services that are not actually required or that are a duplication of another contract. This method is used by employees who have a conflicting financial interest with the contractor.

Thin file syndrome will be evident. The records outlining the specifications will lack information and substance. Reports in consulting or service contracts will also lack substance. The distribution of this material will likely be restricted and will be considered basically useless.

Complaints from the public and, in particular, unsuccessful contractors are an important source of information in identifying Red Flags. As will be detailed in following chapters, equally important is a viable whistle-blowing program that can certainly assist in identifying problem relationships that fellow employees may have with contractors and suppliers of goods and services.

CONCLUSION

We have examined how financial statement and procurement frauds are perpetrated and their attendant Red Flags. We now move on to examining the structural and cultural building blocks in an entity that promote the prevention and early detection of fraud.

9

Bribery and Corruption

INTRODUCTION

This chapter focuses on corruption and on how it can be prevented and detected.

The term "corruption" itself is a linguistic derivative of the Latin word "corrumpere," which translates to "break," "mar," or "seduce."* The *Merriam-Webster Dictionary* defines corruption as "impairment of integrity, virtue, or moral principle...inducement to wrong by improper or unlawful means (as bribery)."†

Earlier in this book, we looked at procurement contracts—an area of business that is among those at highest risk for corruption—and ways in which procurement processes can be corrupted. In the context of business decisions within organizations, corruption often arises from decision-making processes in which agent decision makers do not align their decisions with the interests of their principals.

The misalignment results from external stimulus to the individual decision maker responsible for awarding a procurement contract. It is commonly in monetary form, but often in the form of nonmonetary benefits. In the context of procurement, it leads to purchasing decisions that are detrimental to the principal to an extent that they exceed the benefits accepted by the individual decision maker.

Providing benefits to decision makers with the intent to induce suboptimal decisions for the principal is called bribery. Laws commonly

---

* http://oxforddictionaries.com/definition/english/corruption (accessed July 23, 2013).
† http://www.merriam-webster.com/dictionary/corruption (accessed July 23, 2013).

distinguish between bribery of public officials and bribery in commercial transactions. Bribery in commercial transactions is often called a secret commission. While bribery of public officials is a criminal offense in practically every jurisdiction in the world, albeit often not adequately enforced, bribery in commercial transactions is not a criminal offense in many countries.

The Foreign Corrupt Practices Act (FCPA) of 1977 was the first and, for many years, the only antibribery law of its kind. The FCPA makes it unlawful for a US person, and certain foreign issuers of securities, to make a corrupt payment to a foreign official. Since 1998, it also applies to foreign firms and persons who take any act in furtherance of such a corrupt payment while in the United States.

Over the years, Congress worried that US companies were disadvantaged by foreign ones who paid bribes. At the time, in some countries, the cost of bribes could be deducted as business expense. In 1988, Congress directed the Executive Branch to persuade partners to enact laws like FCPA. In 1997, the United States and 33 other countries signed the Organization for Economic Cooperation and Development (OECD) Convention on Combating Bribery of Foreign Public Officials in International Business Transactions.

Until now, many multinational corporations focused on compliance with FCPA. The UK Bribery Act will add regulatory complexity and has wide jurisdictional reach. Acts of bribery committed by anyone in the UK or, if overseas, by a British citizen or any other person with a close connection with the UK can be prosecuted.

ECONOMIC IMPACT OF BRIBERY

Negative Impact of Corruption at the Global Level

According to research by the World Bank Institute,[*] between $1 trillion and $1.6 trillion is paid every year in bribes between private and public sectors worldwide. This figure does not include embezzled public funds or stolen or misused public assets. It also does not include the resulting losses in investment, private sector development, and economic growth in a country. According to the World Bank, economies grow much faster

---

[*] World Bank. Corruption. http://web.worldbank.org/WBSITE/EXTERNAL/EXTABOU TUS/0,,contentMDK:23272490~pagePK:51123644~piPK:329829~theSitePK:29708,00.html (accessed July 23, 2013).

if corruption is lower and property rights and the rule of law are safe-guarded. It estimates that countries that better control corruption and improve rule of law can expect (on average), in the long run, a fourfold increase in incomes per capita. It further estimates that a country with an income per capita of $2,000 could expect to attain $8,000 per capita in the long run by making strides to control corruption.*

Corruption also has a negative impact on levels of infant mortality, poverty, and inequality. According to the World Bank, countries that better control corruption and improve rule of law can expect (on average), a 75% reduction in child mortality.†

Negative Impact of Corruption—Internal

We would all agree that saying "no" to corruption is the right thing to do, but it also makes commercial and ethical sense. Corruption carries legal, regulatory, reputational, and financial risks.

Legal and regulatory risks are rising annually. This is demonstrated by the sharp increase in the number of corruption-related prosecutions and investigations since the OECD Convention on Combating Bribery of Foreign Public Officials in International Business Transactions entered into force in 1999.

In the United States, between 1999 and 2010, a total of 227 cases were prosecuted. But in 2010 and 2011, some 219 major investigations were under way. In the United Kingdom, between 1999 and 2010, a total of seventeen cases was prosecuted. But in 2010 and 2011, some 54 major investigations were under way. In Canada, between 1999 and 2010, just two cases were prosecuted. But in 2010 and 2011, some 57 major investigations were under way.‡

In addition to reputational costs, the direct legal costs can be significant. The German conglomerate Siemens AG, for example, pleaded guilty in 2008 to conspiring to violate the US Foreign Corrupt Practices Act. The criminal fines, totaling more than $450 million, were supplemented

---

* World Bank. Six questions on the costs of corruption. http://web.worldbank.org/WBSITE/EXTERNAL/NEWS/0,,contentMDK:20190295~menuPK:34457~pagePK:34370~piPK:34424~theSitePK:4607,00.html (accessed July 23, 2013).

† Ibid.

‡ Transparency International. Progress report 2012: OECD antibribery convention. http://www.transparency.org/whatwedo/pub/exporting_corruption_country_enforcement_of_the_oecd_anti_bribery_conventio (accessed July 23, 2013).

by more than $350 million that Siemens agreed to disgorge as part of a settlement in a parallel SEC suit.*

But there are also internal costs. A corporation that pays bribes sets a permissive tone among employees aware of or involved in the payment of bribes. This, in turn, might increase the likelihood that these employees might engage in corrupt activities. This undermining of ethical standards can create a cascading atmosphere in which illegal and/or question-able practices are seen to be tolerated, and the cultural of compliance is degraded.

Former US Assistant Attorney General Lanny A. Breuer has stated:

> FCPA enforcement is…vital to ensuring the integrity of our markets. Our FCPA enforcement program serves not only to hold accountable those who corrupt foreign officials, but in doing so it also serves to make the international business climate more transparent and fair for every-one…rooting out foreign bribery matters. It matters for the health of democratic institutions across the globe and it matters for the strength of international commerce.†

BRIBERY OF PUBLIC OFFICIALS

Large-scale foreign contracts can be highly profitable for any corporation and corruption will often form part of the contract arrangement. In some countries, government officials will demand as much as 10% to 15% of the total value of the contract or value of the benefit granted.

This means the successful corporation that is awarded a foreign contract or such other benefits as mentioned before will be requested to pay these unlawful benefits by setting up a secret system to deliver the benefits to the official(s). These benefits are commonly termed kickbacks because the multinational corporation will likely add these benefit costs to the contract price.

For example, a corporation that has obtained a major construction contract in one of the countries that is deemed to be high risk for cor-ruption is in itself a Red Flag. We already wrote about the annual cor-ruption perception indexes published by Transparency International.‡ In

---

* http://www.justice.gov/opa/pr/2008/December/08-crm-1105.html (accessed July 23, 2013).
† Assistant Attorney General Lanny A. Breuer. 2010. Remarks at the 24th National Conference on the Foreign Corrupt Practices Act, National Harbor, MD, November 16, 2010.
‡ See Chapter 11.

such a situation, there is a high likelihood that the contract was obtained by promising and providing benefits to government officials. As we will show in this chapter, such payments are criminal offenses in most countries of the world where the bribes are being paid, even in countries considered to be highly prone to corruption. Such payments are also criminal offenses in many countries from which such payments originate under foreign corrupt practices legislation.

Bribery is one of the biggest challenges directors of multinational corporations managing and maintaining worldwide operations have to face. Corporations are often dependent on public-sector work both domestically and internationally. In many countries, bribery is an accepted practice and is ingrained as part of the local culture. As a result of a culture of corruption, officers and employees of multinational corporations who carry on business in these high-risk countries have devised complex systems to move the required corrupt payments from their control to the benefit of the public officials.

Bribe payments will be required before the contract is awarded and also during the performance of the contract. Additional bribes will be required for almost every government action that arises during the course of the contract. This would include incidental permits that are required from government authorities. For example, in a major construction project, custom and excise officials will demand bribes to clear equipment that is imported from outside the country, even if all the official fees and taxes have been paid.

Many multinational corporations have strict corporate policies to restrict officers and employees from participating in any activity that would allow the payment of a bribe to a foreign public official.[*] However, many corporations with strict anticorruption policies do not enforce such policies through adequate compliance risk management. In spite of the laws prohibiting bribery and corruption, and in spite of strict corporate antibribe policies, companies continue to pay bribes in order to obtain contracts.

For the same reason that international action and laws have not stopped illicit drug trafficking and use, officers, employees, and directors continue to be driven by huge profits that foreign contracts bring to their corporation and also to them personally. Bonuses, share options, and other financial incentives will drive these corporate officials to continue these

---

[*] Smith and Williamson. 2011. Antibribery and corruption policy, June 2011. https://www.smith.williamson.co.uk/anti-bribery-corruption-policy/

corrupt practices. The enhanced rules, regulations, and laws will serve to devise more complex schemes to provide corrupt benefits to foreign public officials.

COMPONENTS OF ANTIBRIBERY LAWS

Bribery as a Criminal Offense

In 2003, the United Nations adopted a convention that requires member countries that signed on to the convention[*] to establish sanctions for criminal and other offenses to cover a wide range of acts of corruption, if these are not already crimes under domestic law. Such sanctions to be instituted cover domestic as well as foreign corruption and should cover bribery of public officials and private sector bribery. Over 140 countries out of the 160 members[†] have adopted the convention and some have enacted enhanced laws to make it unlawful to bribe officials of government.

In practice, however, bribery and corruption of foreign decision makers are often poorly policed in many countries, which is mainly due to inabilities of law enforcement to investigate the often complex and multinational transactions used to conceal corrupt benefits.

In reviewing the state of corruption enforcement around the world, Transparency International stated:

> The overall level of enforcement remains inadequate. There are still only seven countries (with 28 percent of world exports) with active enforcement, a number that has not changed in three years. To enable the Convention to reach the tipping point—when the prospects for success change from uncertain to favorable—there must be active enforcement in countries with over half of world exports. That will require active enforcement in six to 10 additional countries.[‡]

The seven countries with active enforcement are Denmark, Germany, Italy, Norway, Switzerland, United Kingdom, and United States. In the

---

[*] The Convention against Corruption was adopted by the General Assembly of the United Nations on October 31, 2003, at United Nations Headquarters in New York.

[†] UN signature and ratification status as of December 2012.

[‡] Transparency International. 2012. Progress report 2012: OECD antibribery convention. http://www.transparency.org/whatwedo/pub/exporting_corruption_country_enforcement_of_the_oecd_anti_bribery_conventio (accessed July 23, 2013).

moderate enforcement category are the following 12 countries with 25% of world exports: Argentina, Australia, Austria, Belgium, Canada, Finland, France, Japan, South Korea, Netherlands, Spain, and Sweden.

Transparency International concluded: "The state of enforcement in most of the countries with moderate enforcement is not at a level that provides a credible deterrent to foreign bribery. In countries with little enforcement there is only little deterrent and there is no deterrent in countries with no enforcement."[*]

Many industrialized countries have therefore focused their efforts on criminalizing corruption originating from their territories and have built or are in the process of building law enforcement capabilities to investigate and prosecute foreign corruption.

Legal concepts geared toward preventing foreign corruption should be distinguished based on the following criteria:

- Corporate criminal liability versus individual criminal liability
- Legal entity view versus conglomerate view
- Criminalization of facilitation payments as bribes
- Who is subject to the foreign corrupt practices rules?
- Definition of a public official
- Extent of sentence

Corporate Criminal Liability versus Individual Criminal Liability

Penal codes as they relate to corporate behavior and actions of a corporation's representatives can be distinguished based on whether a corporation as a legal person is criminally liable for the acts and omissions of the natural persons it employs.

Industrialized countries that hold corporate entities criminally liable for the actions of their representatives are the United States, the United Kingdom, Canada, Australia, and Japan. Examples of industrialized countries without corporate criminal liability are Germany and France. It is common, however, that even countries that do not recognize corporate criminal liability impose administrative sanctions. The monetary value of such sanctions tends to be comparatively small, though. Administrative sanctions tend to be based on a conglomerate view.

---

[*] Ibid.

Legal Entity View versus Conglomerate View

The distinction based on the legal entity view refers to the liability of a corporation for actions or omissions in foreign affiliated entities. In essence, legal systems taking a conglomerate view pierce the shield of legal entities. Legal systems that do not recognize corporate criminal liability also tend to limit the liability to actions performed by individuals, who as individuals are subject to the laws of the respective country.

For example, if a non-German national bribes a public official on behalf of a German corporation in a foreign country, Germany has no jurisdiction over the crime. It has, however, the authority to impose administrative financial sanctions up to 1 million Euro on the corporation. The German government is currently contemplating proposing legislation that will increase the maximum administrative sanction to 10 million Euro.

Criminalization of Facilitation Payments

Bribes are commonly distinguished from facilitation payments. While the purpose of a bribe is to influence the outcome of a decision, facilitation payments are made for routine administrative action such as processing papers, issuing permits, and other actions of a public official, in order to expedite performance of duties of a nondiscretionary nature. A facilitation payment is not intended to influence the outcome of the official's action, only its timing. The Foreign Corrupt Practices Act in the United States does not prohibit facilitation payments, but permits them to expedite or to secure the performance of a routine governmental action. The UK Bribery Act makes facilitation payments illegal. Facilitation payments are prohibited under the German Criminal Code. Changes to Canada's antibribery act also prohibit facilitation payments.[*]

Application of Antibribery Laws

All countries with foreign corrupt practices legislation apply these rules to their own citizens, residents, and/or legal entities where there is corporate criminal liability and to crimes committed on their territories.

Some countries go beyond this. In the United States, foreign corporations that have a class of securities registered or are required to file

---

[*] http://blog.bennettjones.com/blog/2013/06/26/tougher-canadian-foreign-corruption-law-raises-the-stakes-for-officers-and-directors/ (accessed July 23, 2013).

reports under the Securities and Exchange Act of 1934 are also subject to the Foreign Corrupt Practices Act.

In the United Kingdom, corporations or partnerships that carry on a business or part of a business in the UK, irrespective of the place of incorporation or formation, are subject to the regulations of the UK Bribery Act. Given that the act was adopted in 2010, there is little if any legislation that could shine a light on whether a non-UK entity can be regarded as carrying on a business or a part thereof in the United Kingdom. A guidance document issued by the Ministry of Finance says:

> The Government would not expect, for example, the mere fact that a company's securities have been admitted to the UK Listing Authority's Official List and therefore admitted to trading on the London Stock Exchange, in itself, to qualify that company as carrying on a business in the UK and therefore falling within the definition of a "relevant commercial organization."*

Amendments to Canada's antibribery act extend its reach to the activities of Canadian companies, citizens, and permanent residents regardless of where the alleged bribery has taken place. The law had limited the prohibited activity to activities that had "a real and substantial connection to Canada."

Definition of a Public Official

Countries with foreign corrupt practices legislation consider a person to be a public official if he or she is serving in an executive role for the government. Some countries, such as the United States and the UK also include members of political parties with the capability to influence a decision by the political party or the individual party member. Some countries, such as Germany, have shied away from defining members of parliament as public officials as they have not found a way to distinguish lobbying from bribery in a legislative concept.

Extent of Monetary Penalties

No prohibition can be successful in deterring unwanted behavior if penalties are tolerable. From a corporate perspective, what counts is not

---

* Ministry of Justice: The Bribery Act 2010. Guidance about procedures which relevant commercial organizations can put into place to prevent persons associated with them from bribing. www.justice.gov.uk/guidance/bribery.htm (accessed July 23, 2013).

the sentence associated with the crime for the individual, but the monetary sentence associated with the crime for the corporation. In legal systems without corporate criminal liability, penalties are limited to the financial consequences of administrative sanctions.

The United States is the one country that has imposed meaningful monetary penalties. Consider the top 10 Securities and Exchange Commission FCPA settlements:

1. Siemens (Germany): $800 million in 2008
2. KBR/Halliburton (US): $579 million in 2009
3. BAE (UK): $400 million in 2010
4. Total S. A. (France): $398 million in 2013
5. Snamprogetti Netherlands B.V./ENIS.p.A (Holland/Italy): $365 million in 2010
6. Technip S. A. (France): $338 million in 2010
7. JGC Corporation (Japan): $218.8 million in 2011
8. Daimler AG (Germany): $185 million in 2010
9. Alcatel-Lucent (France): $137 million in 2010
10. Magyar Telekom/Deutsche Telekom(Hungary/Germany): $95 million in 2011[*]

Given that the UK Bribery Act was instituted in 2010, there is no experience yet with the extent of fines that corporations violating the act will have to face.

So far, the highest fine charged in any Canadian case was a $10 million fine against Griffith Energy of Calgary over a $40 million bribe paid in connection with landing oil rights in Chad.

But monetary penalties are only part of the cost. Companies also face huge bills when investigating themselves for potential violations. Should potential violations turn up, they then provide their findings to law enforcement and regulators in the hope of getting lighter penalties or none at all. The benefits of doing so are clear. Former US Assistant Attorney General Lanny A. Breuer has stated:

> Voluntarily disclose wrongdoing if you discover it. As a former defense lawyer, I understand that the question of whether to self-report is a difficult one. But I can assure you that if you do not voluntarily disclose your organization's conduct, and we discover it on our own, or through a competitor or a customer of yours, the result will not be the

---

[*] See more at: http://www.fcpablog.com/blog/2013/5/29/frances-total-sa-cracks-our-top-10-list.html#sthash.z5wjys5Q.dpuf (accessed July 23, 2013).

same. Of course, voluntary disclosure is not the only factor we consider in deciding how to resolve a particular case. We take into account all the factors set forth in the *Principles of Federal Prosecution of Business Organizations,* and we consider the particular facts and circumstances of each individual case. But there is no doubt that a company that comes forward on its own will see a more favorable resolution than one that doesn't.*

But the costs of internal investigations—especially for a multinational company—can be significant. Siemens, for example, hired more than 300 lawyers, forensic accountants, and support staff over a 2-year period to conduct its own internal investigation. The document review alone cost about $100 million.

As the *Wall Street Journal* reported: "The cost and efforts of conducting internal investigations can seem like punishments themselves. In some cases, the criminal and civil settlements companies pay are dwarfed by their investigative expenses."[†]

Money Laundering to Conceal Corrupt Payments

In addition to anticorruption legislation, laws prohibiting the laundering of money may apply in these bribery cases. Therefore, if payments to government officials were secretly converted from the corporate bank accounts, offenses of laundering of money[‡] may also be applicable to these corrupt payments.

Money laundering has three goals

1. It converts proceeds of crime to another, less suspicious form.
2. It conceals the criminal origins and ownership of funds.
3. It creates legitimate explanation for the source of funds.[§]

Money laundering is, at heart, a process for disguising the proceeds of corrupt relationships. The ultimate goal is to obscure the origins of those funds so that they appear to have been earned legally. If that can be accomplished, the bribes can be used in the legal economy without raising

---

* Assistant Attorney General Lanny A. Breuer. 2010. Remarks at the 24th National Conference on the Foreign Corrupt Practices Act, National Harbor, MD, November 16, 2010.
† *Wall Street Journal.* FCPA Inc.: The business of bribery, October 2, 2012.
‡ The Bank Secrecy Act is codified at 31 U.S.C. §§ 5311 et seq.
§ http://www.rcmp-grc.gc.ca/qc/pub/blanch-launder/blanchiment-laundering-eng.pdf (accessed July 23, 2013).

suspicion. It is for this reason that the most successful money laundering schemes closely mimic legal transactions.

Corrupt payments thus are laundered for two reasons:

- The bribe payer wants to ensure that the illegal payments are not discovered internally by audit departments or externally by regulators and law enforcement.
- The bribe recipients need to be able to conceal the origins of this portion of their wealth so that they can freely enjoy it without coming under suspicion.

In one case, the local agent in Asia for a multinational contractor sought to conceal the payments of bribes by mimicking legitimate ones. To make corrupt payments, he registered a company in the British Virgin Islands (BVI) with the same name as a legitimate supplier and then opened a bank account in another offshore jurisdiction in its BVI name. Thus, a payment to the offshore account would appear to have the characteristics of a legitimate payment to a bona fide supplier.

The beneficial ownership of the BVI company would be very difficult to uncover because shareholder information is kept on file with the local BVI registered agent. Details of a company's beneficial owners, directors, and shareholders are not publicly available.

In another case, senior executives in a multinational corporation concealed corrupt payments by booking the funds against unrelated projects in jurisdictions unconnected to the corrupt projects. Until a detailed internal investigation was conducted, these payments appeared to be legitimate.

Secret Commissions or Bribes to Nonpublic Officials

Bribery of public officials is very often the core focus when discussing corruption. Secret commissions, however, given to officers and employees of competitors or customers, are also significant and common illegal activities in the commercial world.

Corrupt payments to private sector decision makers are made to achieve some corporate objective. Unlawful payments and benefits are often paid to purchasing agents who are responsible for buying goods and services for their entity. Unlawful payments can also be made to competitors who may be involved in a competitive bidding process. These have been outlined in greater detail in Chapter 8.

Unlawful secret commissions can also be paid for trade secrets and other protected information that will enhance the profitability of the company that is paying for them.

In some cases, during a very competitive process to obtain a contract, companies will engage the services of a private investigator or agents to aggressively obtain information that will give them an advantage in the process of being awarded the contract. This can involve anything from using special agents specifically suited to a particular situation to using an organized crime group to intimidate individual officers or employees to provide the desired information.

However, the most common form of unlawful enticement to corporate insiders is to provide money or other financial benefits.

Secret Commissions or Bribes to Nonpublic Officials—Case Examples

A newly appointed buyer for a large national retailer met for the first time with an officer of a large foreign toy manufacturer. He was there to renew a contract to continue to supply the retailer with the manufacturer's product. The officer showed the buyer the facilities and the products. When the tour was over, the officer explained to the buyer that the manufacturer was prepared to continue to offer the buyer a personal cash kickback. It amounted to 5% of the total value of the sales to the retailer.

This secret commission would be paid monthly to a secret offshore bank account that would be completely set up by the manufacturer. The officer recommended that the buyer not use the proceeds until his term of employment with the retailer was over. He should, instead, look at this payment as a retirement benefit that he would use in his retirement years. He was told that by following this procedure, the payment would never be detected, and he could end up with sufficient funds to be able to retire in several years.

The buyer, however, reported this offer to his employer and the retailer terminated the contract with the manufacturer. The retailer then turned attention to the previous employees who had dealt with that manufacturer over the years. It was found that the same arrangement had been made.

In another example, a manufacturer of a highly competitive product was falling behind in market share. Its review of the situation revealed that a competitor's product was superior in terms of the technology that had been developed.

The manufacturer launched a campaign to obtain the details of this technology from the competitor's key employees. The company engaged the services of a private investigative team to obtain the necessary background on the employees. Following extensive surveillance, it found that one key employee was prone to gambling at casinos.

This individual often traveled with gambling junkets to various casino locations. It was also discovered that he was deeply in debt. A special agent was engaged to befriend the employee. Over a relatively short period of time a system of paying funds in return for confidential information was established. The employee in question had access to much of the information that the manufacturer required. This cloak and dagger system of obtaining information is thought to be reserved for government spies. However, it is much more common in the business world than suspected.

Secret Commissions as a Criminal Offense

A corrupt secret commission (i.e., a bribe in commercial transactions) is an offense under the criminal law in most jurisdictions in industrialized countries, but less commonly considered a criminal offense in developing or Third World countries.

It has been included in criminal laws in the United Kingdom and Commonwealth countries such as Canada, Australia, and New Zealand since the early part of the twentieth century. Many states in the United States have also adopted this type of law. Other English-speaking jurisdictions have used the term "bribery" for corrupt payments to both public and nonpublic officials. For the most part, the concepts of corrupt payments to nonpublic officials are similar whether the term used is bribery or secret commission.

In jurisdictions where secret commission criminal laws are in effect, an employee is not legally permitted to accept a benefit for any work-related activity without first seeking permission of the employer. This type of activity, however, is seldom prosecuted in the criminal courts; instead, it more often ends up as a civil dispute between the companies involved.

When a trade secret or confidential information is obtained by deception or intimidation, as opposed to the payment of a benefit, the activity is usually considered to be a criminal offense of theft of information or criminal intimidation.

In addition to the substantive law relating to secret commissions and bribery, many countries have a law of conspiracy, which makes it an offense to conspire with others to give a corrupt secret commission. This conspiracy offense is committed when an agreement is completed, whether the substantive offense (actually, making the payment) is carried out or not.

By applying the laws of conspiracy, it is not necessary that all the conspirators be in any one jurisdiction. In fact, if one conspirator is situated in one jurisdiction and the others are spread around the world in different countries, they could still be subjected to the criminal conspiracy in that one jurisdiction, even if they were never physically in that particular jurisdiction. Sending mail, communicating by telephone, and using other forms of communication may often be deemed sufficient to connect an individual or corporation in the unlawful conspiracy agreement, no matter where the physical location is.

The United States does not have a specific statute at the federal level prohibiting such private sector bribes to foreign private officials, but the US Department of Justice is in a position to charge individuals under the Travel Act for traveling internationally to violate bribery statutes.* This, however, does not result in corporate criminal liability, and bribes paid by non-Americans would largely go unpunished. Each state creates its own criminal laws and there are provisions that make it an offense to provide secret commissions to nonpublic officials of private institutions. While these criminal offenses would have an effect within the United States, they have limited impact on payment to foreign officials from locations outside the country.

Recently, the Securities and Exchange Commission has found a way to charge corporations for bribery based on disclosure laws. Under disclosure laws, investors are entitled to gain a full picture of how a corporation generates its revenue. If revenue is generated with the use of bribes as opposed to the strength of a corporation's products or services, nondisclosure of bribes and even claiming product strength as a key factor to obtaining a major contract is a violation of disclosure rules.

If the payments of bribes or secret commissions are secretly transferred in a manner to hide the true nature of the payment, such activity may also fall under the federal US money-laundering statutes. Also, when the US mail is used to carry out any fraudulent act, a federal offense of mail fraud may apply.

Under the UK Bribery Act, secret commissions paid to any foreign person or private sector or public official are prohibited. Germany, too, prohibits bribery of private sector decision makers.

---

* Move over, DOJ: The SEC can charge private-sector bribery too. 2012. Forbes Online, July 31, 2012, http://www.forbes.com/sites/howardsklar/2012/07/31/move-over-doj-the-sec-can-charge-private-sector-bribery-too/ (accessed July 23, 2013).

Secret Commissions as a Criminal Offense—Case Example

This example involves the use of corrupt payments to acquire a trade secret. The scheme began with an employee of a telecommunication company engaging an agent in another country at the direction of the company's senior vice president. An e-mail between the employee and the senior vice president set out that funds were to be transferred to the agent to pay an officer of a competitor, once a specific trade secret was delivered to the agent.

The agent traveled to a third country to meet the officer near his workplace. The agent outlined the terms and conditions and the officer agreed to deliver the specified information. The agent and the officer agreed to make the payment and receive the information on a specified future date. This information was then relayed by the agent to the employee and in turn to the senior vice president.

The jurisdiction where the telecommunications company was situated had a criminal law that made it an offense to pay secret commissions to an employee of another company in exchange for confidential information without the permission of the employer. This jurisdiction also had criminal conspiracy laws applicable in this situation.

As a result, all of the participants in this case were subject to being prosecuted for conspiring to pay a secret commission to an officer of a competing company. With the e-mail evidence and the potential payment of the benefit, there was sufficient evidence to proceed with a criminal conspiracy prosecution against all the individuals involved.

SCHEMES USED TO PAY UNLAWFUL BENEFITS

Many different schemes have been used over the years to pay secret commissions and bribes in both domestic and foreign contracts. Bribes used to be paid by simply placing cash in an envelope and handing it to the recipient. As a result of more enhanced scrutiny by auditors and regulators, very complex payment systems have evolved, although undoubtedly the cash-in-envelopes system is still utilized.

In order to hide the payment out of the corporation, intricate systems of creating false invoices and entities to convey the benefits have developed.

Regardless of corporate policy, strict and enhanced antibribery laws, or international bribery conventions, there are few reductions in demands for bribes in high-risk jurisdictions. As noted in the previously referenced Transparency International report, many of the 140 countries that have adopted the UN Convention have not adopted significant enforcement changes to deal with the bribery of public officials.* In countries where bribery is part of the culture, local enforcement for this type of activity is often nonexistent.†

Schemes used to provide unlawful benefits to public officials or decision makers in private corporations are most difficult to detect, yet they are often devastating to the parties involved when detected. This type of criminal offense is consensual in nature, involving willing parties. And, as a consequence, it requires considerable skill on the part of directors and management to develop detection systems and then to act on Red Flags that may be the early indicators of this type of corruption.

The challenge for corporations that intend to provide corrupt benefits is to make such funds or goods and services available as off-book means, in particular as undisclosed slush funds or undisclosed asset ownership—for example, in real estate or yachts‡ to be transferred to the recipient of illicit benefits.

The use of cash in envelopes has given way to more sophisticated schemes devised to conceal corrupt payments. Such schemes tend to include the following:

- The use of false and fictitious invoices and contracts
- Payments from secret offshore bank accounts
- The use of offshore corporations in tax haven countries
- Issuance of company shares or debentures at reduced prices
- Transfer of real estate or other major assets at no cost or at a significantly reduced price
- Lavish vacations
- Entering into fictitious contracts with agents acting on behalf of public officials
- Providing scholarships to the family of a foreign government official
- Issuing shares that are undervalued to the benefit of the public official
- Lavish entertainments like box seats to sporting or other public events
- Providing contractors at no cost to renovate a home or build a cottage

Historically, we have found that laws and policy do not prevent aggressive employees from securing lucrative contracts through the payment of bribes. For this reason it is useful to examine the types of schemes that have

---

* ADB/OECD Anticorruption Initiative for Asia and the Pacific—Criminalization of bribery in Asia and the Pacific.
† Libya during the Gaddafi years in power.
‡ These are just examples, albeit popular examples.

been used to convey unlawful benefits to foreign public officials and private sector decision makers in more detail. Given that the monetary value of benefits paid as bribes can range between 10% and 15% of the value of the entire project, bribe payments can be very substantial and require a great deal of ingenuity to develop schemes that cannot easily be detected.

Bribes Paid with Funds under Direct Control of the Corporation—Using Secret Off-Book Funds

Some managers of corporations have secretly placed large pools of corporate funds in offshore tax haven bank accounts so that they can be used to corrupt and influence government officials and others to secure contracts. These funds are not recorded in any of the corporation's consolidated financial statements. Many different systems have been developed to set aside sources of funds for this purpose.

The simplest involves the formation of offshore corporations, whose stated business purpose involves business-consulting services. The corporation or one of its subsidiaries issues a request for an expert opinion to be received from such a consulting entity. The entity either renders a useless report or no report at all. It then bills the corporation or its subsidiary for consulting services often amounting to several hundred thousand dollars. Once the consulting entity receives the funds, they will be retained and accumulated as slush funds. Such action is not limited to tax haven jurisdictions. It may well involve layered invoices and fake services with the first layer service being rendered from an onshore business, which then funnels funds to offshore entities.

In other cases, such funds are skimmed from the sale of equipment that has been depreciated to a lower than market value. When the equipment is sold, it is first sold to an offshore entity under the control of the corporation at or near book value. The offshore entity then sells the equipment to the ultimate buyer at market value. The difference between the actual sale price and the depreciated value is then retained in an offshore bank account. Similar ways to create slush funds include intercompany transactions using nonconsolidated entities as intermediaries between seller and buyer. This allows for a windfall profit to stay with the nonconsolidated entity.

Another path is to funnel funds from the sale of foreign real estate into a secret slush fund applying similar intermediary structures as in the equipment sale example.

There is, of course an additional risk for the corporation. Such funds are not subjected to the transparency control of a regular fund management. Managers who control this type of account may end up keeping the fund or portions thereof for their personal use after those who know about these illegal offshore funds leave the company.

Red Flags include the following:

- Payments to offshore corporations
- Transactions in jurisdictions that appear to be unrelated to where the project or its main suppliers are located
- Transactions that do not appear to have a commercial purpose
- Consultancy services from nonestablished consulting providers
- Intercompany exchange of goods using intermediaries
- Equipment always sold at or near the actual book value

Using Secret Off-Book Funds—Case Example

An international construction company had several subsidiary corporations in various offshore locations. As a normal procedure, the corporation would regularly sell used construction equipment at the conclusion of a construction project. The depreciated book value of the equipment would always be below the actual retail market value. The difference between the book value and the actual sale price would be secretly moved to a bank account in a tax-free jurisdiction.

The employee who handled the sale of all equipment would advise the buyer that payment would be required in two separate amounts. The first would be close to the book value. The balance would be paid by a bank draft payable to the bank where the special account was situated. The buyer was told that the second payment was to pay the part owner of the equipment. The excess funds that were transferred to this account were then used for bribes and secret commissions.

One of the corporation's internal auditors became suspicious when the company always received very close to the actual book value and never more when all the equipment was sold. The auditor reported this finding to corporate management. The auditor's report was placed on file but no action taken. Several years later, when the corporation went bust, the matter was uncovered by the bankruptcy trustee. The special bank account was recovered but no criminal charges concerning this matter were instituted.

Using Lawyers to Channel Corrupt Payments to Public Officials or Private-Sector Decision Makers

Sometimes corporations engage lawyers and solicitors to arrange for the bribe payments to be made. The professionals are often in a close and trusted relationship with the intended recipient of the funds. The initial contract between the corporation and the foreign attorney will relate to providing legal advice in connection with the bidding process in the upcoming contract or other services in connection with the business advantages the corporation intends to achieve. In some cases the foreign company attorney will make the money transfers to a second lawyer, who will then pay the government official.

The use of lawyers can help provide a veneer of legitimacy. The International Bar Association has noted:

> Lawyers are sometimes seen as the authenticity for other professionals when a client is referred to them, confirming their supposed "legitimacy" by association. This in itself represents a unique problem. If lawyers are not obliged to carry out client due diligence checks or report any suspicions they have that the client may be involved in money laundering or terrorist financing efforts, they are potentially allowing an unsuspecting third party, such as a financial advisor, to incur accessory liability.[*]

The Lawyers' Professional Indemnity Company[†] has similarly stated that "...lawyers are in a unique position of trust. A lawyer's professionalism is held in the highest esteem, so their services automatically are imbued with an aura of respectability and confidence."[‡]

In large part, this high-esteem and legitimacy arise from the fact that lawyers, as officers of the court, are supposed to operate in an environment in which

> ...the commercial interests of the client and the lawyer's interest must give way to the overriding duty to the court...this means that the lawyer is in the unenviable position of having to insist that a client refrain

---

[*] International Bar Association, "Lawyers and Money Laundering," http://www.anti-moneylaundering.org/Lawyers_and_Money_Laundering.aspx, accessed July 23, 2013

[†] Provides liability insurance to more than 22,000 members of the Law Society of Upper Canada.

[‡] *LAWPRO Magazine*. 2003. Respecting the "trust" in trust account. March 2003.

from actions that may be in the client's self-interest but which subvert the administration of justice.[*]

Bribe payers are interested in a number of services offered by lawyers. The first is the protection offered by solicitor–client privilege to safeguard the confidentiality of communications by a client with his or her lawyer for the purpose of furnishing or obtaining professional legal advice or assistance. Since legal arrangements such as this will often be viewed as privileged information between the client corporation and the foreign lawyer, there is a belief that the risk of detection will be much lower. The company officials will hide these payments under the general legal expenses comingled with payments for legitimately incurred services in preparing the various stages of the contract.

The second attraction for bribe payers is the use of lawyers' trust accounts that can hold client funds in trust for extended periods of time. Trust accounts are particularly useful to money launderers because they provide quasi-banking services with a high level of confidentiality through solicitor–client privilege. An added layer of anonymity comes from the fact that they are not subject to the same AML/ATF regulations, including record keeping and suspicious reporting requirements, as are other financial intermediaries.

The Lawyers' Professional Indemnity Company has stated:

> For those who prefer not to leave a paper trail, lawyers' trust accounts are an attractive alternative to traditional financial institutions. Among the most vulnerable is the sole practitioner who—perhaps of economic necessity—closes his eyes to the improper ways in which he is being asked to use his trust account, or simply does not understand that his trust account is being used for purposes that have nothing to do with his legal expertise, and everything to do with moving money in inappropriate, and sometimes illegal, ways.[†]

The third attraction for bribe payers is the fact that lawyers provide a wide range of services, including financial and tax advice, creating corporations and trusts in a number of jurisdictions, completing real estate transactions,

---

[*] *LAWPRO Magazine.* 2003. Respecting the "trust" in trust account. March 2003.

[†] David W. Scott, Q. C. 1998. Law Society of Upper Canada Report to Convocation of the Futures Task Force Working Group on Multidiscipline Partnerships (September 1998) cited in an address by the Honorable Patrick J. LeSage, Q. C. on May 13, 2005, at Kingston, Ontario, for the Advocacy Retreat.

and overseeing financial transactions. The kinds of legal services sought by bribe payers are perfectly legitimate and play an important role in the functioning of modern economies. The act of seeking these services does not in itself raise any suspicion. Many people, for example, have the experience of using their lawyer's trust account when buying a home, condo, or cottage.

The intergovernmental, Paris-based Financial Action Task Force (FATF) sets global anti-money-laundering and anti-terrorist-financing policies procedures and processes. It has noted that lawyers

> ...and other similar professionals perform a number of important functions in helping their clients organize and manage their financial affairs. First of all, they provide advice to individuals and businesses in such matters as investment, company formation, trusts and other legal arrangements, as well as optimization of tax situations. Additionally, legal professionals prepare and, as appropriate, file necessary paperwork for the setting up of corporate vehicles or other legal arrangements. Finally, some of these professionals may be directly involved in carrying out specific types of financial transactions (holding or paying out funds relating to the purchase or sale of real estate, for example) on behalf of their clients.
>
> All of these perfectly legitimate functions may also be sought out by organized crime groups or the individual criminal. They may do so for purely economic reasons; however, more important is the desire to profit from the expertise of such professionals in setting up schemes that will help to launder criminal proceeds. This expertise includes both advice on the best corporate vehicles or offshore locations to use for such schemes and the actual establishment of corporations or trusts that make up its framework.[*]

Red Flags include the following:

- An additional lawyer in a foreign-country transaction whose business purpose appears to be unclear or extraneous
- Legal fees charged in the absence of legal services
- Unusually high fees for legal services
- Lack of appropriate level of detail in legal invoices

Using Lawyers to Channel Corrupt Payments to a Public Official or Private Sector Decision Maker—Case Example

A CEO of a large international construction and engineering firm was anxious to increase the revenues of the company. The corporation in question was a public company and the shareholdings were widely

---

[*] FATF. 2004. Report on money laundering typologies 2003–2004, Paris, p. 24.

disbursed among a variety of investors. The company was governed by seven directors, with five outside directors and two from management. The CEO was one of the directors and the CFO the other. The board of directors was chaired by a nonexecutive chairman. The CEO's salary and annual bonus were based on performance and, in particular, on annual profits.

The government of a country in Africa had several large projects in the works that involved the construction of a highway that extended for hundreds of miles. This project was split into three separate contracts. One contract involved clearing and preparing the land, the second was for building the roadway, and the third was for paving and landscaping. The government and country would have been classified as a high-risk fraud and corruption area.

The government was controlled by one person who was suspected of having obtained a great deal of wealth from an enterprising kickback scheme. The information indicated that the CEO had met the head of government on a previous occasion. He traveled to the capital of the country and met the man and they discussed the upcoming project. The CEO was asked by the government official to meet with a local solicitor who would provide him with all the details of the project.

At this meeting the lawyer did provide all the details of the project and suggested that the CEO's company was highly regarded and that there was a very good chance that it could win the upcoming bids for all three contracts. The lawyer stated that the company would first have to incorporate within that country and recommended that all of those details and other matters concerning the bidding process should be handled by the services of another law firm.

The second law firm, which was closely related to the first lawyer, agreed to become the company's legal representative within the country. The CEO was advised that in order to be qualified to bid on this project, a special fee would have to be paid. This fee would ensure that the CEO's company would be awarded the first contract. If everything went according to plan, he would then pay another special fee to be qualified for the other two contracts.

In addition, the CEO was advised that regular periodic special fees would have to be paid throughout the three contracts. All the special fees would be included in the law firm's regular invoices for its legal services. These fees would amount to a sum equivalent to 10% of the value of each of the contracts.

The CEO agreed to the terms and, on his return to his office, he issued instructions to pay the amount of the legal services along with the fees. The first contract was awarded to the company. After paying the two other special fees, together with the cost of the legal services, the other two contracts were awarded. The CEO included the cost of the special fees in the bid price that he submitted to the government.

In reporting to the board of the success of winning these three contracts, the CEO did not mention the additional 10% that was added to the contract. Nor did he report anything about the special fee that was included in the legal invoice from the law firm.

The board of directors never questioned the CEO regarding the awarding of these three contracts. The CEO in turn was awarded a significant bonus for the profits the company secured as a result of these contracts.

This matter would never have surfaced if there had not been a change in government in the country. The new head of government ordered a complete investigation, which uncovered the bribe scheme. Because of the time lapse involved, no criminal charges were instituted.

Arrangements with Foreign Agents and Consultants

Engaging agents or consultants to pay bribes to public officials has been used on many occasions. This system is not as common as it used to be since publicity and the introduction of new laws to combat corruption have made it more recognizable as a corrupt activity. However, in some cases the agents and consultants have represented the public official, thus making it difficult to connect the actual payment as a bribe. In cases where bribe payments are small, this method is still used successfully.

Engaging marketing or lobbying agencies to pay bribes is often difficult to uncover. The goal of the corporation is to comingle bona fide marketing activities and costs related to them and funds intended for bribe payments. When first used, this scheme will produce a spike in marketing expenses related to products, projects, or regional presence.

In a normal and legal course of business, marketing expenses do not tend to fluctuate in the short term as marketing activities follow comparatively steady plans and budgets even when sales cycles show spikes and valleys. When marketing expenses fluctuate with the volume of sales, this might indicate that funds are being expensed in order to win specific projects. When agents are used on a commission basis to sell products and projects, there normally is a close link between volume of sales and commissions paid. When the use of agents to pay bribes is initially introduced, there is an increase in the percentage commission paid for products or projects and/or in specific regions.

Because of the risk posed by agents—especially since corporations may be held responsible for illegal activities of agents—it is important to conduct robust precontract screening and enhanced due diligence of third intermediaries. This will involve determining such things as the following:

- Their reputation
- Whether they have been charged with participation in corrupt activities
- Whether they have been investigated for corrupt activities, since in some countries bribes can be used to "make investigations go away"
- Whether they have a criminal history
- Their civil litigation history
- Whether they have been barred by any country, including the United States, or international organization, like the World Bank, from participation in public contract bidding
- Whether there is adverse media on them, etc.

In addition to appropriate levels of due diligence, corporations also need to ensure that contracts contain sufficiently strong language and penalties to help ensure partners and agents do not commit or attempt to commit any illegal actions on a company's behalf, including bribery. Suitable compliance standards should be included in those contracts, as well as audit and termination rights.

Red Flags include:

- No recognizable service provided by foreign agent or consultant and no record of service delivery
- Unusually high fees paid for the services rendered
- Marked fluctuation in marketing expenses
- Increases in commission expenses when the use of agents is first introduced

Using Local Importers in Foreign Jurisdictions

This scheme is common in procurement processes. Once a bid for the sale of goods has been awarded at a certain price for manufactured goods, the manufacturer arranges with the foreign buyer that the product will be delivered using a local importer. The manufacturer then bills the local importer at a price that has been lowered by the amount of the agreed bribe in addition to a reward for the importer's service. This way, the manufacturer maintains control over the extent of funds paid to win the contract.

This scheme is also common in situations where there is recurring business activity in a particular region or country.

Red Flag:

- Winning bids where products are not invoiced directly to the principal purchaser on record for the tender

Bribes Paid with Funds under the Control of Intermediaries

Retention of control over funds means that Red Flags become visible, which may result in suspicions giving rise to investigations. As a result, some corporations have recognized a need to relinquish control and allow third parties to do the dirty work for them without having control over funds. Their goal is to conceal ties between the bribe paid and the corporation itself. This tends to increase the cost to the corporation, as there is a risk that the funds provided to third parties exceed the bribes they are intended to pay. In a worst-case scenario, third parties can take the money and run.

Using Foreign Subcontractors or Joint Venture Partners to Pay the Bribe

When major construction projects are being offered in a foreign jurisdiction, it will usually be necessary for the corporation to partner with local contractors for many parts of the overall contract. During the early stages of the contract offerings, the relationship will begin with the subcontractors. In these cases of major construction projects, the bribe payments will be large and it might be difficult for the corporation to transfer funds to cover these payments without being discovered by auditors.

In such cases the local subcontractor will agree to make all the bribe payments—in particular, those bribe payments that will be required to secure the contract at the outset of the contract negotiations. Once the contract is under way it will be easier for the contractor to divert funds from the actual contract.

- A Red Flag is the payment of advances to subcontractors or joint venture partners in the absence of contracts, but within a short time of winning a bid

DIRECTORS' OBLIGATIONS

Company officials who participate in bribery carefully conceal their actions so that it is difficult (though not impossible) for corporate auditors or directors to detect them.

The first and clearly most important line of defense at the board level is to ensure that a corporation has a compliance risk management program in place. Such a program should be adequate for the size of the corporation, the industry, and its current and future markets. New markets, especially in countries where corruption is endemic, present an especially significant risk.

Nonexistence of a compliance risk management program is a very obvious Red Flag accessible to every member of a board of directors. Directors must insist on the existence of a compliance risk management program and function within a corporation.

Adequacy tends to require more detailed assessments. Directors either on the full board level, or definitely at the audit committee level, need to require periodic reports by compliance and ethics executives on key factors affecting their corporations such as violations and risks. The minimum topics on which to require reports are the following:

- Organizational structure of the compliance risk management department
- Number and types of violations during the reporting period
- Violations by category, business unit, severity, and geographic area
- Identified risks by category, business unit, severity, and geographic area

Directors are commonly not involved in assessing individual projects and thus are not in a position to observe the Red Flags referred to in this chapter, unless the size of such projects exceeds approval thresholds. Therefore, directors need to ask compliance and ethics executives and senior executives in charge of high-risk regions, products, and markets what they observed with respect to the common Red Flags.

It is important that directors not allow themselves to be intimidated by the executives, officers, and fellow directors as they attempt to discover details of suspicious transactions. Subtle intimidation may often lead directors to develop a culture of willful blindness during board or committee meetings. This is the type of culture that has been present in all of the cases where major fraud has driven the corporate share prices to disastrous levels and in some cases put the company into bankruptcy.

CONCLUSION

Avoiding corruption not only is the right thing to do, but also makes commercial and ethical sense. Corruption carries legal, regulatory, reputational, and financial risks—risks that are rising annually. Corporations are well advised to implement and monitor robust systems for the prevention and early detection of corruption.

10

Fraud and Money Laundering

INTRODUCTION

This chapter focuses on money laundering and how it can be used to conceal the proceeds of fraud.

THE KOOP FRAUD*

In 1997, William H. Koop, a US citizen from New Jersey, began to represent himself as an experienced investment advisor. Even though he had no financial credentials or education beyond high school, Koop, a retired contractor, began selling a high-yield investment program that he claimed could produce returns as high as 489% over a 15-month period, allegedly with little or no risk.

In fact, it was nothing more than a fraud that bilked investors of millions of dollars. As part of the fraud, Koop, who pleaded guilty in 2000 to conspiracy to commit money laundering, used offshore banks and investment entities to both launder $13 million and advance his fraudulent activity. The investment vehicles, for example, were registered on the Caribbean island of Dominica. In 2000, Dominica was blacklisted by the Financial Action Task Force (FATF)† because, among other things,

---

* The details in this case are drawn from the following document: Minority Staff of the US Senate Permanent Subcommittee on Investigations: Report on correspondent banking: A gateway to money laundering. Washington, DC: February 5, 2001.
† The Financial Action Task Force (FATF) is an intergovernmental body whose purpose is the development and promotion of policies, both at national and international levels, to combat money laundering and terrorist financing.

the offshore sector appeared to be largely unregulated. That same year, it was strongly criticized for being "attractive to international criminals and money launderers" in the US State Department's annual International Narcotics Control Strategy Report.*

According to a US Senate subcommittee that investigated Koop's fraud, he used four Caribbean-based banks to further his fraudulent activities in four ways:

1. To establish offshore companies to conduct business transactions
2. To open offshore accounts where coconspirators and investors could send funds and he could start to launder them
3. To generate revenue and perpetrate his fraud by offering investors the opportunity, for a fee, to open their own offshore bank accounts where promised investment returns could be deposited
4. To increase his wealth by earning interest on deposits or using the offshore banks' investment programs†

DEVELOPMENT OF MONEY LAUNDERING LAWS

In the early 1980s huge sums of money were being generated by organized crime in the illicit drug trade at the international level. Billions of dollars that flowed from the illegal sale of illicit drugs at the street level had to be moved upward to the international drug traffickers who produced, manufactured, and distributed the illicit drugs. This money distribution system inspired many ingenious money laundering systems. At that time they were primarily developed to hide the identity of the recipients who were involved in drug trafficking. Money laundering in itself was not a crime.

Some organized crime groups were established for the sole purpose of converting the criminal street level funds to funds that appeared to be generated by legitimate business. Every conceivable business model was used. Business fronts were established to make it appear that the illicit drug money was being generated by a certain business entity. Banks

---

* State Department, Bureau of International Narcotics and Law Enforcement Affairs. 2000. 1999 International narcotics control strategy report. Washington, DC: March 2000.
† Minority Staff of the US Senate Permanent Subcommittee on Investigations: Report on correspondent banking: A gateway to money laundering. Washington, DC: February 5, 2001.

and financial institutions along with some of their employees became corrupted in their attempt to assist in the movement of these funds.

The first step in curbing this money conversion activity came as a result of a United Nations Convention* finalized in 1985 and adopted in 1988. This convention brought changes within all member countries to adopt measures to seize and forfeit the proceeds of illicit drug trafficking.[†] Most member countries[‡] adopted this convention and enacted laws to make it an offense to launder the proceeds derived from drug trafficking. Some of the countries, like the United States, United Kingdom, Canada, and others, extended this provision and made it an offense to launder the proceeds of all major crime at a time when the convention was first finalized. This added provision in their criminal law included all major crime including fraud and corruption.

In 2000 the United Nations adopted a second convention[§] against transnational organized crime, which requires member countries to

---

* United Nations Convention against laundering the proceeds of illicit drug trafficking.
† Article 5: CONFISCATION: 1. Each Party shall adopt such measures as may be necessary to enable confiscation of: (a) Proceeds derived from offenses established in accordance with article 3, paragraph 1, or property the value of which corresponds to that of such proceeds; (b) Narcotic drugs and psychotropic substances, materials and equipment or other instrumentalities used in or intended for use in any manner in offenses established in accordance with article 3, paragraph 1. 2. Each Party shall also adopt such measures as may be necessary to enable its competent authorities to identify, trace, and freeze or seize proceeds, property, instrumentalities or any other things referred to in paragraph 1 of this article, for the purpose of eventual confiscation. 3. In order to carry out the measures referred to in this article, each Party shall empower its courts or other competent authorities to order that bank, financial or commercial records be made available or be seized. A Party shall not decline to act under the provisions of this paragraph on the ground of bank secrecy.
‡ 160 member countries of the United Nations.
§ The United Nations Convention against Transnational Organized Crime, adopted by General Assembly resolution 55/25 of 15 November 2000, is the main international instrument in the fight against transnational organized crime. It opened for signature by member states at a high-level political conference convened for that purpose in Palermo, Italy, on December 12–15, 2000, and entered into force on September 29, 2003. The convention is further supplemented by three protocols, which target specific areas and manifestations of organized crime: the Protocol to Prevent, Suppress and Punish Trafficking in Persons, Especially Women and Children; the Protocol against the Smuggling of Migrants by Land, Sea and Air; and the Protocol against the Illicit Manufacturing of and Trafficking in Firearms, Their Parts and Components and Ammunition. Countries must become parties to the convention itself before they can become parties to any of the protocols.

include provisions to curb money laundering* within their territory as it relates to organized crime groups.

Again, many jurisdictions extended these requirements in this convention to other conspiratorial acts involving offenses of fraud, bribery, and corruption. The United States, Canada, United Kingdom, and European Union countries have adopted this convention.

With the adoption of the United Nations Convention on Corruption[†] in 2003, the member countries that have signed and ratified this convention were required to enact laws that would make it an offense to launder the proceeds of corruption.[‡] Now, most countries of the world[§] have enacted laws against money laundering for most serious criminal activity, which includes all the offenses related to fraud and corruption.

---

* Article 6: Criminalization of the laundering of proceeds of crime: 1. Each State Party shall adopt, in accordance with fundamental principles of its domestic law, such legislative and other measures as may be necessary to establish as criminal offenses, when committed intentionally: (a) (i) The conversion or transfer of property, knowing that such property is the proceeds of crime, for the purpose of concealing or disguising the illicit origin of the property or of helping any person who is involved in the commission of the predicate offense to evade the legal consequences of his or her action; (ii) The concealment or disguise of the true nature, source, location, disposition, movement or ownership of or rights with respect to property, knowing that such property is the proceeds of crime; (b) Subject to the basic concepts of its legal system: (i) The acquisition, possession or use of property, knowing, at the time of receipt, that such property is the proceeds of crime; (ii) Participation in, association with or conspiracy to commit, attempts to commit and aiding, abetting, facilitating and counseling the commission of any of the offenses established in accordance with this article.

† United Nations Convention against Corruption. General Assembly resolution 58/4 of October 31, 2003.

‡ Article 23. Laundering of proceeds of crime: 1. Each State Party shall adopt, in accordance with fundamental principles of its domestic law, such legislative and other measures as may be necessary to establish as criminal offenses, when committed intentionally: (a) (i) The conversion or transfer of property, knowing that such property is the proceeds of crime, for the purpose of concealing or disguising the illicit origin of the property or of helping any person who is involved in the commission of the predicate offense to evade the legal consequences of his or her action; (ii) The concealment or disguise of the true nature, source, location, disposition, movement or ownership of or rights with respect to property, knowing that such property is the proceeds of crime; (b) Subject to the basic concepts of its legal system: (i) The acquisition, possession or use of property, knowing, at the time of receipt, that such property is the proceeds of crime; (ii) Participation in, association with or conspiracy to commit, attempts to commit and aiding, abetting, facilitating and counseling the commission of any of the offenses established in accordance with this article.

§ 140 countries of the 160 member countries of the United Nations.

WHAT IS MONEY LAUNDERING?

The Paris-based Financial Action Task Force (FATF), which sets global anti-money-laundering and anti-terrorist-financing policies, procedures, and processes, uses the following definition for money laundering:

> The goal of a large number of criminal acts is to generate a profit for the individual or group that carries out the act. Money laundering is the processing of these criminal proceeds to disguise their illegal origin. This process is of critical importance, as it enables the criminal to enjoy these profits without jeopardizing their source.[*]

The General Assembly of Interpol, the international police organization, adopted the following working definition of money laundering: "any act or attempted act to conceal or disguise the identity of illegally obtained proceeds so that they appear to have originated from legitimate sources."[†]

Law enforcement defines money laundering as follows:

1. It converts proceeds of crime to another less suspicious form.
2. It conceals the criminal origins and ownership of funds.
3. It creates legitimate explanation for the source of funds.[‡]

Whatever the definition, money laundering is, at heart, a process for disguising the proceeds of criminal activity. The ultimate goal is to obscure the origins of those funds so that they appear to have been legally earned. If that can be accomplished, the proceeds of fraud and other crimes can be used in the legal economy without raising suspicion. It is for this reason that the most successful money laundering schemes closely mimic legal transactions.

From a technical standpoint, money laundering schemes generally have three stages: placement, layering, and integration. The FATF provides the following description of the three stages:

> In the initial—or placement—stage of money laundering, the launderer introduces his illegal profits into the financial system. This might be done by breaking up large amounts of cash into less conspicuous smaller sums that are then deposited directly into a bank account, or by purchasing a series of monetary instruments (checks, money orders, etc.) that are then collected and deposited into accounts at another location.

---

[*] http://www.fatf-gafi.org/pages/faq/moneylaundering/ (accessed July 23, 2013).
[†] http://www.interpol.int/Public/FinancialCrime/MoneyLaundering/default.asp
[‡] http://www.rcmp-grc.gc.ca/qc/pub/blanch-launder/blanchiment-laundering-eng.pdf (accessed July 23, 2013).

After the funds have entered the financial system, the second—or lay-ering—stage takes place. In this phase, the launderer engages in a series of conversions or movements of the funds to distance them from their source. The funds might be channeled through the purchase and sales of investment instruments, or the launderer might simply wire the funds through a series of accounts at various banks across the globe. This use of widely scattered accounts for laundering is especially prevalent in those jurisdictions that do not co-operate in anti-money laundering investigations. In some instances, the launderer might disguise the transfers as payments for goods or services, thus giving them a legiti-mate appearance.

Having successfully processed his criminal profits through the first two phases the launderer then moves them to the third stage—integration—in which the funds re-enter the legitimate economy. The launderer might choose to invest the funds into real estate, luxury assets, or business ventures.[*]

The three stages are not necessarily found in all money laundering schemes, however. The techniques in simple money laundering schemes tend to be low-tech and the three stages (i.e., placement, layering, and integration) are compressed into one or two stages.

The auditor general of Canada has noted:

The simplest forms of laundering take place close to where the origi-nal crime was committed. For example, money laundering may involve purchasing and then cashing in casino chips. In this way, the criminal profits are changed into what appears to be legal gambling profits. More complex examples can involve the purchase and sale of stocks, commod-ities, or property.

These techniques are best suited to relatively small and/or occasional sums. When the criminal activity is continuous, cash-based retail busi-nesses such as car washes and laundries, video-game arcades, video rentals, and bars and restaurants have been used. Proceeds of crime are mixed with legal funds and the total reported as legitimate busi-ness earnings. Any additional tax that may be due is treated as a cost of doing business.[†]

More complex cases generally have an international component and may involve a variety of financial instruments; intermediaries, includ-ing lawyers; and more than one jurisdiction, possibly including financial

---

[*] http://www.fatf-gafi.org/pages/faq/moneylaundering/ (accessed July 23, 2013).
[†] Report of the Auditor General of Canada, April 2003, Chapter 3, p. 9.

secrecy havens. With regard to complex money laundering cases, the auditor general of Canada has explained:

> Bulk cash has been carried or shipped out of the country, or transferred through formal or informal financial systems. Alternatively, funds have been moved through companies that engage in international trade in goods and services and thus have credible explanations for moving funds abroad.
>
> An offshore corporation or trust may then receive the funds and place them within the international financial system. At that point, the owner of the funds may be protected by bank secrecy, corporate secrecy, and possibly solicitor–client privilege, which also provides secrecy.
>
> There are a number of techniques that criminals have used to access these funds from home: from a debit or credit card issued by an offshore bank, through domestic accounts of a foreign bank, as profit from real estate sales or securities trading, as salary or business income from a foreign company, or as a business loan.[*]

FRAUD AND MONEY LAUNDERING

While most of the media attention on money laundering has focused on the washing of drug trafficking proceeds, it is also an equally important facet of frauds—after all, swindlers like Koop want to be able to enjoy the fruits of the crimes—and of fraud investigations. Virtually all fraud investigations focus, to some extent, on a scheme's money laundering features. This is done in order to

- Document that a fraud has occurred and that the loss was not due to some other reason, including incompetence
- Identify how the scheme was undertaken so that gaps in internal controls can be filled
- Quantify how much was taken, which may be important for making an insurance claim, for filing a damages claim against the fraudster, for use in an asset recovery legal action, etc.
- Trace how the funds were spirited away, which may help to identify coconspirators and to locate defalcated assets for a recovery legal action

---

[*] Report of the auditor general of Canada, April 2003, Chapter 3, p. 10.

CREATING AND OPERATING UNDISCLOSED OR OFFSHORE CORPORATIONS

With globalization, corporations can be easily incorporated or created in many countries where the names and identities of the shareholders and owners are held in secret. These companies are referred to as offshore corporations. They are often operated through local people who are called nominees. These nominees operate the entities on behalf of the real shareholder or owners. In this way a transfer of funds or assets to these companies can appear to be done with a party who is not connected or related. In many cases all the members of a board of directors of a corporation are not aware that this foreign entity belongs to their company.

Payments for bribes of foreign officials or benefits to senior managers can be made without disclosing details to the members of the board and shareholders. It also allows the company not to disclose the transaction in the financial statement or to auditors and regulatory institutions. The transfer of assets can also be done to evade income tax or to avoid sanctions in domestic laws and regulations.

CREATING AND OPERATING UNDISCLOSED OR OFFSHORE TRUSTS

Many countries allow trusts to be formed to hold real or personal property, including other assets such as money in a bank account, within their jurisdiction. A trust is simply a formal document that names a local company, bank, or person as a trustee to act as the legal owner of the named property. The trustee carries out the duties and authority outlined in the trust document and holds that property in accordance with the terms specified, for the real or beneficial owner. In this way the name of the real owner is held in secret. The trust document is sometimes filed with an agency of government or is held by the trustee and the beneficial owner under the laws and regulations of the country. A trust can be less flexible than a corporation and as a result is primarily used to hold property in order to avoid or evade taxes.

CREATING AND OPERATING UNDISCLOSED OR OFFSHORE BANK ACCOUNTS

A number of countries have enacted laws to protect the identity of foreigners who open bank accounts within their jurisdiction. These secret offshore accounts are then used to hold funds that have been the subject of bribery, corruption, and tax evasion. Once an account has been opened and funds deposited, the foreign owner may use a variety of systems to use the funds in a normal manner outside that country. He may obtain a credit card from the bank where the account is held. When the credit card is used for a purchase somewhere in the world, the invoice is automatically returned to the bank where it is paid with an automatic charge to the account. All records are maintained solely by the bank. The secret bank account can also be used in conjunction with an offshore corporation or a trust.

UNDISCLOSED INSIDER BENEFICIAL RELATIONSHIPS

Most of the countries that permit offshore corporations, secret trusts, and bank accounts have companies, law firms, accounting firms and individuals that specialize in managing these specific entities and accounts. They act on behalf of the foreign owner and carry out directions in a protected environment where it is almost impossible to obtain information on the real owners of the property that is under their control. Local government laws and regulations protect them from disclosing the names and information and, in some cases, make it a criminal offense to do so.

CREATING FICTITIOUS RECORDS
TO ENHANCE THIS OFFSHORE ACTIVITY

In order to transfer funds to these offshore facilities, fictitious budgets, contracts, and supporting documents such as invoices are the most popular schemes to transfer money and other assets to or from these countries. Many of the companies that are created in these offshore jurisdictions are named to resemble trades and services consistent with the issuing of an invoice that would minimize suspicion when presented for payment. Systems have evolved where fictitious contracts and invoices can be put in place and regular payments made. In this manner funds may be transferred in what is deemed to be a legitimate transaction.

CONCLUSION

This chapter has introduced the reader to the nature and characteristics of money laundering and outlined the most commonly used schemes to launder the proceeds of fraudulent activity.

11

High-Risk Corporate Activities and Market Manipulation

INTRODUCTION

In previous chapters we discussed a variety of issues facing directors in searching for Red Flags indicating fraud, corruption, and other improper activity within their organization. This chapter focuses on high-risk corporate activities, including those involving start-ups and manipulations of securities markets.

HIGH RISK WITH START-UP CORPORATIONS

Start-up public corporations have unusual risks for members of the board. In these cases, a private corporation, partnership, or sole proprietorship operated by a promoter or a group of promoters decides to go public. They may have an ongoing business that has been successful on a small scale or they may simply have a concept or a plan to launch a new business. In either case they are seeking capital investment to continue their perceived operational enterprises. The most common of these business concepts have included:

- Mineral claims—gold, silver, etc.
- Computer software
- Biomedical research developments
- Newly patented products
- Product manufacturing and distribution

By their nature, new corporate business ventures always have a certain amount of risk. Raising capital is a major challenge and potential failure always hangs over the heads of management.

Although financial collapse will have an impact on the future income and profits for everyone associated with the corporation, directors often feel that they are not at risk. They are protected from personal liability for the debts of the company. They will likely have liability insurance to protect them from financially related lawsuits. Share options are the standard method of rewarding directors for company success. If the corporation fails, it simply means that the options cannot be redeemed. Directors will therefore feel that the risk-reward factor is in their favor.

There are, however, a number of risks that directors face if things go wrong. Directors can be held liable if they are negligent in the performance of their duties. However, directors whose corporations participate in criminal activity will also be implicated. This may occur as they passively agree to support an aggressive CEO who is pursuing a criminal act to enhance his or her personal income.

MARKET MANIPULATION

Market manipulation schemes and insider trading—intended to create a false price for traded securities or to provide an unfair advantage to a class of shareholders—are very high-risk issues for directors as well as management. These activities are criminal offenses in most jurisdictions. While market manipulation is not restricted to corporate insiders, the involvement of insiders has a very negative impact on the corporation.

The opportunities to become involved in a manipulation scheme are much greater for managers and directors since they have operational control of the company and therefore can best predict the impact that corporate operational activity will have on the market price of shares. For example, if some action will have a positive or negative impact on the share price, an insider with this knowledge can profit through the purchase or sale of shares in the public market.

The laws of most jurisdictions prohibit this type of activity. However, the leak of this kind of confidential information is very difficult to prove, especially when the shares are beneficially held by others on behalf of the insider.

The case examples that follow will serve to demonstrate some pitfalls that may face directors in the performance of their duties as they serve on the board or on corporate committees. These are actual cases that have occurred. Some have been resolved successfully by quick action on the part of the board of directors; others have ended up with the company bankrupt, members of management prosecuted, and civil action against the directors.

Case Example—Problems with Taking Over an Existing Company

In this case Robert had been working successfully over the years in the development of a unique computer software program. He sought the assistance of a colleague to bring the program to a stage where it could be marketed to an established software company. In seeking advice from legal and accounting friends, they were encouraged to set up this software program in their own publicly financed corporation. In this way they could market the program directly to the public. The software program, they were told, had a greater potential to earn them more income. Again they consulted a legal friend who encouraged them to acquire an existing corporation that had been already trading on a public market, but was now in a dormant state.

There are many public companies that have gone through the stages of incorporation and structuring that have not succeeded operationally, are now inactive, and are available for new management to take over. This type of approach requires that a due-diligence program be carried out to ensure that all liabilities are identified and background checks made on the former directors and management. The old management can be paid by way of a share transaction from the new management (Newcorp).

The old board of directors and management resigned and a new board was elected. All the outstanding shares held by the old board and management were canceled. The new board then appointed the CEO and managers of Newcorp.

Newcorp issued shares to the new board and management in return for the software program, which then became the property of Newcorp. Robert, the managers, and directors, as well as other former shareholders, held the majority of the outstanding shares of Newcorp. The widely held minority shares remained in the possession of the former shareholders since there were insufficient shares to influence the makeup of the board of directors of Newcorp.

All these transactions occurred simultaneously, so Robert could now organize a board meeting to authorize that Newcorp issue a new public offering of shares to be sold to the public. The company shares had been traded on the over the counter (OTC—Pink) market at a high of $1.15 and a low of $0.05. They had been relatively inactive for over 6 months.

The board of directors, with advice from Robert, decided to engage the former company's underwriters to handle the new public offering. A prospectus was prepared for the new offering. The underwriter advised Robert that several offshore companies, who were already shareholders in the company, were potential buyers. Robert asked for details on the ownership of these companies. This underwriter refused. Robert became suspicious and the company engaged an independent forensic accounting firm to carry out a further background investigation on the underwriter and the offshore shareholders of the company.

The investigation revealed that insider trading had previously occurred with the shares of the old company. Neither Robert nor the board members realized that the former board and management had been involved in a market manipulation scheme using offshore corporations that held shares in the old company. The manipulation scheme involved artificial share trades between the offshore shareholders to bump up the price. With the price of the shares at the highest point, the insiders sold and the share price subsequently dropped. The underwriter was aware of the manipulation scheme. Further background checks on the offshore companies revealed that they were controlled by a known organized-crime family. The Newcorp board canceled all further transactions with the underwriter. A new team was organized and, with a new underwriter on board, a new public offering was completed.

This example shows how close Robert, management, and the board came to being criminally involved with a market manipulation scheme and an undesirable relationship with organized crime.

Case Example—An Exploration Company Involved in a Pump and Dump Market Manipulation Scam

A publicly traded exploration company's shares were unlisted and had been trading as a penny stock in the over-the-counter market at the 25-cent level for a long time. When the company had gone public 7 years earlier, they issued an initial public offering (IPO) for one million shares. Because the company did not carry out any exploration activities over a period of 2 years, investment interest virtually disappeared. Without funds and a less than viable future, the share price dropped to 5 cents asked and 2 cents offered. There had been no trades recorded for over a year. The company was virtually dormant.

A new group acquired control through negotiation with the old board of directors. A new board was elected and the company acquired several gold claims that had been developed by a prospector years earlier. The claims, however, were close to being revoked for lack of exploration work that was required by regulation.

To avert this, the claims were acquired by an individual and further exploration work was carried out. The claims were in a gold-producing region and had been worked up, by the prospector and former owner, to a point where a surface geological report was prepared. The report indicated that the property had the potential to justify further exploration.

The new owner of the claims then took over this dormant exploration company. He transferred the claims to the company and arranged a controlling share interest through a new company stock issue. In addition he began purchasing company shares on the market for less than 10 cents a share. He also convinced four prominent individuals to serve as board members. They received stock options in the corporation. He became the CEO and board chairman.

The company then engaged an underwriter and issued a new public share offering at a price of 50 cents. With the issuance of a prospectus and positive publicity regarding the new claims, the company generated enough interest in the marketplace to sell the new issue and raise the much needed funds for the corporation.

The corporation then engaged a geologist and workers to continue the exploration work on the claims. The new CEO took charge of the exploration group and within a 6-month period generated some very positive results concerning the viability of this property.

A new report was issued showing that the results were so encouraging that they would commence a drilling program. With this positive news, the share price steadily increased to over $1.00 a share.

The CEO engaged a group of Internet marketers who put out more positive information on finding sufficient gold on these claims to support a mining operation. The share price climbed to its highest level at $1.75. The CEO had connections to a boiler room operation situated in an offshore location and was able to use this channel to sell a great number of shares at a significant profit. The other shareholders lost their opportunity to sell their shares in the company at a profit, as the value dropped back to its original starting price of less than 5 cents a share.

The board members were not specifically aware of the CEO's secret market manipulation scam. The CEO did, however, convince them to sell a significant number of their shares at the top end of the market price. As a result, the directors were now implicated in the unlawful market manipulation fraud.

Case Example—Insider Trading

Providing confidential information for the purpose of profiting by buying or selling stock on the public market is known as insider trading.

This case example involves a board director who had personal financial difficulties and was a member of the board of a public company whose shares were traded on a major stock exchange. He decided to use confidential corporate information to profit from the sale of his company's shares. The company itself also faced serious financial problems and senior managers were negotiating with a legal and accounting team to prepare a proposal that would put the corporation into a Chapter 11 bankruptcy protection.

The company's shares had been trading at price ranges between $8.00 and $10.00 a share. The director knew that when the news of the impending Chapter 11 bankruptcy reached the public, the price would drop. The director met with his stockbroker and they devised a plan to short sell* as many shares as the market would bear. The trader was a friend of the broker and not connected to the director.

The broker, using the services of his friend, was able to short sell 15,000 shares over a period of 5 days at an average price of $7.50 per share. When the news of the Chapter 11 proposal became public knowledge, the stock price plummeted to less than $1.00 per share. The broker's friend then purchased 15,000 shares to cover his margin. This scheme produced a profit of over $90,000, which was distributed among the three parties.

Case Example—Professional Market Manipulators

GUNS FOR HIRE

Jim and Sam had been in the brokerage business for a number of years when they came up with the plan to make more money. Jim was a floor trader on a major stock exchange and Sam was a broker with a large brokerage. Both quit their jobs and devised a plan to set up a partnership that would manipulate share prices on the public markets for corporate insiders.

---

* Short selling: "Selling short is the opposite of going long. That is, short sellers make money if the stock goes down in price. This is an advanced trading strategy with many unique risks and pitfalls. Novice investors are advised to avoid short sales." Source: Investopedia at http://www.investopedia.com/terms/s/shortselling.asp (accessed July 23, 2013).

They both had many friends in the securities industry. They recruited a number of stockbrokers and floor traders to participate in their scheme. The brokers and floor traders would be compensated for their assistance because they would receive their commissions on the various share transactions that would be made through this scheme. Jim and Sam would profit by buying and selling the shares that they would control through this scheme.

The scheme involved receiving an assignment of a block of shares from a client who was an insider of a public company. With the assistance of the team of floor traders and brokers, they began to sell and buy the stock to give the illusion of a positive material development within the corporation. They then released significant positive information concerning the operational activity that would affect corporate earnings. With this combined action, the shares begin to increase rapidly in the market price. When the price reached the predetermined high, the client's block was offered for sale.

The floor traders favored the client's sell order over those offered by other shareholders as the sell orders came in on the down side. The block was unloaded to unsuspecting new buyers. As soon as the price dropped back to the premanipulated level, the client repurchased the shares to replenish the block. The scheme provided considerable profit to clients, the floor trader, and the brokers. Jim and Sam made their own profits by also buying and selling the same stock as the prices increased and then dropped in the process.

Jim and Sam found many clients, who participated in their scheme over a period of several years. It was only when a group of organized criminals decided to use this scheme that law enforcement began a criminal investigation. This investigation resulted in many officers and directors of public companies facing prosecution. Most were convicted and sentenced to fines and imprisonment.

MARKET MANIPULATION AND START-UP CORPORATIONS—RED FLAGS

- Promoters of a start-up company using friends instead of seasoned professionals to guide the corporation through the early stages of development
- Promoter failing to carry out extensive and comprehensive due diligence on planned takeover of new company
- Fellow company insiders involved in excessive trading of company shares on the public market

- High-trading volumes of shares before confidential information is released to public; share price increase before forthcoming positive information is released
- Short selling and share price drop before negative information is released to public
- Significant share price fluctuations on the public market without reason

CONCLUSION

This chapter has focused on high-risk corporate activities, including those involving start-ups and manipulations of securities markets. It has demonstrated that they represent a noteworthy, if little noticed, fraud risk.

12

Pyramid Schemes

INTRODUCTION

A pyramid scheme is devised basically to take funds from many people for the benefit of a few at the top of the so-called pyramid. Modern business pyramid schemes are usually bundled up in some type of investment scam that produces millions of dollars through the sale of investment certificates, territory, or products. Only the promoters really benefit from this type of scheme.

Here is an example of a simple version of how this particular scam works. The promoter mails a letter to ten people asking them to contribute a small amount of money to the promoter and then mail a similar letter to ten other people. They, in turn, are asked to send the same amount to the promoter and the second sender's name is then placed on a list under the promoter's name. A list of names is then developed as the different levels in the pyramid are generated through the distribution chain. The promoter of this chain letter will succeed in receiving funds from this chain. On occasion the second and third level may also benefit to some extent. But as the levels increase it is impossible that there will be enough people to participate and benefit everyone.

As we can see from Figure 12.1,* a pyramid scheme cannot be sustained beyond the very few at the top level. Level 13 exceeds the earth's population.

---

* http://www.sec.gov/answers/pyramid.htm (accessed July 23, 2013).

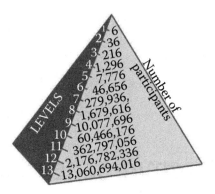

Figure 12.1 Pyramid base. (http://www.sec.gov/answers/pyramid.htm [accessed July 23, 2013].)

Another type of pyramid scheme, which has often been referred to as a Ponzi scheme, involves a variety of fraudulent investment scams. This scheme often begins by the promoter promising investors a very high rate of return on investments. To encourage new people to participate, the first investors are paid a very high profit on their investments. This so-called profit actually comes from their own investment funds or from funds paid by subsequent investors. There comes a point in this type of scheme when too many investors demand a return of either the profits or their initial investment. Since there simply are not enough funds available in the fund, the entire system eventually collapses. The promoter is the only person who will profit, and even then, only for a finite period. Ponzi schemes cannot operate indefinitely.

CHARLES PONZI

Ponzi schemes are named after Charles Ponzi, who used this scheme to defraud thousands of people in the United States in the early twentieth century.

Ponzi immigrated to the United States from Parma, Italy, in 1902. He came from a wealthy Italian family and was a graduate of the University of Rome La Sapienza. He first settled in Boston, but in 1907 he moved to Montreal, Canada, where he became manager of Banco Zarossi. A bank that catered to Italian immigrants, it also imposed a higher rate of interest on loans and mortgages. The bank failed and Ponzi found himself without funds. He found someone's checkbook and ended up forging a check in an amount of approximately $400. He was charged with the offense of forgery, and this resulted in a prison term of 3 years. On his release from the Canadian prison, he returned to the United States in 1911 and again took up residence in Boston.

Ponzi started a business involving the purchase and sale of international postal reply coupons called IRCs. These coupons could be exchanged for postage stamps in different countries. Ponzi discovered that if he purchased IRCs in various foreign countries like Italy, he could convert them in the United States for a much higher value. Through this conversion process he could make huge profits. This business venture was so profitable that he made over 400% on his initial investments.

While the business concept was legal and initially produced significant income for Ponzi, he found that he could turn it into an investment organization and make even more money. He incorporated what became known as the Security Exchange Company and he began offering investment opportunities to others in the IRC business, with promises of high rates of return on the funds that were invested. He promised investors a return of over 50%, when interest rates were 6%. A huge number of investors immediately appeared at Ponzi's office with thousands of investment dollars. Ponzi received so much money that he purchased the Hanover Trust, a local Boston bank. He also hired agents around the world to buy and sell the IRCs.

Ponzi used a number of other banks in the area to hold the investment proceeds. Publicity in new reports indicated that the early investors made $750 on a $1,200 investment over a 45-day period. As news of this success spread throughout the northeastern United States, more investors poured into Ponzi's investment scheme.

Then the *Boston Post* newspaper carried a story suggesting that Ponzi's business was a scam. Ponzi sued the newspaper and was awarded $500,000 in damages. Following some additional positive publicity on his investment business, more investors flooded his office requesting investment opportunities. Ponzi's business grew rapidly. He used the funds to purchase large homes and assumed the lifestyle of a multimillionaire.

The *Boston Post*, still suspicious about Ponzi's ability to promise and pay such lucrative returns on investment over a short period of time, launched a more in-depth investigation. The investigation revealed that Ponzi would need 160 million IRCs in circulation to support the investments already made in the Security Exchange Company, but that the company actually only had 27,000. A number of investigations by state authorities then followed. The result clearly showed that Ponzi was operating an illegal pyramid scheme and there was no possibility that the investors would recover their investment.

Ponzi was charged with eighty-six counts of mail fraud. He pleaded guilty to one count on November 1, 1920, and was sentenced to 5 years in federal prison. Four banks that Ponzi had used in this scheme went into receivership because of the publicity over this scam. Ponzi's bank, the Hanover Trust, went into bankruptcy. Investors lost over $20 million. Ponzi was later charged again under state criminal law for mail fraud and in 1922 was convicted and sentenced to an additional 7 to 9 years. This conviction was later upheld by the Supreme Court of the United States.

BERNARD L. MADOFF

More recently, a Ponzi scheme was used by Bernard Madoff in what has been termed one of the largest investment scams in US history. It resulted in a net loss to investors of approximately $10 billion. By comparison, Ponzi's scam netted a mere $20 million loss to the investors, which could exceed $250 million in today's value.

Bernie Madoff was a former nonexecutive chairman of the NASDAQ stock exchange in the United States. Highly respected in the financial world prior to his downfall, his clients were a Who's Who from the worlds of finance and entertainment.

He had previously been a financial advisor and stockbroker and was chairman of Bernard L. Madoff Investment Securities LLC, from 1960 until his arrest in 2008. Madoff was considered reputable and trustworthy by investors across the country. Because of this reputation he was able to entice hundreds of wealthy people to invest, in some cases their life savings, into his care.

Again, he promised a high rate of return to each of his investors and was able to pay investment returns to some investors, who would then entice new investors. He established a very sophisticated system of reporting earnings to the investors to keep them happy. The investors believed that he was investing their money in hedge funds that had a very high rate of return through stock and commodity trading, dividends, and capital appreciation.

In fact, Madoff did not establish a real hedge fund. Instead, he simply deposited much of the investors' money in his corporate bank accounts. He did, however, record fictitious entries of purchases and sales of stocks, bonds, and other securities in his company's books and records. This was done so that his outside auditor could prepare positive financial statements based on those false entries.

In turn, Madoff could then report those positive results to the individual investors. Madoff's outside auditor was a small, three-member accounting firm that had only one active accountant and was not qualified to audit an investment company of this magnitude. Whenever any particular investor required funds from his investment account, Madoff would simply pay that amount from the funds that had been pooled in the bank accounts. As new investors came on board, he could use their money to pay those that requested a payout. He also used those pooled funds for his personal use.

In 1999 Harry Markopolos, a financial analyst, reported to the US Securities and Exchange Commission that it was not possible for Madoff to sustain the kinds of gains that he promised his investors. Markopolos claimed, at that time, that he attempted to replicate Madoff's claims on financial returns on his investment and was unable to do so. In 2000 and 2001, he made allegations to the Boston office of the SEC that Madoff was a fraud. He repeated his claim to the New York office of the SEC again in 2005 and 2007. Other major trading companies refused to deal with Madoff as well because they felt that his promises to his investors just did not add up.

Finally, in 2008, the Federal Bureau of Investigation began its investigation of Madoff. It quickly found that Madoff was operating a classic Ponzi scheme. He was arrested and charged with securities fraud, mail fraud, wire fraud, money laundering, and perjury. On March 12, 2009, he entered pleas of guilty and was sentenced to 150 years in US federal prison. The US Securities and Exchange Commission carried out an investigation into Markopolos's complaints following Madoff's confession, arrest, and conviction, and found that Markopolos had been right all along.[*]

HOLIDAY MAGIC

Many other pyramid schemes have been detected and prosecuted over the years. Several of these schemes have focused on recruiting people to sell products. The products are, in effect, only a selling point to recruit individuals who supposedly become distributors for the product. Each

---

[*] US, SEC Office of Investigation. http://www.sec.gov/news/studies/2009/oig-509.pdf (accessed July 23, 2013).

person pays a fee to become an exclusive distributor in a specific territory. The new distributor is then expected to recruit other distributors and a pyramid type network evolves. The fees for the distributor recruitment are then distributed upward. The problems occur when there are more distributors than people in a given area. The sale of distributorships produces more revenue than the sale of the product.

An example is Holiday Magic,[*] a US-based corporation that manufactured and distributed cosmetic products. It was established in 1964 and structured as a pyramid type multilayered distribution system where distributers at the top earned more from the sales than those at the lower levels did.

The company maintained offices throughout the United States and Canada. Holiday Magic developed a very aggressive pyramid selling scheme involving the recruitment of distributers as the main objective as opposed to the sale of the cosmetic products.

Following a class action lawsuit, a court in Florida issued an injunction to prevent the company from continuing operating a pyramid sales scheme. In Canada, a senior vice president was prosecuted for operating this illegal pyramid scheme.

This case was considered as one of the largest and most aggressive pyramid schemes in its day. Leadership Dynamics[†] was another pyramid sales scheme that followed and was connected with Holiday Magic.

KUBUS

The Kubus pyramid scheme is another notorious scam that cost participants a lot of money that went to the benefit of the promoter Adriaan Neuwoudt. He used the distribution of a milk culture-based skin product in a classic pyramid scheme. This product and scheme began in South

---

[*] United States Court of Appeals, Ninth Circuit. Frank I. Marshall and Howard S. Myers, Plaintiffs and Cross-Defendants-Appellees,v. Holiday Magic, Inc., et al., Defendants, Dora Popa and Perry Marshall, Defendants and Cross-Plaintiffs-Appellants. No. 74-2773. March 8, 1977. Holiday Magic is a cosmetic company which distributes its product via a "pyramid sales" scheme. Distributorships are purchased from the corporation and arranged in a hierarchy. Those at higher levels earn larger profits, thereby encouraging all participants to enlist other distributors into the plan. Continued upward mobility in the hierarchy depends on an infinite supply of distributors.

[†] Leadership Dynamics, also known as Leadership Dynamics Institute (LDI), was a company incorporated in the United States that focused on executive training, personal development, and self- improvement.

Africa in 1984 and then spread to the United States, where two corporations took over and carried on this scam throughout the country for several more years.

THE BENNETT FUNDING GROUP

The Bennett Funding Group out of Syracuse, New York, was another pyramid scheme that involved investments into an implement-leasing Ponzi scheme. Before Madoff, this scam was the largest Ponzi scheme in US history, involving losses of over $1 billion.

Patrick R. Bennett was the founder and CEO of the various companies that were involved in this scam that was operational between 1990 and 1996. Bennett and other company executives were charged and convicted of criminal fraud and money laundering. Patrick Bennett was sentenced to a 30-year prison term.

WHY PYRAMID SCHEMES ARE A CONCERN

A variety of products have been the subject of pyramid sales schemes. Some pyramid sales organizations remain within the legal framework. These organizations can be profitable over a long period of time. However, when revenue eventually begins to slip and pressure to maintain profit increases, management will often turn to a more aggressive sales program. New sales teams are brought in to improve corporate sales. At this stage there is a real possibility that the existing sales program will become an illegal pyramid scheme.

So why is the pyramid scheme an important issue for directors of corporations?

Let us examine a hypothetical situation that has been the scenario in almost every public pyramid selling structure.

A major international publicly traded company distributes a variety of legitimate products through individual agents. The revenues drop off and the company comes under pressure to increase corporate profit. The board then hires a new dynamic CEO, who in turn brings in a high-pressure sales team. The declining revenue from the sale of their product suggests that a new idea and concept is needed. The CEO recommends to the board that additional distributors and new territories are required.

141

This new program for recruiting new distributors is put into effect. In order to generate rapid expansion and growth, a significant incentive to existing agents to recruit new subdistributors is put into place. The plan requires each new agent to pay a fee to become a distributor. The program provides for a generous sharing of these fees with the existing distributors.

In addition, the distributors are promised a commission on all of the product sales from the subdistributors. Since each new distributor is required to pay a fee to the company, this fee becomes the most significant source of income to both the agents and the company. As the recruitment fee begins to generate more revenue than actual sales of the product, an unlawful pyramid scheme evolves.

The shareholders, directors, and management will benefit financially with this newfound wealth in the short term. However, when the pyramid collapses, the company will become bankrupt, the shareholders will lose their investment, the directors will be assessed significant civil penalties, and managers will be prosecuted. Their short-term gain will certainly turn into long-term pain. Just look at Madoff and Bennett.

If history holds true, one day there may be another Ponzi scheme that will make the Madoff scheme the second largest in US history.

RED FLAGS—PYRAMID SCHEMES

1. When corporations report more revenue from the recruitment of agents and distributers than from the sale of their product
2. Commissions paid to recruit agents or distributors
3. Disproportionately large commissions paid for marketing investments
4. Interest rates on investments higher than the average for the same level of risk; in particular, interest rates on "safe deposits" that exceed market rates for equivalent certificates of deposit with insured banks
5. Investment plans are secret
6. Rapid growth programs
7. Promoters failing to meet obligations and asking for unreasonable delays
8. Lack of disclosure of specific assets held by a company even for investments in publicly traded securities
9. Promoter's business plan relates to new hi-tech or unregulated markets

10. Many interlocking and/or affiliated corporate entities
11. Engagement of small public accounting firms unable to service a large operation with complex legal structure
12. Small group of tightly bonded senior managers, consisting predominantly of family members and friends
13. Lack of proven expertise and track record of senior managers
14. Lavish lifestyle of principal senior managers
15. Media releases and reports publishing all or some of the aforementioned inconsistencies

13

Fraud and the Absence of Good Governance

INTRODUCTION

This chapter focuses on good governance, because the fraud and corruption detected in major corporate scandals in recent years can, in many ways, be directly attributed to the failures of good governance. In fact, the absence of good governance is the single factor that caused the downfall of major public companies such as WorldCom,[*] Enron,[†] Tyco,[‡] Bre-X Gold,[§] and Health South.[¶] Numerous other examples can be added to this list.

---

[*] In June 2002, WorldCom's internal auditors uncovered approximately $3.8 billion of the fraud. It was later estimated that the company's total assets had been inflated by around $11 billion. See Report of Investigation by the Special Investigative Committee of the Board of Directors of WorldCom, Inc., May 31, 2003.

[†] Enron's annual revenues reached $100 billion in 2000, making it the sixth largest energy company in the world. In December 2001, Enron filed for bankruptcy protection.

[‡] Between 1996 and 2002, Bermuda-based Tyco inflated its operating income by at least $500 million as a result of improper accounting practices related to a number of acquisitions.

[§] A Canadian public company, Bre-X, was the subject of a $1 billion scandal when its gold find in Indonesia was shown to be fraudulent in 1997.

[¶] Once the largest operator of rehab hospitals, Health South allegedly overstated earnings by $2.5 billion.

GOVERNANCE AND GOOD GOVERNANCE

Many books, articles, and reports have been written about these cases, and in identifying a root cause most point to the absence of good governance. First, let us discuss what governance entails.

Governance, on its own, is the authority exercised within a corporation and how that authority is exercised from the top down across the corporation. This authority comprises a system of rules and relationships that is coordinated with the desire to achieve certain results in order for the corporation to be successful, This is the case whether the entity is a corporation striving for profits for its investors and shareholders, a nonprofit organization that has specific objectives to achieve, or a publicly owned corporation providing services to a community.

What, then, comprises "good governance"?

Good governance—recognized as a fundamental building block to achieve success in managing fraud and corruption risks—is based on the following principles:

- Ethical leadership as reflected in the tone at the top
- Structured and reliable decision-making processes
- Accountability and transparency

The absence of good governance on the part of a board of directors has the most disastrous consequences on the future viability of any corporation. The board that fails to check corporate greed at the management level by ensuring there is good governance will soon find the company spiraling downward in a destructive path to bankruptcy. Loss of investments by shareholders and loss of jobs by employees can always we traced back to that failure in the boardroom. Over one hundred public company CEOs have been sued over the last 5 years for committing white-collar crimes.[*]

DUTIES AND RESPONSIBILITIES
OF A BOARD OF DIRECTORS

To further understand what comprises good governance, let us take a brief look at the duties and responsibilities of a board of directors. A more detailed outline is covered in Chapter 14.

---

[*] Association of Certified Fraud Examiners. Tone at the top: How management can prevent fraud in the workplace. See http:// http://www.acfe.com/uploadedFiles/ACFE_Website/ Content/documents/tone-at-the-top-research.pdf (accessed July 23, 2013).

Elected by shareholders, the board of directors manages the overall direction of a corporation, sets its objectives, and makes its strategic decisions. The directors choose the officers—usually a president, chief executive officer, vice presidents, chief financial officer—whose responsibility it is to run the day-to-day operations of the corporation.

Discharging their responsibilities through the board and a number of committees, directors approve and monitor the organization's budgets, financial accounts, core initiatives, projects, and business strategy. This is consistent with the leadership role set out in the quality management principles embodied in ISO 9000,* which states that "leaders establish unity of purpose and direction of the organization. They should create and maintain the internal environment in which people can become fully involved in achieving the organization's objectives."†

Directors have a fiduciary duty to the organization. They are entrusted by shareholders with the control and responsibility of the organization's assets and reputation.‡

When large companies first emerged in the nineteenth and twentieth centuries, they were often family owned and operated and did not have boards of directors. The owners and operators were one and the same. With large numbers of investors becoming involved, the concept of limited liability came into the corporate legal system and with it came the formal appointment of a board of directors. Increasingly in the twentieth century and continuing into the twenty-first, the dominant corporate model changed to one of public ownership.

Entrepreneurs realized that it was in their corporation's best interests to raise capital by selling shares to the public and listing their shares on stock exchanges. Listings help ensure the liquidity of stock and thus make it attractive to investors.

Because share ownership was no longer concentrated in the hands of a founder or proprietor, public ownership led to the separation of the duties and responsibilities of ownership and management. It was no

---

* The eight quality management principles are customer focus, leadership, involvement of people, a process approach, a systems approach to management, continual improvement, a factual approach to decision making, and mutually beneficial supplier relationships. See ISO's "quality management principles" at http://www.iso.ch/iso/en/iso9000-14000/understand/qmp.html

† See ISO's quality management principles at http://www.iso.ch/iso/en/iso9000-14000/understand/qmp.html

‡ "The duties of a fiduciary include loyalty and reasonable care of the assets within custody. All of the fiduciary's actions are performed for the advantage of the beneficiary." Source: *West's Encyclopedia of American Law*. Copyright 1998 by the Gale Group, Inc.

longer considered appropriate for a single individual or family to look after the interests of both shareholders and managers.

This led to creation of a new type of corporate hierarchy, in which directors represented shareholders and stakeholders and oversaw officers who managed the operations of the corporation.

There are basically two types of directors. Inside directors are also officers of the corporation. Independent, or outside directors are not officers, and they are expected to provide an unbiased and impartial perspective.

In practice, many boards, as highlighted by the Enron, WorldCom, and other financial scandals, acted frequently at the direction of the chief executive officer, who either chaired the board or controlled the agenda of board meetings. Independence and accountability were sacrificed. Shareholders and stakeholders, including employees, paid a big price.

As Arthur Levitt, Jr., former chair of the US Securities and Exchange Commission, remarked:

> When this independence and accountability are absent, markets cease to work properly. Capital is allocated poorly. And, eventually, someone pays the price. We saw this during the scandals at the beginning of this decade at Enron, WorldCom, and several other now infamous companies. ... Corporate board members stayed silent in exchange for big paydays or not to offend their friend in the CEO suite.[*]

GOOD GOVERNANCE AND TONE AT THE TOP

A common thread running through Enron, WorldCom, and the other major frauds of recent years is a lack of an ethical corporate culture. Their officers and directors sent a message to management by their actions, but mostly by their inaction, that unethical behavior allowed the top managers to carry out a series of fraudulent acts to enrich themselves to the detriment of the corporation and the shareholders.

There is a rule of thumb among fraud investigation professionals that 20% of people tend to be honest and 20% tend to be dishonest; thus, the remaining 60% are as honest as the situation provides. Although these percentages are based on anecdotal assessments, rather than empirical research, their tendencies appear intuitively acceptable. The key is

---

[*] Arthur Levitt, Jr., former chairman, US Securities and Exchange Commission. 2007. Remarks to dialogue with the OSC, November 27, 2007.

persuading the 60% to emulate their honest colleagues and not come under the influence of the dishonest ones. A culture of greed is more likely to sway the 60% to the dishonest side.

The Committee of Sponsoring Organizations of the Treadway Commission has identified a number of factors that create optimal conditions for preventing fraud. Among the most important is the example set by an organization's directors and officers: "According to the Commission, the tone at the top plays a crucial and influential role in creating an environment in which fraudulent financial reporting is ripe to take place."[*]

One of the important lessons of Enron and other major financial frauds is that directors and officers must not only be sufficiently vigilant for the signs of fraud, but also must make sure their corporation's culture is sufficiently oriented to ethical behavior. Among antifraud professionals, this is known as setting the right "tone at the top." The Association of Certified Fraud Examiners defines it as follows:

> Tone at the top refers to the ethical atmosphere that is created in the workplace by the organization's leadership. Whatever tone management sets will have a trickle-down effect on employees of the company. If the tone set by managers upholds ethics and integrity, employees will be more inclined to uphold those same values. ... Employees pay close attention to the behavior and actions of their bosses, and they follow their lead. In short, employees will do what they witness their bosses doing.[†]

Creating the right ethical atmosphere can help a corporation avoid the fate of the Enrons and WorldComs. As Stephen Cutler, director, Division of Enforcement, US Securities and Exchange Commission, stated: "Once the recent scandals recede from our collective memories, it's corporate culture that will serve as the bulwark against the eruption of a new scandal."

At another time and in another context, abolitionist Wendell Phillips said: "Eternal vigilance is the price of liberty. ..." Eternal vigilance is sound advice in this time and in this context.

By soundly endorsing the values of honesty and integrity, by rewarding employees who adhere to those values, and by providing avenues for employees to report ethical lapses, you can cultivate a healthy, thriving ethical climate in your company. By setting a tone of integrity at the top,

---

[*] Association of Certified Fraud Examiners. Tone at the top: How management can prevent fraud in the workplace. See http:// http://www.acfe.com/uploadedFiles/ACFE_Website/ Content/documents/tone-at-the-top-research.pdf (accessed July 23, 2013).
[†] Ibid.

you can create a climate for long-term success, a climate in which every-one gets it right.[*]

How to set the right tone at the top? Fraud experts have recommended the following kinds of initiatives:

- Create a culture of doing the right thing.
- Set an ethical tone at the top: Upper management has to lead by example and actions. These actions should include rewarding ethical behavior while punishing unethical actions. There should be sanctions for engaging in, tolerating, or condoning improper conduct.
- Establish a code of ethics: Organizations should produce a clear statement of management philosophy. It should include concise compliance standards that are consistent with management's ethics policy relevant to business operations. This code of ethics should be given to every employee, who will be required to read and sign it. It should also be given to contractors who work on behalf of the organization for their review and signature.
- Carefully screen job applicants: According to the Association of Certified Fraud Examiner's *Fraud Examiners Manual,* one of the easiest ways to establish a strong moral tone for an organization is to hire morally sound employees.
- Assign proper authority and responsibility: In addition to hiring qualified, ethical employees, it is important to place these individuals in situations where they are able to thrive without resorting to unethical conduct.[†]

Chapter 15 will provide additional in-depth insights into the role of the control environment, including the role of the tone at the top as part of enterprise-wide risk management.

---

[*] Tone at the top: Getting it right. 2004. Speech by Stephen Cutler, director, Division of Enforcement, US Securities and Exchange Commission, to the Second Annual General Counsel Roundtable, Washington, DC, December 2004.

[†] These fraud prevention best practices are derived from Management antifraud programs and controls: Guidance to help prevent and deter fraud, which was issued jointly by the American Institute of Certified Public Accountants, Association of Certified Fraud Examiners, Financial Executives International, Information Systems Audit and Control Association, Institute of Internal Auditors, Institute of Management Accountants, and Society for Human Resource Management.

STRUCTURE AND RELIABLE
DECISION-MAKING PROCESSES

A common phenomenon of the prominent fraud cases in recent years was the lack of structured and reliable decision-making processes—in particular, reward systems. WorldCom, for example, was strongly dominated by the persona of its CEO, Bernie Ebbers. He is said to have rewarded top-performing employees, who enabled or recorded the fraudulent accounting entries, with discretionary rewards in addition to WorldCom's remuneration and bonus regulations. Such rewards attack the foundations of good governance.

ACCOUNTABILITY AND TRANSPARENCY

The terms "accountability" and "transparency" refer to reporting mechanisms between management and the board of directors. Internal and external auditors play a key role in ensuring reliable reporting mechanisms—a fundamental component of good governance. Their failures, intentional or unintentional, were key components of the great corporate failures in the recent past.

CONCLUSION

Good governance is an essential building block to an entity that wishes to reduce its fraud vulnerabilities and enhance its ability to detect fraud early in the scheme's life.

14

The Board of Directors and Its Responsibility to Safeguard the Organization

INTRODUCTION

This chapter outlines the responsibilities of boards of directors to safeguard their organizations from fraud—responsibilities that are essential to the effective functioning of the Red Flag System. In particular, this chapter will outline the individual responsibilities of members of the board with respect to private corporations and public companies as well as nonprofit corporations and government agencies.

GOVERNANCE STRUCTURES

The role of boards of directors can be traced to the "agency theory" put forward by the Scottish economist Adam Smith:

> Smith had already figured out that markets work best when everyone can pursue his own self-interest, so he had to ask himself what would prevent a manager of one of those joint stock companies from pursuing that personal interest when it was contrary to the interest of stockholders. In a free market, Smith concluded, these newfangled stock companies would work only in a few small and simple market niches, where the

manager's actions could be readily routinized and his decisions easily monitored. That way, the manager would have to think about the shareholders, because they could keep close tabs on him.[*]

That is, Smith believed that the goal of organizing a governance structure is to optimize the allocation of scarce resources (i.e., money) to their most efficient uses (ideas). Shareholders are principals providing money. They appoint boards to steward the agents, who have the ideas and skills to put the money to its best use. The board in turn monitors the agents and reports back to the principals.

Over time, governance structures have developed on two separate paths with either single- or two-tier systems. In one-tier systems, the directors form one board, which delegates its responsibilities to the executive officers. All board members are responsible for the company's general course of affairs. In two-tier systems, the shareholders elect a management board, sometimes also referred to as an executive board, and a supervisory board. None of the members of a supervisory board can be members of the executive board. The supervisory board is not responsible for the company's role of affairs; it is solely tasked with monitoring the management board and reporting to the shareholders.

In the United States, Canada, and the United Kingdom, governance structures for corporations are one-tier systems. Germany, Austria, Denmark, Finland, some counties of Asia, Mexico, and most of South and Central America require two-tier governance structures.

More and more countries are moving toward permitting both types of systems, including Belgium, France, Portugal, Spain, and the Netherlands.

DIRECTORS' DUTIES AND RESPONSIBILITIES

Legal concepts regarding directors' duties and responsibilities differ from country to country and often within territorial substructures in each country. However, a number of common concepts apply in most countries governed by both common law and civil law principles.

In most countries, directors are appointed annually at a meeting of shareholders or members of the corporation. Once appointed they become separate and distinct from the shareholders. The shareholder does not retain any right to manage or control the corporation directly. The directors are required to meet subsequently at specified occasions as an entity

---

[*] Slate. The options problem, July 31, 2002.

called the board of directors. The board as a whole becomes the legal entity that provides direction to the officers and employees of the corporation with respect to their day-to-day operations.

In most jurisdictions with a one-tier system, the board may also be required to appoint committees to deal with specific issues based on statutes or based on best-practice principles for corporate governance. The committees must include members of the board and also meet as a distinct entity. Board and committee members have no individual authority except as a member of the board or committee. The committee is a creature of the board and must report back to the board for any binding decisions affecting the corporation.

Committees have specific mandates that have been delegated by the board. In many jurisdictions public companies are required by statute to appoint certain committees to provide oversight on various matters including finances. The most common committees are the following:

- Audit—finance
- Compensation
- Governance
- Management
- Environmental, nominating, and other specified committees that are appointed as required

The audit/finance committee is responsible for all financial matters concerning the corporation. It has direct oversight over the independent auditors and is required to have sufficient expertise to deal with budgets, financial statements, and all financial reporting.

The compensation committee is usually responsible for reviewing and approving all salaries and bonuses to officers and employees.

The governance committee is responsible for examining the general governance of the corporation, which includes the appointment, performance, promotion, and welfare of the officers and employees of the company.

The management committee often includes the chairman of the board, the CEO, and other senior officers, who deal with the issues affecting the day-to-day operation of the corporation.

Every board and committee elects a chairperson, who will be responsible to set the agenda along with dates of meetings. The chairman of the board will be responsible to report to the annual general meeting of the shareholders. The chairman of the committee will, in turn, be responsible to report to the board.

Again, what is important to note is that members of the board may only act as a member of the board as a whole and may not act in an individual capacity within the corporation.

Board members, who are also officers or employees of the company, are known as inside or managing directors. They then wear two "hats": one as a director and another with a specified duty as an officer or employee of the company. This is a common practice in a private corporation. Companies can even be required to have a certain number of inside directors in jurisdictions where the composition of boards is regulated to include a certain number of representatives for employees and unions.*

Most countries and jurisdictions have specific legislation that deals with the duties and responsibilities of corporate directors. Historically, directors of public corporations were treated in much the same way as directors of private companies and nonprofit organizations. However, many jurisdictions have significantly increased the responsibilities of directors of corporations whose shares are publicly traded. This was done to protect the interests of shareholders and investors. In addition, some jurisdictions will have statutory rules and regulations that deal with specific corporations like banks, railroads, airlines, and other institutions that have a public service relationship. These statutory provisions often call for specific requirements that will create additional liability on the directors that goes far beyond the common law requirements.

The duties and responsibilities of directors serving on government agencies and corporations are generally governed by specific statute law. These entities include organizations like municipal services, universities, hospitals, and other public service organizations.

We will now outline some of the jurisdictions that have enhanced regulations concerning the duties and responsibilities of directors.

COMMON LAW AND CIVIL LAW SYSTEMS

Common law legal systems place great emphasis on the precedential weight of court decisions and are theoretically based on the notion that it is unfair to treat similar facts differently in comparable situations. Civil law legal systems, on the other hand, are codified legal systems that evolved from Roman law, which was based on written civil code.

---

* This is the case in Austria, Czech Republic, Denmark, Finland, Germany, Hungary, Luxemburg, the Netherlands, Norway, Slovakia, Slovenia, and Sweden.

While in civil law systems the judiciary's role lies in the interpretation of laws, the judiciary in common law systems can create law by setting precedents.

The judiciary has a similar role in civil law systems.

Although rulings in one case are not binding for another similar case even if such ruling occurred in a higher court, courts tend not to deviate from higher court rulings, because such deviating rulings would most likely be overturned on appeal. Thus, when the need to interpret terms used in statutes occurs, the judiciary's role in civil law systems is similar.

Many common law systems have, over time, been mixed with civil law concepts. In particular, the field of business law is often based on statutes such as the Canada Business Corporations Act (CBCA), the Ontario Business Corporations Act (OBCA), or the California Corporations Code, to name just a few examples.* Nevertheless, where statutes leave voids, the judiciary can fill such voids with binding precedents.

Mixed law concepts originating from common law are the basis for most corporate laws in the United States, Canada, United Kingdom, Australia, New Zealand, India, South Africa, and other Commonwealth countries and territories including Hong Kong.† Common law principles have evolved through court decisions over the years. Together with corporate laws, they effectively lay out the duties and responsibilities of the corporation, shareholders, and directors.

Common law principles are the rules that courts are willing to adopt in a civil action involving the management of a corporation by its board of directors, including the duties and responsibilities of the board members. In civil law jurisdictions as well as in mixed law jurisdictions, the core duties and responsibilities have been codified, namely:

- The duty to act honestly and in good faith with a view to the best interests of the corporation
- The duty to exercise the care, diligence, and skill that a reasonably prudent person would exercise‡

When it comes to determining what constitutes care, diligence, and skill, common law principles provide the answers in mixed law jurisdictions and recurring jurisdiction provides the answers in civil law jurisdictions.

---

* http://www.law.cornell.edu/wex/table_corporations (accessed July 23, 2013) provides a comprehensive overview about statutes governing corporations
† http://www.hklii.hk/eng/hk/legis/ord/32/
‡ See, for example, section 122 CBCA, section 309(a) California Corporations Code, section 116, in conjunction with section 93 of the German Corporation Code (Aktiengesetz).

CORPORATE LAW—UNITED STATES

In the United States, every state regulates corporations. The statutes provide for the creation of corporations along with the duties and responsibilities of directors. In most cases these duties and responsibilities follow the common law principles providing that a director does not require any specific skills and has a fiduciary duty to act in the best interest of the corporation.

There are some specific requirements that affect the duties of a director, but most are very general in nature and have not provided many sanctions to a director who only participated in board decisions that ultimately resulted in fraud on the corporation.

In many cases the board decision actually facilitated an officer of the corporation to gain personal advantage through fraud and corruption and yet the directors were never held liable.*

As a result of a number of major public company frauds in the late 1990s and early 2000s, as outlined in Chapter 5, the US Congress passed a federal statute commonly referred to as the Sarbanes–Oxley Act on July 30, 2002.†

Significantly, it provided for the first time some significant measures to ensure corporate accountability and responsibility. The statute increased significantly the responsibility of officers and directors of publicly traded companies in the United States. In particular, the law provides that the corporation through the board of directors must implement the following:

- All members of the audit committee must be independent.
- Audit committees must be appointed by the board and the committee must include a member with financial expertise.
- The audit committee shall have exclusive control over the external auditors and over the auditors' reports.
- The CEO and chief financial officer must certify all financial statements, including providing statements of evaluation and the effectiveness of internal audit procedures and controls.
- Regulations and controls over insider trading by officers and directors of the corporation must be provided.
- Limitations and controls over corporate loans to executives must be provided.

---

* Enron, Tyco, WorldCom
† Public Company Accounting Reform and Investor Protection Act (Senate) and the Corporate and Auditing Accountability and Responsibility Act (House), commonly called Sarbanes–Oxley or SOX.

- There should be new and enhanced rules for retaining corporate records and documents and regulations providing for the protection of whistle-blowers.

In addition, the statute requires that the Securities and Exchange Commission* (SEC) adopt new rules and regulations to:

- Enhance standards for public accounting firms
- Ensure that board members and management maintain an acceptable standard of honesty and trust to avoid the scandals that cost the investors billions of dollars when companies collapsed because of corporate fraud

These enhanced provisions apply only to corporations that are publicly traded. However, other companies incorporated in the United States also have laws and regulations consistent with the general common law rules regarding the duties and responsibilities of directors. These include private companies as well as all of the other nonprofit organizations.

CORPORATE LAW—CANADA

In Canada, directors' duties and responsibilities are established by common law. They are also regulated by statutes passed by federal government and by statutes passed by each of the provincial governments. Corporations may be created as federal corporations as well as provincial entities based on corporation laws of each of the provinces and territories.

Federal as well as provincial business corporation acts define qualifications, powers, duties, and liabilities of directors as well as many other aspects of corporate governance.

In principle, directors are required to manage the business and affairs of a corporation.[†] While the term "manage" encompasses delegation of authority[‡] and thus requires supervision, some provincial statutes task directors explicitly with management and supervision.[§]

---

[*] It is the responsibility of the SEC to interpret and enforce federal securities laws; issue new rules and amend existing rules; oversee the inspection of securities firms, brokers, investment advisers, and ratings agencies; oversee private regulatory organizations in the securities, accounting, and auditing fields; and coordinate US securities regulation with federal, state, and foreign authorities.

[†] Canada Business Corporations Act (CBCA) s. 102(1).

[‡] See later discussion.

[§] For example: Ontario Business Corporations Act (OBCA) s. 115(1).

In reality, directors are not expected to manage a corporation personally. As a matter of fact, most directors have neither time nor expertise to engage in management functions. The statutes explicitly authorize the delegation of directors' powers to a managing director or committees of directors and permit directors to appoint officers and to delegate to them "powers to manage the business and affairs of a corporation."*

The implementation of delegation structures does not mean an abdication of responsibility. Rather, it requires due diligence in the appointment of managers and in monitoring their performance. Directors remain ultimately responsible for a corporation's business and affairs.

Typically, a Canadian corporation has a number of regular committees tasked to deal with ongoing particular areas. Examples are the environment committee, compensation committee, nominations committee, pension plan committee, and audit committee. While the establishment of these committees is generally a decision of the board of directors, the establishment of an audit committee is mandatory.†

Audit committees have statutory obligations to review a corporation's annual financial statements prior to their submission to the board of directors for approval. Provincial and territorial securities legislation requires the audit committee to review financial statements included in prospectuses prior to the approval by the full board of directors. Many audit committees are tasked with additional duties relating to financial matters such as budget decisions, monitoring continuous disclosure obligations, and ensuring the functions of the internal control/enterprise risk management systems.

Commonly, the audit committee is also tasked with reviewing large-scale single transactions—that, based on an individual corporation's by-law, may require approval by the board of directors—prior to such transactions being presented to the full board of directors for decision.

It must be reiterated that delegation of reviews to committees does not relieve the full board of directors from its ultimate responsibility for its decisions: Delegation requires monitoring.

The standards by which directors' duties are measured are set out in the following manner. They must act honestly and in good faith with a view to the best interests of the corporation and exercise the care, diligence, and skill that a reasonably prudent person would exercise in comparable circumstances.‡

---

* Canada Business Corporations Act (CBCA)—that is, 121 (a) and 115 (1).
† CBCA s. 171.
‡ CBCA section 122 (1).

CORPORATE LAW—EUROPEAN UNION

The European Union has the option for companies in Europe to incorporate as "Societas Europaea" (SE).* The SE is a public limited-liability company similar to those incorporated under US, UK, and Canadian laws. Each member country has, in addition, its own company laws.

Although some European countries have enhanced laws resembling the Sarbanes–Oxley Act,[†] all countries are required to treat SE companies as if they were incorporated under their own laws.[‡] Consequently, the UK, which is a common law jurisdiction and has comprehensive laws regulating public liability companies (PLC), will apply all its company laws and regulations to the SE corporation. The SE, however, may be managed as a one-tier system as those corporations in common law jurisdictions or as a two-tier style, which is prominent in many civil law jurisdictions. All EU countries, with the exception of the UK and Ireland, are civil law jurisdictions.

The duties and responsibilities of directors are primarily governed by the laws of each jurisdiction and are very similar to those outlined in this chapter.

DUTY OF CARE, DILIGENCE, AND SKILL

A corporation is a legal person or entity that is managed by individuals.

With the exception of statutory requirements concerning audit committee members of public corporations, most jurisdictions do not provide any detail with respect to what skill is required from a director. Basically, a director is not required to have any particular knowledge or expertise. There is consensus, however, that directors are obliged to apply the knowledge and skills that they do have.[§]

---

[*] European Public Limited—Company (amendment regulations) regulations 2009 (statutory instrument no. 2009/2004); European Public Limited-Liability Company Regulations 2004 (statutory instrument no. 2004/2326); Council regulation (EC) no 2001/2157 on the statute for a European company (the "regulation"); and Council directive 2001/86/EC supplementing the statute for a European company with regard to the involvement of employees (the "directive").

[†] Italy.

[‡] International Bureau of Fiscal Documentation, Survey on the Societas Eureopaea, http://ec.europa.eu/taxation_customs/resources/documents/survey.pdf (accessed July 23, 2013).

[§] Tëtrault McCarthy and M. Patricia Richardson. 1997. *Directors' and officers' duties and liabilities in Canada*, Chapter 2:1220.

When it comes to the level of care, the statutes provide no guidance as to what is considered an adequate level of care. The standard applied by courts will focus on what level of care a reasonably prudent person would exercise in comparable situations. *Black's Law Dictionary** defines "care" to include "watchful attention and concern as opposed to negligence or carelessness." There appears to be consensus that a higher standard of care is expected for persons, who possess greater knowledge or skill. Therefore, members of audit committees with specifically relevant financial skills, for example, bear a somewhat higher responsibility for the financial conduct of a corporation than other members of the board of directors. *Black's Law Dictionary* defines "diligence" to mean "attentive and persistent in doing a thing; steadily applied; active, sedulous; laborious; unremitting; untiring."

What do these standards mean for decision processes faced by directors in the normal course of business? To begin, directors must exercise care in selecting officers in order to ensure competency. Such care, however, does not relieve directors from their obligations to supervise.

Of particular importance is the so-called business judgment rule. Courts are principally reluctant to interfere with business judgments and generally do not hold directors liable for errors in judgment as long as they acted honestly and carefully. The important aspect of this is that despite the fact that directors may generally not be held liable for errors, they are obliged to ensure honest and diligent decision-making processes with an orientation toward the best interests of a corporation.

ROLES AND RESPONSIBILITIES IN PRACTICE

The term "roles" refers to the capacities in which an individual or body of individuals serves. "Responsibilities" comprise the duties and tasks that an individual or bodies of individuals are expected to perform.

Roles and role distributions vary from jurisdiction to jurisdiction and economic culture to economic culture. The core distinction between the various systems relates to the responsibility of strategic direction. One-tier governance systems tend to allocate this responsibility, often also referred to as "leadership and stewardship," to boards of directors, who may delegate their responsibilities to management. Two-tier governance systems place strategic leadership responsibility into the hands of

---

* *Black's Law Dictionary*, standard 9th ed.

the management board and reserve the role of supervision to the board of directors. It is important to note, however, that no matter what the distinction regarding leadership roles is, boards of directors have a supervisory role in every jurisdiction. Also, boards of directors have supervisory roles in public sector corporations, nonprofit organizations, and nongovernmental organizations.

The question, then, is which responsibilities go with the role as supervisor or overseer. Typical oversight responsibilities of boards of directors include[*]:

- Monitoring corporate performance
- Reviewing and approving financial statements and financial reporting
- Approving certain decisions of management, in particular material transactions and material communication
- Reviewing and approving the budget
- Reviewing and approving major financial decisions
- Safeguarding the corporation's resources
- Ensuring effective strategic risk management
- Using performance measures and verifying their integrity
- Assessing the integrity of information and controls
- Evaluating committee performance

DUE DILIGENCE IN OVERSIGHT ROLE

Boards of directors and their committees depend heavily on management to provide accurate information that is sufficient for the directors to fulfill their duties. In practice, directors discharge their responsibilities intermittently. Their engagement is usually part-time, although the statutes do not prescribe specific amounts of time to be spent on board matters. The distribution of available information is highly asymmetric, with management controlling most of the information and boards receiving condensed information. Under these conditions, how do boards ensure that the information they receive is complete, adequate, and correct?

---

[*] For a list of typical responsibilities of the board covering all roles (i.e., leadership, stewardship, oversight, and reporting), see David A. H. Brown and Debra L. Brown. 2000. *Who does what? A practical guide to the roles, responsibilities and relationships of directors, executives and shareholders*, 267–299. Toronto: Conference Board of Canada.

When looking at a director's statutory duties—the duties of care, diligence, and skill—one might gain the impression that there are contradictions implicit in these duties. For example, one statute from Canada states that a director will have exercised his duties of care and loyalty if and when

> … the director relied in good faith on (a) financial statements of the corporation represented to the director by an officer of the corporation or in a written report of the auditor of the corporation fairly to reflect the financial condition of the corporation; or (b) a report of a person whose profession lends credibility to a statement made by the professional person…*

The difference between this "good-faith reliance defense" and the duty of diligence seems to be that diligence implies active attention and persistence—that is, the requirement not to be satisfied with the face value of statements made by management or external experts. This discrepancy between the good-faith reliance defense and the duty of diligence remains unresolved. Basically, the good-faith reliance defense only covers the duty of care and loyalty, while it does not cover the duty of diligence. However, statutes generally provide that directors will have discharged their duties if they exercise the care, diligence, and skill that a reasonably prudent person would have exercised in comparable circumstances, including reliance in good faith on financial statements or expert reports.

It should be noted, though, that this provision exclusively deals with a director's liability in connection with certain aspects of issuing and redeeming shares and liability for payment of employee wages in certain circumstances.

Would a reliance defense mean that as long as the opinion of an expert is sought, directors have satisfied their duties? Is there due diligence in respect to expert reports and financial statements prepared by management?

The statutory and judicial encouragement of reliance on experts provides incentives to directors to focus on process by obtaining reports and conducting consultations in order to establish a record of due diligence. This would be opposed to directing attention to the answers to be obtained and their quality. Reliance, however, should not be passive. Rather, due diligence includes an obligation on each director to pursue inquiries actively.

---

* This is from the Canadian Business Corporations Act, section 123(5). Most Western jurisdictions have similar sections in their laws.

When relying on expert reports, a separate set of diligence requirements applies. They relate to the selection of the expert, the assessment of the expert's reports, and, when appropriate, the adequacy of follow-up.

In this regard, directors need to

- Determine the issue that needs to be addressed
- Determine the qualifications needed to solve the issue
- Ensure that the expert's knowledge meets the qualification requirements
- As a board, hire the expert directly, as opposed to delegating the relationship to management
- Ensure the expert's independence from management
- Ensure that the expert has unfettered access to information
- Understand the expert report in its entirety, not only its conclusion
- Understand the report's assumptions and assess adequacy for the issue at hand
- Ensure that conclusions logically result from the expert's findings
- Understand unresolved contradictions within the report and in comparison to common industry facts and knowledge

The trend in recent court decisions regarding directors' liability is to place greater responsibility, and hence liability, on directors. Nevertheless, courts still show deference to good-faith decisions made after a reasonable process. The establishment of rules, policies, and protocols with effective follow-up monitoring is essential for proving due diligence.* The emphasis is on effective follow-up monitoring.

INTERNAL CONTROL OVER FINANCIAL REPORTING

Assessing the integrity of information and controls is considered one of the typical tasks of boards of directors. In order to discharge it, boards typically rely on management, external auditors, and consultants. However, the question as to the extent of documentation needed to consider the effectiveness of internal controls over financial reporting needs to be addressed on the level of the audit committee and the full board of directors.

---

* John Finnigan. Director's due diligence: Tips and traps. http://www.tgf.ca/Libraries/Publications/Directors_Due_Diligence_Tips_and_Traps.sflb.ashx (accessed: July 23, 2013).

In its guidance, COSO states:

Controls performed below the senior-management level can be monitored by management personnel or their objective designees. However, controls performed directly by senior management, and controls designed to prevent or detect senior-management override of other controls, cannot be monitored objectively by senior management or its direct reports. In these limited circumstances, monitoring should be performed by the board—often through the audit committee—and its resources (e.g., internal audit).

The board is also in the best position to evaluate whether management has implemented effective monitoring procedures elsewhere in the organization. It makes this assessment by gaining an understanding of how senior management has met its responsibilities.

In most organizations, it is neither feasible nor necessary for the board to understand all of the details of every monitoring procedure, but the board should have a reasonable basis for concluding that management has implemented an effective monitoring system. Boards obtain persuasive information in support of their conclusions through inquiry, observation, and oversight of management; the internal audit function (if present); hired specialists (when necessary); and external auditors. They might also consider the output from ratings agencies and financial analysts. Finally, in some circumstances, boards might make inquiries of nonmanagement personnel, customers, and/or vendors.*

Internal control over financial reporting (ICFR) has been defined by the Securities and Exchange Commission as:

A process designed by, or under the supervision of, the registrant's principal executive and principal financial officers, or persons performing similar functions, and effected by the registrant's board of directors, management and other personnel, to provide reasonable assurance regarding the reliability of financial reporting and the preparation of financial statements for external purposes in accordance with generally accepted accounting principles and includes those policies and procedures that:

    (1) Pertain to the maintenance of records that in reasonable detail accurately and fairly reflect the transactions and dispositions of the assets of the registrant;

    (2) Provide reasonable assurance that transactions are recorded as necessary to permit preparation of financial statements in accordance with generally accepted accounting principles, and that

---

* COSO: Guidance on monitoring internal control systems, 2009.

receipts and expenditures of the registrant are being made only in accordance with authorizations of management and directors of the registrant; and

(3) Provide reasonable assurance regarding prevention or timely detection of unauthorized acquisition, use or disposition of the registrant's assets that could have a material effect on the financial statements.[*]

The responsibilities regarding ICFR vary depending on the size of a corporation and whether a corporation is a public or private corporation.

Both Sarbanes–Oxley, Section 404, and Canadian National Instrument 52,-109 9 (Certification of Disclosure in Issuer's Annual and Interim Filings), which apply to public corporations, make management primarily responsible for ICFR. The CEO and CFO must certify their evaluation of the effectiveness of ICFR and that they disclosed in the annual management discussion and analysis (MD&A) their conclusions about the effectiveness of ICFR at the end of the financial year. This evaluation must be completed using a control framework. Each material weakness related to ICFR has to be disclosed in the MD&A, including plans or actions to remediate such weaknesses. Further, certification by CEO and CFO is required on a quarterly basis that they have designed disclosure controls and procedures (DC&P) and ICFR and that they have disclosed material changes to ICFR.

The responsibilities of the board of directors result from the fact that approval of the annual MD&A, which includes DC&P and ICFR, is a responsibility of the board of directors. Therefore, the board of directors needs to understand the basis for the certification by the officers and becomes co-responsible.

FRAUD AND COMPLIANCE CONTROLS

One of the typical oversight responsibilities of boards of directors is the safeguarding of a corporation's resources. Fraudulent and noncompliant activity negatively impacts a corporation's resources and thus falls into the set of responsibilities of the board of directors.

Controlling activities in fraud and compliance risk management consists of three steps[†]:

---

[*] Securities and Exchange Commission: Final rule: Management's report on internal control over financial reporting and certification of disclosure in exchange act periodic reports, http://www.sec.gov/rules/final/33-8238.htm#i (accessed July 23, 2013).

[†] This will be elaborated in detail in Chapter 15.

1. Prevention
2. Detection
3. Response

Prevention is based on controls designed to reduce the risk of fraud against the corporation or criminal misconduct on behalf of the corporation (in particular, bribery and money laundering) from happening. Detection encompasses all the measures taken to discover fraud or criminal misconduct. Fraud response refers to controls designed to take corrective action and remedy damage caused by fraud or misconduct on behalf of the corporation.

Sarbanes–Oxley, Section 404, as well as Canadian National Instrument, 52-109 9, require officers to inform external auditors and the board of directors of any fraud that involves management or other employees who have significant roles in ICFR.

The question is, "Who controls the officers?"

Controls below the senior-management level can be monitored by officers and management structures reporting to the officers on fraud issues. The board needs to understand the design of fraud and compliance risk management as the basis for management's reporting on the occurrence, or absence, of material fraud against the corporation or violations on behalf of the corporation.

Controls performed directly by senior management—in particular, controls designed to prevent or detect senior-management override—cannot be monitored reliably by officers and therefore require monitoring by the board of directors and/or the audit committee.

HIGH-RISK PROCUREMENT AND SALES CONTRACTS

Approval of material transactions and material communication is typically reserved for the board of directors and/or the audit committee. Such transactions may generally be covered by fraud risk management policies. Nevertheless, large-value individual procurement contracts (e.g., the acquisition of airplanes by an airline, the construction of turnkey factory operations, etc.) require the individual attention of the board of directors. The thresholds for involvement of the board of directors are commonly set based on the individual corporation's business, industry, and size.

While board responsibility is easily understandable on procurement by the corporation, it is less easily accepted in large-value sales contracts.

The risk to be managed by a board of directors results from a possible use of illegal means, e.g., bribery, in obtaining such large-scale contracts.

Sales contracts obtained by manipulation of the customer's procurement procedures imply criminal liability for the corporation. Proceeds of sales from manipulated procurement processes can be qualified as proceeds of crime and can therefore be subject to asset forfeiture and civil liability. Large-volume contracts won by illegal means can jeopardize a corporation's survival.

BUDGETS

Periodic budgets and project budgets often require review and approval by the audit committee and the board of directors. Although not required by law, boards of directors tend to adopt the review of budgets under their principal responsibilities for a corporation's financial performance and for major financial decisions. The thresholds vary depending on the nature and size of the corporation.

Case Examples

The following cases show how directors serving on the board of directors and the audit and financial committees failed to identify obvious Red Flags while examining budgets and financial statements.

As global enterprises continue to expand, corporations have developed subsidiary entities in many jurisdictions. Several mining companies have operations extending from the Amazon region of South America to the far reaches of Tibet in Asia.

Structurally, to operate in such diverse environments, corporations are created in the operating countries and profits are disbursed to numerous tax haven jurisdictions and everything is managed from the parent head office.

Directors on the board at the head office must often sift through huge volumes of complex budget and financial documents to approve the various operations.

Every subsidiary company in the chain will have nominal directors and auditors. However, with such a fragmented and complex operation, no one, except the head office board of directors, will have a complete picture of any issue. The head office board, however, must be provided with many complex details in order to understand the nature of any line on a budget or financial statement.

Often the details of the procurement process in the various subsidiary entities are not provided and directors frequently have no option but to rely on the work of the internal auditors and their reports. Internal auditors are often sent out to these remote locations to review the operational work. The locations may be remote and the language in the local area may be a problem for the auditor.

In one case an internal auditor from the North American head office traveled to a remote mining site in a South American country. The auditor had scheduled 4 days to complete the audit of this site, which had several office locations. Travel from one location to another was difficult and the language and procedures were unfamiliar.

The auditor found that many of the key employees were related to each other and there was no organizational structure to the operation. The local manager had complete soup-to-nuts control over everything from the janitors to the accounting staff and controller.

The operation involved shipping ore from a country where the mine was located to another that housed the smelter. A number of tax and royalty issues affected both countries. Yet, there was no other operational supervision in place to review the manager's activities.

Since there were no checks and balances in place, this should have been flagged by management. In this kind of instance, management would be focused on the bottom line and determining if this operation is producing income consistent with their expectations.

In many instances, if the financial side of this picture is deemed to be acceptable, no action will likely be taken. And since no issue surfaced to the external auditors or the audit committee, no further action would likely occur. But this situation is clearly open to major fraud, which could result in a significant impact on the corporation if large-scale corruption were detected and publicized. Members of the audit committee and the board of directors at head offices should clearly look at this issue as a significant Red Flag.

This was certainly the case with a large North American international construction and engineering company. Corporate executives were accused of bribery and corruption with respect to their construction operations in countries in Africa and Asia with high corruption risks. Senior officers of the company were found to have hidden evidence and information concerning millions of dollars in cash payment to government officials in one country.

Senior officers have been arrested and charged for crimes related to this activity. The members of the board of directors, who were at the head office in a major Western country, were not prosecuted but they were criticized for failing to detect these corrupt practices and payments.

This matter has given an otherwise reputable international public company some very bad publicity and has affected the share price of the company on the stock exchange. Board members said they had been deceived by some individuals in senior management. They claimed that since the board met less than twelve times each year, it was difficult to stop officers and employees determined to commit fraud. But a number of professional critics have stated that when members of a board receive 85% of their information directly from management, they must put processes in place so that they are able to detect fraud and corruption.

These critics go on to say that while many board members are taking a more active role in examining the management of their companies, there are many who are reluctant to dig too deeply into the day-to-day operations of the corporation. However, this practice must change as corporations become more global, with their corporate operations spanning the world and reaching jurisdictions where fraud and corruption are the way of doing daily business.

FRAUD DIAGNOSTIC TOOLS

Fraud prevention experts have developed a number of diagnostic tools and techniques that officers and directors can use to determine their organizations' vulnerability to fraud. This section is intended to introduce the reader to the nature and characteristics of these fraud prevention diagnostic tools and techniques—especially their strengths and their weaknesses.

These fraud prevention diagnostic tools and techniques provide a broad idea of an organization's performance with respect to fraud prevention. It is not a detailed evaluation or an audit. There is no guarantee that there is no fraud in an organization. They cannot be relied upon to provide assurances that fraud does not or will not exist.

They are intended to (a) review, at a high level, an organization's current fraud prevention status; (b) pinpoint possible areas for improvement; and (c) set out a blueprint for cost effectively implementing those improvements on a prioritized basis.

Depending on the findings of such an assessment, an organization may wish to implement best practices like the enterprise risk management (ERM) strategy outlined in the next chapter.

This section contains an amalgam of fraud prevention diagnostic tools and techniques drawn from the authors' own experience and the following resources:

171

- The Association of Certified Fraud Examiners' ACFE Prevention Checkup*
- The guideline entitled "Managing the Business Risk of Fraud," sponsored by the Institute of Internal Auditors, the American Institute of Certified Public Accountants, and the Association of Certified Fraud Examiners[†]
- The fraud examiner's manual of the Association of Certified Fraud Examiners

In general, fraud prevention diagnostic tools and techniques involve a collaborative process between

- Internal stakeholders responsible for a corporation's direction, operations, and/or strategy
- Outside experts who are independent and have unique and proven expertise to identify and mitigate fraud risks

Fraud prevention diagnostic exercises usually involve a questionnaire that reflects fraud prevention best practices and a series of interviews—based on the questionnaire—of a number of directors and senior management. The results are generally analyzed by the outside experts, reviewed by the internal stakeholders, and summarized in a written report submitted to the audit committee and/or the whole board of directors.

It is important to understand the limitations of fraud prevention diagnostic tools and techniques. They are general in nature and do not have the scope or breadth of an audit. They do not guarantee that there is no fraud in an organization or that an organization will not become a victim of fraud in the future. And it is important to keep in mind that if an assessment identifies a possible material weakness in internal controls, it may represent a reportable condition under securities regulations. Anyone undertaking this type of assessment may wish to consider obtaining independent advice on the possible regulatory implications of scoring significantly less than the maximum score.

Many experts also recommend that consideration be given to conducting this type of assessment under the direction of general counsel to protect the organization's legal rights. The benefit is that they provide

---

* http://www.acfe.com/uploadedFiles/ACFE_Website/Content/documents/Fraud_Prev_ Checkup_DL.pdf (accessed July 23, 2013).
[†] http://www.acfe.com/uploadedFiles/ACFE_Website/Content/documents/managing-business-risk.pdf (accessed July 23, 2013).

a high-level status report, generating a broad idea of an organization's performance with respect to fraud prevention. This report will pinpoint areas for improvement and help set out a blueprint for cost effectively implementing those improvements on a prioritized basis.

While there are many types of fraud diagnostics tools, one of the simplest is the Association of Certified Fraud Examiners' (ACFE) Prevention Checkup, which is available free of charge from the website.* The ACFE checkup focuses on the following seven elements:

- **Fraud risk oversight:** This section of the ACFE checkup asks the following kinds of questions:
  - To what extent has the entity established a process for oversight of fraud risks by the board of directors and others charged with governance (i.e., the audit committee)?
  - Is there a written policy to convey the expectations of the board of directors and senior management regarding managing fraud risk?
  - Does the board of directors maintain oversight of the fraud risk assessment by ensuring that fraud risk has been considered as part of the organization's risk assessment and strategic plans? According to best practices, this responsibility should be addressed under a periodic agenda item at board meetings when general risks to the organization are considered.
  - Has the board of directors established mechanisms to ensure that it is receiving accurate and timely information from management, employees, internal and external auditors, and other stakeholders regarding potential fraud occurrences?
- **Fraud risk ownership:** This section of the ACFE checkup asks the following kinds of questions:
  - To what extent has the entity created fraud risk ownership— not just at the CEO level, but across the entity?
  - According to best practices, an organization's culture plays an important role in preventing, detecting, and deterring fraud. Has a culture been created through words and actions where it is clear that fraud is not tolerated, that any such behavior is dealt with swiftly and decisively, and that whistle-blowers will not suffer retribution?

---

* http://www.acfe.com/uploadedFiles/ACFE_Website/Content/documents/Fraud_Prev_Checkup_DL.pdf (accessed July 23, 2013).

- Have entity-level controls that establish the tone at the top and corporate culture been documented in the organization's values or principles, code of conduct, and related policies?
- **Fraud risk assessment:** This section of the ACFE checkup asks the following kinds of questions:
  - To what extent has the entity created an ongoing process for identifying its significant fraud risks?
  - Does the risk assessment include the following phases: risk identification, risk likelihood, and impact assessment and risk mitigation response?
  - Is the risk assessment integrated within an overall organization risk assessment or is it performed as a stand-alone exercise?
- **Fraud risk tolerance and risk management policies:** This section of the ACFE checkup asks the following kinds of questions:
  - To what extent has the entity identified and had approved by the board of directors a policy on how it will manage fraud risks?
  - To what extent has the entity ensured that the fraud risk tolerance of management and of the board is aligned? Have they ensured that fraud prevention is a significant consideration when making major business decisions?
  - To what extent has the organization ensured that the risk tolerance of management is aligned with that of the board of directors?
  - Has the corporation identified fraud risks that may pose a catastrophic risk of financial or reputational damage?
- **Process level controls/antifraud reengineering:** This section of the ACFE checkup asks the following kinds of questions:
  - To what extent has the entity implemented measures to reduce each of the significant fraud risks identified in its risk assessment through process initiatives designed to reduce/remove fraud opportunities and controls to prevent, deter, and detect fraud?
  - Has the organization's structure been reviewed to identify and eliminate unnecessary entities that might be used for inappropriate purposes or that might enable less than arms-length transactions or relationships?
  - Have all overseas and decentralized operations been scrutinized to ensure that they have fraud preventive controls in place to conform with the strictest legal standards and highest ethical principles?

- **Environment level controls:** This section of the ACFE checkup asks the following kinds of questions:
  - To what extent has the entity implemented a process to promote ethical decisions, deter wrongdoing, and facilitate two-way communication on difficult issues?
  - Is there a code of conduct based on the company's core values that gives clear guidance on what behavior and actions are permitted and which ones are prohibited?
- **Proactive fraud detection:** This section of the ACFE checkup asks the following kinds of questions:
  - To what extent has the entity established a process to detect, investigate, and resolve potentially significant fraud?
  - Does the organization have a fraud response plan in place on how to respond if there is a fraud allegation? According to best practices, the fraud response plan considers such issues as who should perform the investigation, how the investigation should be performed, and how to determine the remedial action.

CONCLUSION

This chapter outlines the responsibilities of boards of directors to safeguard their organizations from fraud—responsibilities that are essential to the effective functioning of the Red Flag System. In the next chapter, we will introduce the reader to an enterprise-wide approach to ensuring that organizations have appropriately effective internal controls.

15

Enterprise Risk Management, Fraud Risk Management, and Compliance Risk Management

INTRODUCTION

This chapter sets out the three building blocks—enterprise risk management, fraud risk management, and compliance risk management—necessary to ensure that appropriately effective internal controls are in place on a consistent basis across the enterprise.

ENTERPRISE RISK MANAGEMENT

As a consequence of major corporate failures in the 1970s and 1980s—some resulting from fraudulent financial reporting and others as victims of high inflation and interest rates—the Committee of Sponsoring Organizations of the Treadway Commission (COSO) was founded in 1985.[*] Its mission was to develop an internal control framework, which was released in 1992 and titled "Internal Control—Integrated Framework."

Enron, WorldCom, and the other huge financial scandals of the early twenty-first century suggested it was not enough to have good internal controls to prevent fraud. Rather, it became clear that companies would need a more encompassing approach to identifying, assessing, and managing all risks, including fraud risks.

The result was the development of an important new tool by COSO for boards of directors and senior management to manage their entities' risks, including fraud risks. The tool is called enterprise risk management (ERM). COSO stated:

> The period of [ERM] development was marked by a series of high-profile business scandals and failures where investors, company personnel, and other stakeholders suffered tremendous loss. In the aftermath were calls for enhanced corporate governance and risk management, with new law, regulation, and listing standards. The need for an enterprise risk management framework, providing key principles and concepts, a common language, and clear direction and guidance, became even more compelling.[†]

The COSO standard for enterprise risk management

> ...serves as the broadly accepted standard for satisfying those reporting requirements. This *Enterprise Risk Management—Integrated Framework* expands on internal control, providing a more robust and extensive focus on the broader subject of enterprise risk management. While it is not intended to and does not replace the internal control framework, but rather incorporates the internal control framework within it, companies may decide to look to this enterprise risk management framework both to satisfy their internal control needs and to move toward a fuller risk management process.[‡]

---

[*] An independent private-sector initiative COSO, and its internal control guidance, proved to be highly influential, developing recommendations for public companies and their independent auditors, for the SEC and other regulators and for educational institutions. COSO was sponsored jointly by five major professional associations headquartered in the United States: the American Accounting Association (AAA), the American Institute of Certified Public Accountants (AICPA), Financial Executives International (FEI), the Institute of Internal Auditors (IIA), and the National Association of Accountants (now the Institute of Management Accountants [IMA]). Wholly independent of each of the sponsoring organizations, the commission included representatives from industry, public accounting, investment firms, and the New York Stock Exchange.

[†] Committee of Sponsoring Organizations of the Treadway Commission (COSO). Enterprise risk management—Integrated framework.

[‡] Ibid.

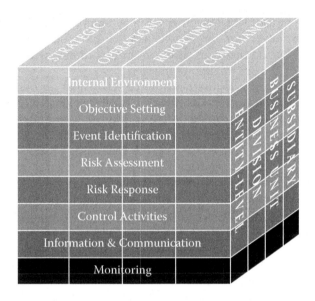

Figure 15.1 Enterprise Risk Management Matrix.

What Is ERM?

Enterprise risk management is more than a set of rules. It is a process effected by an entity's board of directors, management, and other personnel that is applied in strategy setting across the enterprise. It is designed to identify potential events that may affect the entity, manage risk to be within its risk appetite, and provide reasonable assurance regarding the achievement of entity objectives.[*] A cube illustrates this process[†] (Figure 15.1).

The Width Dimension of ERM

The COSO process takes four categories of objectives into consideration:

1. Strategy
2. Operations
3. Reporting
4. Compliance

---

[*] Ibid.
[†] Reprinted with permission from the American Institute of Certified Public Accountants.

Strategy: As an ERM objective, strategy stands for managing the risks of not, or not completely, achieving the strategic goals as defined by the board of directors in accordance with and supported by the organization's mission.

Operations: This is focused on the objective that an organization runs effectively and makes efficient use of its resources. Operations level risks cover a broad range of industry- and organization-specific risks and are commonly broken down into the components of an individual organization's value-generating processes. Typical examples are management risks, personnel qualification risks, information security risks, manufacturing process risks, quality risks, receivables collection risks, business interruption risks, technology risks, liability risks, and fraud risks, to name just a few.

Reporting: The goal of reporting risk management is to ensure that an organization reports accurately and reliably. This not only covers external financial reporting, but also internal financial reporting as well as reporting for controlling purposes and other nonfinancial reports.

Compliance risk management as originally defined by COSO deals with ensuring that an organization complies with applicable laws and regulations. Applicable laws can be of a prohibitive nature, such as anticorruption laws, or of an obliging nature, such as laws requiring maintenance of work safety or health standards. Compliance risk management typically has certain overlaps with other risk management objectives. True and fair financial reporting is a legal requirement as much as it is a reporting objective. Manipulating procurement processes is a fraudulent activity and thus falls under the category of compliance risks. At the same time, procurement manipulation can lead to loss of reputation and may thereby pose a risk to an organization's marketing and sales strategy. This explains why compliance is often not just limited to legal and regulatory compliance, but also extends to cover compliance with stakeholder expectations.

The Height Dimension of ERM

The height dimension, which forms the face of the COSO cube, covers specific activities required for effective risk management. ERM identifies eight specific risk management components:

1. Internal environment
2. Objectives setting
3. Event identification
4. Risk assessment
5. Risk response
6. Control activities
7. Information and communication
8. Monitoring

Managing the **internal environment** relates to the tone of an organization and forms the basis for how risk is viewed and addressed by an entity. This covers diverse topics such as risk management philosophy, risk appetite, and attitudes of boards of directors and senior management as well as attitudes toward integrity and ethical values. It also relates to the organizational setup, leadership culture, and human resource standards. The tone of an organization should not be mistaken for the mere aspect of "tone at the top." The internal environment is relevant throughout an organization's structure. Risk management philosophy should permeate every fiber of an organization homogenously, thereby avoiding silo approaches with incoherent attitudes toward risks. Nevertheless, the tone at the top is an important component of the internal environment as it shows and communicates the risk management philosophy of the board of directors and senior management. It is on that level where risk appetite is set for the organization as a whole.

Risk appetite refers to the level of risk that an organization is willing to accept as well as the ratio between risk and reward. The common view on the concept of risk appetite is that it is an interesting subject of theoretical discussions about risk management, but the concept rarely finds its way into the conscious process of risk management.[*] Yet, decision makers within an organization need guidance as to how much risk is acceptable. Risk appetite has immediate implications on risk response.

Risk appetite needs to be developed by making principled choices on the basis of understanding the trade-offs involved with different levels of risk appetite. Once developed, risk appetite needs to be communicated by way of an overall risk appetite statement. Communication also needs to address risk appetite for specific organizational objectives and different risk categories.

---

[*] The Committee of Sponsoring Organizations of the Treadway Commission (COSO): Understanding and communicating risk appetite, January 2012.

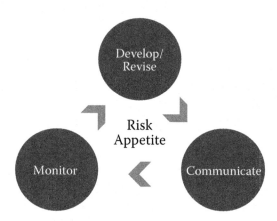

Figure 15.2 Risk appetite process.

A third component of risk appetite setting is the monitoring of activities for consistency with risk appetite and as a basis for reviewing and revisiting risk appetite development. Figure 15.2 illustrates this process.[*]

Examples of deficiencies in risk management philosophy in the recent past are the actions of so-called rogue traders at multinational financial institutions:

- In 2012, for example, Britain's Financial Services Authority fined UBS the equivalent of $47.6 million because serious weaknesses in the internal controls of its investment banking unit failed to prevent a $2.3 billion loss caused by a former trader.[†]
- In 2008, the French bank Société Générale discovered a $7.2 billion fraud. Its internal controls were, in themselves, effective, identifying nearly one hundred operational anomalies, or Red Flags, over a 2-year period. The problem appears to have been that no one took notice.[‡]
- This seems to all have started with Nick Leeson, who, acting out of Singapore, single-handedly caused the collapse of Barings Bank in 1995.[§] Leeson could conceal his activities from his superiors

---

[*] Ibid. Reprinted with permission from the American Institute of Certified Public Accountants.

[†] http://dealbook.nytimes.com/2012/11/26/ubs-fined-47-5-million-in-rogue-trading-scandal/?_r=0

[‡] *Wall Street Journal.* Once again, the risk protection fails. January 25, 2008 (accessed July 23, 2013).

[§] http://news.bbc.co.uk/2/hi/business/375259.stm (accessed July 23, 2013).

because, in a gross violation of basic internal controls, he was responsible for both the trading and the settlement sides of the Singapore operations.*

In these three cases, deviations in risk management philosophy and risk appetite may have led to silo approaches in risk management philosophy and risk appetite. These traders or their departments took more aggressive, riskier, and unhedged positions than what their organizations had determined was acceptable and adequate for their business models.

Responsibilities for infusing risk management philosophy into the depth of an organization need to be allocated to leadership and specialists in business entities and hierarchical levels supported by specialists where appropriate.

Table 15.1 provides a model for allocation of responsibilities.

Table 15.1   Risk Management Responsibilities

Position/Role	Responsibilities
CEO	• Determine strategic approach to risk (limits, thresholds, risk appetite, risk tolerance, risk capacity) • Establish organization and procedures for risk management • Understand the most significant risks • Consider implications of poor risk management decisions • Manage the organization during crisis
Senior management of business entities	• Build a risk-aware culture within the entity • Agree on risk management performance targets for the entity • Evaluate risk management reports from employees • Ensure implementation of risk improvement recommendations • Identify and report changed circumstances/risks
Individual employees	• Understand, accept, and implement risk management processes • Report inefficient, unnecessary, or unworkable controls • Report loss events and near-miss incidents • Cooperate with management in incident investigations • Ensure that business partners comply with procedures

continued

---

* Wolfgang H. Reinicke. 1998. *Public policy: Governing without government?* Washington, DC: The Brookings Institution.

Table 15.1 (continued)   Risk Management Responsibilities

Position/Role	Responsibilities
Risk officer	• Develop and maintain risk management policy • Facilitate a risk-aware culture within the organization • Establish internal risk policies and structures • Coordinate risk management activities • Compile risk information and prepare reports for the board of directors
Specialist risk management functions	• Assist the organization in establishing specialist risk policies • Develop contingency and recovery plans • Keep up to date with developments in the specialist area • Support investigation of incidents and near-misses • Prepare detailed reports on specialist risks
Internal audit manager	• Develop a risk-based internal audit program • Audit the risk processes across the organization • Provide assurance on the management of risk • Support and help develop the risk management processes • Report on the efficiency and effectiveness of internal controls

Source: Paul Hopkin. 2010. *Fundamentals of risk management—Understanding, evaluating and implementing effective risk management.* London: Kindle edition locations 3243-3282. Reprinted with permission from Koganpage Books.

Management has to establish a process to **set objectives,** which ensures that the chosen objectives support and align with the entity's mission and are consistent with its risk appetite. In accordance with the distinction of objectives, there are four categories of objectives—namely,

- Strategic objectives
- Operating objectives
- Reporting objectives
- Compliance objectives

Once again, the emphasis is on "process." Not only does an organization need to set its overarching objectives as high-level goals for its strategies, operations, reporting, and compliance, but it also needs to put a process in place to develop subsets of objectives for the various components of ERM in all business units (see "Depth Dimension" later in the chapter).

The most important guidance for such processes is the mission statement. It allows an organization to both develop high-level strategic objectives and guide the development, selection, and implementation of operations, reporting, and compliance subobjectives.[*]

COSO defines an event as an incident or occurrence emanating from internal or external sources that affects implementation of strategy or achievement of objectives. Events may have positive or negative impact, or both. Internal and external **events** affecting achievement of an entity's objectives must first of all be **identified** and distinguished between risks and opportunities. The COSO framework's event categories are shown in Table 15.2.

Table 15.2 Event Categories

External Factors	Internal Factors
Economic	**Infrastructure**
• Capital availability	• Availability of assets
• Credit issuance, default	• Capability of assets
• Concentration	• Access to capital
• Liquidity	• Complexity
• Financial markets	
• Unemployment	
• Competition	
• Mergers/acquisitions	
Natural environment	**Personnel**
• Emissions and waste	• Employee capability
• Energy	• Fraudulent activity
• Natural disaster	• Health and safety
• Sustainable development	
Political	**Process**
• Governmental changes	• Capacity
• Legislation	• Design
• Public policy	• Execution
• Regulation	• Suppliers/dependencies
Social	**Technology**
• Demographics	• Data integrity
• Consumer behavior	• Data and system availability
• Corporate citizenship	• System selection
• Privacy	• Development
• Terrorism	• Deployment
	• Maintenance

continued

---

[*] Robert R. Moeller. 2007. *COSO enterprise risk management—Understanding the new integrated ERM framework*. Hoboken, NJ: John Wiley & Sons.

Table 15.2 (continued)   Event Categories

External Factors	Internal Factors
Technological	
• Interruptions	
• Electronic commerce	
• External data	
• Emerging technology	

Source: Committee of Sponsoring Organizations of the Treadway Commission (COSO). *Enterprise Risk Management—Integrated Framework.* Reprinted with permission from the American Institute of Certified Public Accountants.

How to identify events is, in itself, a process warranting close attention. The International Standard Organization (ISO) lists the methods that can be used for event identification in its ISO 31010 risk management standard (accessed July 23, 2013 from http://www.iso.org/iso/news.htm?refid=Ref1266). Methods deemed strongly applicable to the event identification process are shown in Table 15.3.

Table 15.3   Event Identification Processes

Method	Description
Brainstorming	Brainstorming involves stimulating and encouraging free-flowing conversation among a group of knowledgeable people to identify potential failure modes and associated hazards, risks, criteria for decisions, and/or options for treatment. The term "brainstorming" is often used very loosely to mean any type of group discussion. However, true brainstorming involves particular techniques to try to ensure that the thoughts and statements of others in the group trigger people's imagination.
Structured and semistructured interviews	In a structured interview, individual interviewees are asked a set of prepared questions from a prompting sheet, which encourages the interviewee to view a situation from a different perspective and thus identify risks from that perspective. A semistructured interview is similar, but allows more freedom for a conversation to explore issues that arise.

186

Table 15.3 (continued) Event Identification Processes

Method	Description
Delphi	The Delphi technique is a procedure to obtain a reliable consensus of opinion from a group of experts. Although the term is often now broadly used to mean any form of brainstorming, an essential feature of the Delphi technique, as originally formulated, was that experts expressed their opinions individually and anonymously while having access to the other experts' views as the process progressed.
Checklists	Checklists are lists of hazards, risks, or control failures that have been developed, usually from experience, either as a result of a previous risk assessment or as a result of past failures.
PHA (primary hazard analysis)	PHA is a simple, inductive method of analysis whose objective is to identify the hazards, hazardous situations, and events that can cause harm for a given activity, facility, or system.
HAZOP	HAZOP is the acronym for *haz*ard and *op*erability study and is a structured and systematic examination of a planned or existing product, process, procedure, or system. It is a technique to identify risks to people, equipment, environment, and/or organizational objectives. The study team is also expected, where possible, to provide a solution for treating the risk.
Hazard analysis and critical control points (HACCP)	HACCP provides a structure for identifying hazards and putting controls in place at all relevant parts of a process to protect against the hazards and to maintain the quality, reliability, and safety of a product. HACCP aims to ensure that risks are minimized by controls throughout the process rather than through inspection of the end product.
Structured "what-if"-technique (SWIFT)	SWIFT was originally developed as a simpler alternative to HAZOP. It is a systematic, team-based study, utilizing a set of "prompt" words or phrases used by the facilitator within a workshop to stimulate participants to identify risks. The facilitator and team use standard "what-if" type phrases in combination with the prompts to investigate how a system, plant item, organization, or procedure will be affected by deviations from normal operations and behavior. SWIFT is normally applied more at a systems level, with a lower level of detail than HAZOP.

continued

Table 15.3 (continued) Event Identification Processes

Method	Description
Scenario analysis	Scenario analysis is a name given to the development of descriptive models of how the future might turn out. It can be used to identify risks by considering possible future developments and exploring their implications. Sets of scenarios reflecting (for example) best case, worst case, and expected case may be used to analyze potential consequences and their probabilities for each scenario as a form of sensitivity analysis when analyzing risk.
Failure modes and effects analysis (FMEA) and failure modes and effects and criticality analysis (FMECA)	FMEA is a technique used to identify the ways in which components, systems, or processes can fail to fulfill their design intent. FMEA identifies: • All potential failure modes of the various parts of a system (a failure mode is what is observed to fail or to perform incorrectly) • The effects that these failures may have on the system • The mechanisms of failure • How to avoid the failures and/or mitigate the effects of the failures on the system FMECA extends an FMEA so that each fault mode identified is ranked according to its importance or criticality.
Cause and effect analysis	Cause and effect analysis is a structured method to identify possible causes of an undesirable event or problem. It organizes the possible contributory factors into broad categories so that all possible hypotheses can be considered. It does not, however, by itself, point to the actual causes since these can only be determined by real evidence and empirical testing of hypotheses.
Human reliability assessment	Human reliability assessment (HRA) deals with the impact of humans on system performance and can be used to evaluate human error influences on the system.
Reliability-centered maintenance	Reliability-centered maintenance is a method to identify the policies that should be implemented to manage failures so as to achieve the required safety, availability, and economy of operation efficiently and effectively for all types of equipment.
Consequence/ probability matrix	The consequence/probability matrix is a means of combining qualitative or semiquantitative ratings of consequence and probability to produce a level of risk or risk rating.

Source: International Standard Organization. 2009. Risk management-risk assessment techniques, p. 22 and annexes B1 through B29. Reprinted with permission from the International Standard Organization.

Once identified, risks need to be assessed regarding the likelihood of their occurrence and the extent of their impact. Risk assessment is not a one-time event, but rather a continuous process reflecting and taking into account the evolution of an organization.

Inherent risk is the risk of a certain event prior to, and in the absence of, mitigating measures. The risk remaining after such mitigation is the residual risk. If a risk is not managed at all, its residual risk equals its inherent risk. The relationship between inherent and residual risks varies as a consequence of risk appetite. The higher the risk appetite is, the higher is the acceptable residual risk.

Uncertainty of potential events has two components:

1. The extent of an event's impact
2. The likelihood that an event will materialize

Risk assessments require complex judgments and such judgments can vary depending on the individual assessor.

To be truly effective, an organizational entity needs to find a way to optimally amalgamate data sources and individual perspectives into an entity assessment. Typical approaches are benchmarking, probabilistic models, and nonprobabilistic models. The techniques range from interviews to workshops and moderated self-assessment processes.

The result of the risk assessment is commonly visualized in a risk matrix. It is a two-dimensional graph. One axis reflects the magnitude of impact from an event. The second reflects the likelihood that an event is expected to occur. Typically, the magnitude of impact and likelihood are set out in one of five levels. The risk management system applied by NASA provides a good example of a generic risk matrix (see Figure 15.3).

Likelihood	Safety (Estimated likelihood of safety event occurrence)	Technical (Estimated likelihood of not meeting performance requirements)	Cost/Schedule (Estimated likelihood of not meeting cost or schedule commitment)
5 Very High	$(P_{SE} > 10^{-1})$	$(P_{TE} > 50\%)$	$(P_{CS} > 75\%)$
4 High	$(10^{-2} < P_{SE} \leq 10^{-1})$	$(25\% < P_T \leq 50\%)$	$(50\% < P_{CS} \leq 75\%)$
3 Moderate	$(10^{-3} < P_{SE} \leq 10^{-2})$	$(15\% < P_T \leq 25\%)$	$(25\% < P_{CS} \leq 50\%)$
2 Low	$(10^{-6} < P_{SE} \leq 10^{-3})$	$(2\% < P_T \leq 15\%)$	$(10\% < P_{CS} \leq 25\%)$
1 Very Low	$(P_{SE} \leq 10^{-6})$	$(0.1\% < P_T \leq 2\%)$	$(P_{CS} \leq 10\%)$

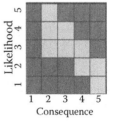

Figure 15.3 Risk matrix. (From NASA. 2009. Goddard Space Flight Center, risk management reporting, May 2009, http://standards.gsfc.nasa.gov/gsfc-std/obsolete/gsfc-std-0002.pdf (accessed July 23, 2013).)

Table 15.4 Consequence Categories

Risk	1 Very low	2 Low	3 Moderate	4 High	5 Very high
Safety	Negligible or no impact	Could cause the need for only minor first-aid treatment	May cause minor injury or occupational illness or minor property damage	May cause severe injury or occupational illness or major property damage	May cause death or permanent disabling injury or destruction of property
Technical	No impact to full mission success criteria	Minor impact on full mission success criteria	Moderate impact of full mission success criteria; minimum mission success criteria is achievable with margin	Major impact to full mission success criteria; minimum mission success criteria is achievable	Minimum mission success criteria is not achievable
Schedule	Negligible or no schedule impact	Minor impact to schedule milestones; accommodates within reserves; no impact to critical path	Impact to schedule milestones; accommodates within reserves; moderate impact to critical path	Major impact to schedule milestones; major impact to critical path	Cannot meet schedule milestones
Cost	<2% increase over allocated and negligible impact on reserve	Between 2% and 5% increase over allocated and can handle with reserve	Between 5% and 7% increase over allocated and cannot handle with reserves	Between 7% and 10% increase over allocated and/or exceeds proper reserves	>10% increase over allocated and/or cannot handle with reserves

The five categories for likelihood as well as magnitude of impact (or consequences) are labeled 1 (very low), 2 (low), 3 (moderate), 4 (high), and 5 (very high). Likelihood is expressed as a percentage probability. Impact is determined on the basis of organization-specific criteria. In the case of NASA, safety, technical, scheduling, and cost risks are taken into account when expressing consequences of events (see Table 15.4).

A crucial component of risk assessment involves considering relationships between events. Events that are seen as unrelated are referred to as stochastic[*] risks. Related events are called systematic risk.

The collapse of the financial markets in 2007 and 2008 was predominantly caused by the assumption that mortgage and other credit default risks were unrelated. That is, if one mortgage defaulted, other mortgages would still have unaltered default probabilities.

The design of two types of debt securities that were prominent in the collapse—collateral mortgage obligations (CMOs)[†] and collateral debt obligations (CDOs)[‡]—was based on the assumption of stochastic risk distributions. The fact, however, was that these risks were not stochastic. The default of even a limited number of mortgages led to increased supplies in the real estate markets. The resulting decline in real estate values, in turn, led to even more defaults. The risks were systematic as opposed to stochastic. This led to default of countless CMOs and CDOs and this mistaken assessment brought the world financial systems to the brink of collapse.

The range of responses to any given risk assessment encompasses avoidance, acceptance, reduction, and sharing:

- Risk **avoidance** describes the strategy of not incurring or walking away from the risk by selling the activity determined to be avoided or shutting it down. Avoidance is an approach for risks with high impact and high probability that do not lend themselves to mitigation or cost-efficient mitigation.

---

[*] *Merriam-Webster Dictionary.* Involving a random variable. http://www.merriam-webster.com/dictionary/stochastic

[†] As defined by the SEC, these are "bonds that represent claims to specific cash flows from large pools of home mortgages. The streams of principal and interest payments on the mortgages are distributed to the different classes of CMO interests, known as tranches, according to a complicated deal structure. Each tranche may have different principal balances, coupon rates, prepayment risks, and maturity dates (ranging from a few months to twenty years)." See http://www.sec.gov/answers/tcmos.htm (accessed July 23, 2013).

[‡] "An investment-grade security backed by a pool of bonds, loans and other assets. CDOs do not specialize in one type of debt but are often non-mortgage loans or bonds." http://www.investopedia.com/terms/c/cdo.asp (accessed July 23, 2013).

- Risk **reduction** can be achieved through a myriad of business decisions and often entails steps to diversify processes or to establish backup processes or early intervention responses.
- Risk **sharing** is commonly achieved through insurance or hedging strategies. Joint ventures can serve this purpose and, in the insurance industry itself, reinsurance is a method of risk sharing.
- Risk **acceptance** is the strategy of no action, which can lend itself to situations where sharing or reduction lead to costs exceeding the probability-weighed impact of the event itself.

These four types of risk responses can serve as an overlay in a risk matrix, as shown in Figure 15.4.

Risks that lend themselves to sharing have a low likelihood and high impact, typically a five-to-one configuration. Risks might be accepted when both likelihood and impact are low, typically a one-to-one configuration. Risks to avoid relate to events with high probability and high impact, typically between four-to-four and five-to-five configurations. All other combinations of likelihood and impact should be managed by applying adequate control activities. Thus, a risk matrix with a response overlay could look like the one shown in Figure 15.5.

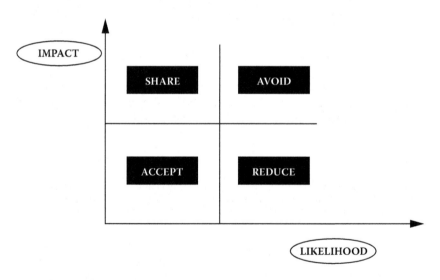

Figure 15.4 Types of risk responses.

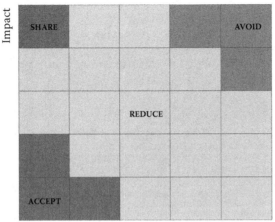

Figure 15.5 Risk response overlay.

It is at the assessment stage that cost–benefit considerations are assessed. Costs have to be compared to the benefits of mitigation and should ideally be optimized. This is illustrated in Figure 15.6.

Response intensity does not refer to any single risk response. Any given risk may lend itself to a portfolio of responses with each response portfolio having different response intensity.

Control activities (i.e., control policies and procedures) need to be established and implemented to help ensure that risk responses are effectively carried out. To achieve this, an understanding of the desired responses and suitable control procedures needs to be established. There is obviously a strong link to the development of risk responses. Once the procedures have been determined, they have to be tested for effectiveness and efficiency. This involves creation of testing approaches and subsequently the actual testing. Depending on the results of such tests, the control procedures will need to be tweaked. Typical control procedures are

- Separation of duties
- Authorization of transactions
- Ensuring availability of audit trails
- Retention of records
- Physical safeguards
- Data processing safeguards

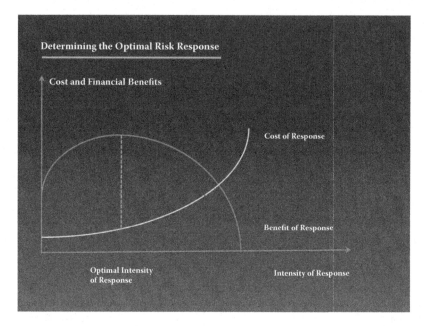

Figure 15.6 Optimal risk response.

- Disabling override by creating process integrity
- Supervision of operations
- Reviews of results
- Reports to compare actual results to expected and planned results

COSO defines **information and communication** as a separate component of the risk management process. Yet, information and communication is required at each stage of the risk management process as well as between its stages. For example, the results of risk identification need to be provided to those members of the organization tasked with assessing these risks. Their input needs to be communicated to personnel in charge of determining risk responses.

As simple as this may sound, the flow of information and communication is often structured inadequately. In particular, IT environments need to be designed and programmed with the goal of providing all relevant information and avoiding the distractions of irrelevant information. Communication should develop a commonly understood risk management language throughout the organization and a clear understanding of roles and responsibilities.[*] The interdependence of information flows is shown in Figure 15.7.[†]

The role of **monitoring** as part of the risk management process is perpetually to determine that the risk management processes are working as expected. Given the frequent changes in approaches to operations such as modifications in manufacturing processes, changing marketing approaches, and rapidly changing IT environments, to name just a few, the monitoring task needs to be defined and redefined on an ongoing basis. Not only does monitoring ensure that deviations from once considered effective and efficient processes are noted, but it also serves to flag necessary adaptations to processes.

Monitoring activities can generally be distinguished into ongoing monitoring activities, which are primarily geared toward ensuring that the enterprise risk management is carried out as designed and separate evaluations deal with specified suspected deficiencies.

The Depth Dimension of ERM

The depth dimension of the COSO cube covers substructures within an organization. This is shown along the right side of the cube. The fourfold objective setting and the eightfold risk management activities should apply to all units and activities of the organization.

FRAUD RISK MANAGEMENT

The risk of losses due to fraudulent activity is a risk jeopardizing the operational objectives of a corporation. Fraud risk management as part of an integrated enterprise risk management needs to look at the eight components of the height dimension for all substructures of an organization.

---

[*] Robert R. Moeller. 2007. *COSO enterprise risk management—Understanding the new integrated ERM framework.* New York: John Wiley & Sons.
[†] The Committee of the Sponsoring Organizations of the Treadway Commission. 2004. Enterprise risk management—Integrated framework, application techniques. Reprinted with permission by the American Institute of Certified Public Accountants.

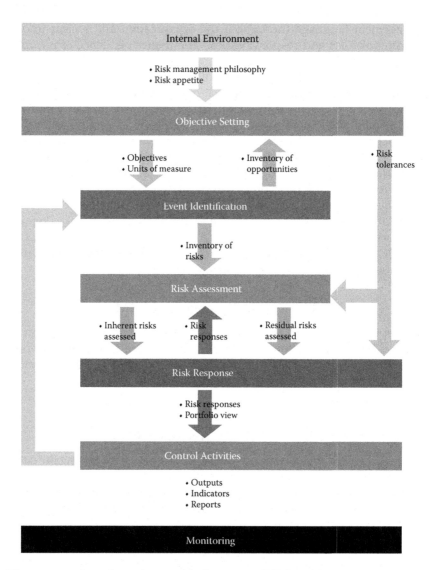

Figure 15.7 Interdependence of information flows. (The Committee of the Sponsoring Organizations of the Treadway Commission. 2004. Enterprise risk management—Integrated framework, application techniques. Reprinted with permission from the American Institute of Certified Public Accountants.)

196

Internal Environment

The internal environment as it relates to fraud is largely integrated into the overall internal environment of the organization. The tone of an organization as far as fraud risk management is concerned needs to be one of honesty, integrity, and corporate ethical behavior.

The term "tone" not only refers to what is being said and published as corporate guidelines such as ethics policies, but also includes the way such ethical values are integrated into day-to-day business activities. Actions speak louder than words. From the outset, a corporate environment that fosters honest and ethical business behavior reduces the likelihood of fraud as an inherent risk.

Promoting open communication and the free exchange of ideas as well as ethical behavior not only serves to manage the risk of fraud, but also is a key ingredient in sustainable management of operations across all activities of an organization.

Designing the internal environment also involves determining the risk appetite—in this case the fraud risk appetite. Appetite appears to be an unfortunate term when it comes to fraud, but organizations that actually have a risk management process in place tend to define their fraud risk appetite in terms of budgets and targets for expected losses.*

Although actions speak louder than words, words are necessary to communicate expected actions and behavior. Senior executives should communicate the tone from the top and live the tone at the top, leading by example. While a code of conduct describes a set of standards designed to promote ethical conduct beyond fraud, a fraud policy specifically communicates an organization's approach to fraudulent behavior. The responsibility for this lies with the board of directors, the audit committee, and senior management. A fraud policy communicates core elements and results of the enterprise risk management policies.

The city of Toronto, for example, states in its Fraud Prevention Policy†:

> The City of Toronto is committed to protecting its revenue, property, proprietary information and other assets. The City of Toronto will not tolerate any misuse or misappropriation of those assets.
>
> The City of Toronto Fraud Prevention Policy is established to provide guidance to employees when misuse or misappropriation of City assets is suspected.

---

* Financial Services Authority. 2006. Firms' high-level management of fraud risk. www.fsa.gov.uk/pubs/other/fraud_risk.pdf (accessed July 23, 2013).
† www.toronto.ca/audit/fraud_policy.pdf (accessed July 23, 2013).

It is the City's intent to fully investigate any suspected acts of "fraud," as it is defined in this Policy, in an impartial manner regardless of the suspected wrongdoer's length of service, position, title or relationship to the City.

Any act of fraud that is detected or suspected must be reported immediately and investigated in accordance with this Policy.

The City will make every reasonable effort, including court ordered restitution, to recover or receive compensation from any appropriate source for City assets obtained by fraud.

This policy applies to all Members of Council, the Mayor, City Manager, City Clerk, Auditor General, City Solicitor and all employees of the City of Toronto.

Whistle-blowing is often seen as an element of control activities against fraudulent activity. While this will be addressed further, there also is an aspect of "tone of an organization" to it. This relates to protection of whistle-blowers from disciplinary or harassing actions by safeguarding those who bring dishonest actions to the attention of management from consequences such as reprisals. By standing behind whistle-blowers, management endorses its commitment to the policies it communicates.

The City of Toronto, for example, states in its Fraud Prevention Policy[*]:

No person covered by this policy shall:

- Dismiss or threaten to dismiss an employee
- Discipline or suspend or threaten to discipline or suspend an employee
- Impose any penalty upon an employee
- Intimidate or coerce an employee, because the employee has acted in accordance with the requirements of the policy

Objective Setting

In setting the objectives of fraud risk management, the organization needs to go beyond the simple desire to avoid all frauds. Rather, it needs to consider the range of costs related to fraud, including actual losses and reputational issues, as well as the actual costs of prevention and detection. In addition, objectives need to address the real cost of avoiding a threat to the very existence of an organization.

---

[*] Ibid.

Event Identification

Identifying potential fraud events requires an understanding of "what can happen." To that end, a useful guideline—titled the "Occupational Fraud and Classification System"—was published by the Association of Certified Fraud Examiners in its 2012 Report to the Nations on Occupational Fraud and Abuse (http://www.acfe.com/uploadedFiles/ACFE_Website/Content/rttn/2012-report-to-nations.pdf).

The ACFE distinguishes fraud into three main categories: asset misappropriation schemes, corruption schemes, and financial statement schemes. Those three categories and their related subschemes are set out in the ACFE's fraud tree in Figure 15.8. The fraud tree is a very helpful tool

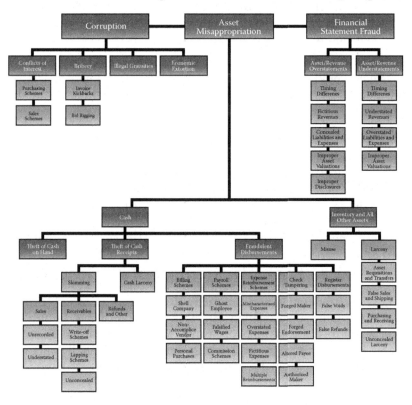

Figure 15.8 ACFE's fraud tree. (Reprinted with permission from the Association of Certified Fraud Examiners.)

for the identification of fraud risks pertaining to an organization and its substructures. Not every fraud scheme is a risk to every type of business unit. Using the fraud tree allows those tasked with event identification to ensure completeness of the event definitions.

FRAUD RISK ASSESSMENT

Assessing the risks of fraud requires the consideration of the type of impact and the likelihood that the fraud occurs. Becoming a victim of a fraud can impact an organization in three ways:

1. Immediate loss as a result of the fraud
2. Loss of reputation and productivity as a result of the fraud
3. Legal and regulatory consequences

Table 15.5 is a fictitious and simplified example of what a fraud risk assessment could look like. When plotted graphically in a matrix with impact and likelihood axes, the risks in Table 15.5 would look like those in Figure 15.9.

In this simplified example, only two identified risks would not fall into the "reduce" category: theft of stationery would be accepted or handled as part of day-to-day business. An attentive board of directors should primarily mitigate the risk of kickbacks to senior management during M&A negotiations. Given a board's limited insight into negotiations, however, the remaining risk could potentially be insured through directors' and officers' liability insurance.

The immediate loss resulting from a fraud is commonly measured based on its worst-case amount. This amount does not necessarily relate to an individual transaction by itself, but rather the total of fraudulent transactions under a particular scheme.

Losses of reputation and productivity can result from publicity surrounding a fraud investigation—in particular, when law enforcement action leads to the execution of search warrants. This can generate a reduced level of trust in an organization, affecting potentially all spheres of an organization from loss of human capital to loss of suppliers to loss of customers.

Regulatory impact from fraud happens when the occurrence of a fraud leads to regulatory action. One example of such a scenario is fraud in the health care industry, where late discovery of a collusive billing fraud scheme can lead to increased frequency of audits.

Table 15.5   Fraud Risk Assessment

ID	Identified Event	Business Process	Magnitude of Impact (Scale of 1–5)	Likelihood (Scale of 1–5)
A	Payments to fictitious vendors	Accounts payable	4	4
B	Duplicate payments	Accounts payable	4	4
C	Overpayments to vendors	Accounts payable	3	4
D	Loss of receivables	Sales/accounts receivable	3	1
E	Falsified sales	Sales/accounts receivable	3	2
F	Improper sales cutoff	Sales/accounts receivable	5	3
G	Cash and check theft	Cash and cash equivalents	2	2
H	Unauthorized bank accounts	Cash and cash equivalents	3	4
I	Sale of products for cash without recording of sale	Cash and cash equivalents	2	3
J	Password theft	Access security	4	4
K	Corporate espionage	Access security	5	2
L	Hacking	IT security	4	3
M	Electronic eavesdropping	IT security	5	2
N	Fictitious employees	Payroll	3	3
O	Falsified wages	Payroll	3	3
P	Former employees continuing on payroll	Payroll	3	3
Q	Expense report fraud	Payroll	1	5
R	Use of insider information	Financial reporting/controlling	4	3
S	Charge personal purchases to company through misuse of purchase orders	Purchasing	2	3

continued

Table 15.5 (continued)   Fraud Risk Assessment

ID	Identified Event	Business Process	Magnitude of Impact (Scale of 1–5)	Likelihood (Scale of 1–5)
T	Purchase goods at inflated prices	Purchasing	2	3
U	Theft of inventory combined with falsification of inventory records	Inventory	3	5
V	Redirect returned goods for personal use	Inventory	2	3
W	Theft of stationery	Inventory	1	1
X	Kickbacks on acquisition of real estate	Fixed assets	4	2
Y	Kickback payments to senior management in connection with M&A activity	Fixed assets	5	1

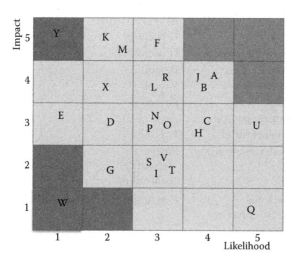

Figure 15.9   Fraud risk assessment matrix.

FRAUD RISK RESPONSE

Most business processes that lend themselves to fraudulent transactions are essential for value generation of an organization. Thus, risk avoidance is not an option for a risk response. Risk acceptance can be considered for events with very low financial significance and low probability of occurrence. Very few, if any, fraud schemes fall into this category. Risk sharing is a possibility against a number of fraud schemes such as computer fraud, credit card fraud, and funds transfer fraud to name a few. There are industry-specific solutions for some industries—for example, the health care industry and financial industry.

The previous fictitious example contains only one acceptance scenario (theft of stationery) and one sharing scenario (kickback payments to senior management). Sharing in such cases could potentially happen through directors' and officers' liability insurance. All other fraud risk scenarios would be considered in need of steps to mitigate the fraud risks.

Risk reduction through control activities is the most applicable response to fraud risks.

Fraud Risk Control Activities

The term "control activities" refers to the totality of policies and procedures designed to PREVENT, DETECT, and RESPOND TO fraudulent actions by individuals or organizations inside and outside the corporation.

Prevention

Preventive control activities aim at deterring and hampering transactions through procedural requirements for day-to-day operations. Naturally, detection and responses to fraud occurrences, too, are in themselves deterrents, but their primary aim is to catch losses to the organization and recover such losses. Preventive activities include:

- Authorization
- Documentation
- Reconciliation
- Security
- Separation of duties

Authorization does not exclusively serve the purpose of fraud prevention. Proper authorization also ensures that activities are carried out by individuals with adequate knowledge and range of control. Observing authorization protocol, however, not only protects from operational errors, but also hampers the completion of fraudulent transactions. Setting adequate authorization policies encompasses defining roles, actions to be performed in such roles, and setting privileges.

Documentation can be electronic or on paper. Documentation ensures accountability. Documentation for each transaction should allow the determination of the nature of the transaction, who performed it, who authorized it, and when the transaction was executed.

Reconciliation involves comparison of transactions or transaction reports. Its purpose is to ensure accurateness, completeness, and validity of financial information. A reconciliation procedure should also include a timely error correction process. Reconciliation activities need to be documented as well.

Security involves all steps to safeguard assets. They can be physical, electronic (IT security), and administrative in nature.

Separation of duties ensures that nobody has sole control over the entirety of a transaction. Ideally, responsibilities for any one transaction should be divided into initiation, submission, processing, authorization, and review. Depending on the size of an entity, not all responsibilities can be separated in accordance with an ideal risk management scenario. In such cases, the level of risk associated with any specific type of transaction should lead to the best possible separation regimen.

Why do preventive control activities aim at hampering and not disabling fraud? The term "prevention" easily provides a false sense of security. Can, for example, separation of duties truly make it impossible to commit a fraud? The obvious answer is "no." Separation of duties makes it harder to commit fraud because, instead of requiring just one individual to manipulate a transaction, two or more people need to collaborate. In issuing a purchase order, delivery documentation and invoice approval could be handled by one individual. A single individual could easily approve payment of a false invoice for a nonexisting or substandard delivery to a collaborating entity, maybe even to himself or herself under the guise of a corporate entity owned by such an individual. The more these approval processes are separated, the more individuals would need to collaborate—that is, to conspire—to commit such a fraud. However, it is entirely possible that the purchasing manager and the accounts payables clerk collaborate with someone in warehousing to commit the fraud and share the proceeds. This is not only possible; it has happened more than once.

Control activities increase the risks and cost of committing a fraud. The larger the number of collaborators is, the bigger is the risk of detection and they reduce the proceeds of a fraudulent transaction for any given individual participant in a fraud scheme.

Detection

Control activities are often not sufficiently well designed for optimal fraud prevention. This may be due to financial and size constraints. But it may also be because even a well-designed system of control activities cannot make fraud impossible. Because of these limitations of control activities, organizations need to implement policies and procedures for detecting fraud.

The detection of fraud allows recovery of embezzled assets, fine-tuning of control activities, and deterrence of fraud by increasing the level of consequences a would-be fraudster may wish to take into consideration before he or she commits a fraud.

The first step to fraud detection is the development or existence of an allegation. Allegations can happen as a result of passive recording processes or as a result of active analyses. The difference between the two is that passive systems do not require specific measures to develop such allegations. Examples of active measures to develop fraud allegations are targeted audits of vulnerable processes, internal audit findings, and the analysis of management accounting reports.

The most well-known example of a passive recording process is the whistle-blower hotline. Whistle-blower hotlines are mandatory mechanisms to receive complaints in some jurisdictions, including the United States. Even where they are not mandatory, such hotlines are part of best practice and a vital component of an effective fraud risk management program. Information obtained through hotlines has consistently proven to be the most common method by which frauds are detected. A whistle-blower hotline—organized as a telephone, e-mail, or web-based reporting mechanism—is a tool that enables individuals inside and outside an organization to report information about potential fraudulent activity.

Stakeholders, in particular employees, should not only have the possibility to report observations, but they also they need to trust that information provided via a hotline will be treated confidentially. They need to be assured that they will not suffer adverse consequences from legitimate reports of observations. It is advantageous for any organization to be in a position to deal with allegations internally and then to investigate and respond on the basis of its fraud prevention policy.

Confidential reporting mechanisms should[*]

- Have an appointed executive leader responsible for implementing and championing it
- Allow for anonymous and confidential tips, where permitted by law
- Be designed to receive tips from employees, customers, vendors, and other third parties
- Be well publicized through a variety of means, such as employee training sessions, posters in break rooms and other common areas, and discussion in employee newsletters
- Provide a variety of options for incoming tips, such as telephone interviews, online forms, e-mails, and in-person reports
- Be openly and genuinely supported by the board and management
- Be backed by an enforced whistle-blower protection policy
- Be accessible 24 hours a day, 365 days a year, because many hot-line reports are made during nonbusiness hours
- Be staffed by individuals trained in sensitively eliciting information from whistle-blowers, as well as in spotting potentially fake reports

Fraud allegations, whether obtained via hotlines or through active procedures, should record the following details[†]:

- What is the alleged matter of concern or suspicion?
- Who knows about this?
- How can we ensure the confidentiality of this information?
- What are the particulars, such as timing, location, etc.?
- What is the relationship to the organization's operations?
- What issues are raised?
- What are known/suspected elements of deceit or dishonest conduct?
- What breaches may have occurred?
- What benefits might be sought?
- How much of the information is established facts?
- What evidence or witnesses are there likely to be?
- Are the witnesses and evidence adequately safeguarded?
- Has anything been done administratively yet in relation to the matter?

---

[*] Andi McNeal. 2011. The role of the board in fraud risk management, The Conference Board, *Director Notes*, 3, no. 21, October 2011, Reprinted with permission by The Conference Board.

[†] Based on Australian government, the attorney general's department: Fraud control in Australian government agencies, Canberra, 2004, p. 38.

- Is there any evidence to indicate that the suspects are already alerted?
- What courses of action are open?
- Who might be able to assist/advise?
- What practical risks are involved?
- What might inhibit further investigation?

Once an allegation is seen as credible, detection requires an investigation. When it comes to investigations, organizations need to decide who will conduct the investigation. Generally, the choice is between internal departments, such as internal audit or corporate security; external qualified fraud investigators; and/or law enforcement institutions.

The attorney general's department of the Australian government has developed a helpful example of an appropriate escalation model (Table 15.6). Escalation criteria are complexity, extent of potential damage, nature of the alleged offense, status of evidence, scope of the investigation, and availability of evidence.

Table 15.6   Australian Government Escalation Model

	Involve Law Enforcement Agencies	**Use Qualified Investigators**	**Handle in House**
Complexity	Requires detailed analysis of large amounts of evidence, both paper and computer based. Use of sophisticated technology.	Requires detailed analysis of evidence, both paper and computer based.	Analysis of relevant evidence straightforward.
Potential damage	High monetary loss. Significant damage to the reputation of the corporate group.	Medium monetary loss. Significant damage to the reputation of the corporate entity.	Minor monetary loss. Minor damage to the reputation of the corporate entity.
Nature of offense	Elements of criminal conspiracy. Serious breach of trust by senior management.	Likely to involve action before a court or tribunal.	Likely to be limited to administrative action within the corporate entity.

continued

207

Table 15.6 (continued)   Australian Government Escalation Model

	Involve Law Enforcement Agencies	Use Qualified Investigators	Handle in House
Status of evidence	Preliminary analysis indicates strong possibility of proof beyond reasonable doubt.	Preliminary analysis indicates possibility of proof to the level of proof beyond reasonable doubt or balance of probabilities.	Preliminary analysis indicates strong possibility of proof to the level of balance of probabilities.
Scope	Involves known or suspected criminal activities in a number of corporate entities and/or jurisdictions. Collusion between a number of parties.	More than one party suspected of being involved in the case.	Isolated incident
Availability of evidence	Evidence is required that can only be obtained by exercise of a search warrant or surveillance.	Evidence is required that can be obtained within the corporate entity or corporate group.	Evidence is required that can be obtained within the agency.

Note: Based on Australian government, the attorney general's department: Fraud control in Australian government agencies, Canberra, 2004, p. 43.

Response
Responding to a fraud that has been detected should not be mistaken for risk response, but should be viewed as a component of risk response. A fraud risk management policy needs to be clear about corrective actions and remedies as a result of a finding of fraudulent action. Remedies can be

- Counseling
- Greater scrutiny/increased controls
- Loss of privileges
- Transfer to another department
- Demotion
- Suspension
- Termination

- Transfer of case to law enforcement
- Recovery action

These remedies can be chosen cumulatively. In all cases, the quality of evidence to select them does not need to be beyond reasonable doubt. These criteria are reserved for the criminal courts. Rather, if the evidence under consideration indicates with a balance of probabilities that a fraud has been committed against the company, any of the aforementioned actions can be chosen.

When making a decision whether to seek criminal remedies by transferring and reporting a fraud case to the authorities, some jurisdictions reward organizations for cooperating with authorities. This can be of importance if a fraud committed against an organization also affects third parties as victims.

The SEC, in particular, considers in its decisions on prosecutorial consequences against an organization the self-policing activities of an organization.

Information and Communication

As stated earlier, information and communication are not stand-alone steps, but will need to occur throughout all the steps of the risk management process. The organization's fraud prevention policy[*] is the foremost tool to communicate the importance of the fraud risk management program and the organization's position on fraud risk.

Communication does not stop there. The individual steps in designing and maintaining the fraud risk management program usually involve different staff and departments. The objectives as well as the level of risk appetite need to be communicated to those charged with risk responses. When it comes to risk appetite, however, such information and communication should be on a need-to-know basis.

---

[*] An example policy was described previously in Chapter 1; a more generic example of a fraud prevention policy can be found in the Institute of Internal Auditors, American Institute of Certified Public Accountants, and Association of Certified Fraud Examiners. 2010. Managing the business risk of fraud: A practical guide, http://www.aicpa.org/forthepublic/auditcommitteeeffectiveness/guidanceandresources/downloadabledocuments/managing_the_business_risk_of_fraud.pdf (accessed July 23, 2013, Appendix I).

Communicating that there is a level of fraud risk appetite might otherwise be misunderstood by some that fraud or some forms of it can be somewhat tolerated. This might inadvertently invite fraud schemes to be pursued at elevated intensity, thus altering the precommunication risk profile of such a scheme.

Zero tolerance toward fraud and risk appetite are not incompatible, because zero tolerance relates to frauds uncovered as part of the risk response level based on risk appetite.

An important format of information and communication beyond the fraud prevention policy is fraud awareness training, which needs to be developed by those in charge of designing prevention concepts and is commonly delivered in seminar and e-learning formats. Making all members of an organization understand the existence, importance, and quality of a whistle-blowing hotline is a communication component necessary for the adequate functioning of the hotline process.

Monitoring

Monitoring a fraud risk management process has two benefits. It provides periodic evaluation of antifraud controls as well as independent evaluations of the fraud risk management program by internal or external audit functions.

The metrics to be monitored for evaluation of proper functioning of the fraud risk management program are the number of allegations of fraudulent conduct received via whistle-blower hotlines or otherwise; the number of resolved and unresolved fraud investigations and the ratio between resolved and unresolved case investigations; the level of recurrence of fraud allegations; the extent of financial resources spent on investigations; the number of employees, vendors, and customers who have not signed or otherwise accepted the organization's code of ethics; the extent of participation in ethics training seminars, industry-specific fraud risks as published in fraud surveys; and results of integrity surveys taken within the organization.*

Some of these metrics can be tracked electronically to aid in continuous monitoring and detection activities.

---

* The Institute of Internal Auditors, American Institute of Certified Public Accountants, and Association of Certified Fraud Examiners. 2010. Managing the business risk of fraud: A practical guide, http://www.aicpa.org/forthepublic/auditcommitteeeffectiveness/ guidanceandresources/downloadabledocuments/managing_the_business_risk_of_ fraud.pdf (accessed July 23, 2013); also: Andi McNeal. 2011. The role of the board in fraud risk management. Conference Board, *Director Notes* 3(21), October 2011.

COMPLIANCE RISK MANAGEMENT

Having completed our examination of enterprise risk management and fraud risk management, we now proceed to the third building block: compliance risk management.

Internal Environment

The internal environment as it relates to compliance is largely integrated into the overall internal environment of the organization just like the internal environment as it relates to managing the risk of fraud. The tone of an organization as far as compliance risk management is concerned needs to be one of honesty, integrity, and corporate ethical behavior. We mentioned before that the tone of an organization does not stop at the top. It is conceivable that the tone at the level of senior management is one that emphasizes compliance, but that leaders in marketing divisions or subsidiaries have a different view.

Corruption and procurement manipulation are prime examples for how deficiencies at any level can negatively impact the compliance attitude on subsequent levels of an organization's hierarchies. If, for example, the marketing manager of a Chinese subsidiary is convinced that he can only achieve his budget targets using bribes, chances increase that his subordinate managers will adopt the policies of corruption including manipulation of procurement processes. Such situations need to be managed so that the tone at the top becomes the tone in the middle, too.

Where does the term risk appetite find its justification in compliance risk management? Is compliance not a dichotomous concept? Are there degrees of compliance? Clearly, there are no degrees of compliance and the term itself is dichotomous. However, it is virtually impossible to rule out that violations occur. Rather, an organization can have more or less intense control activities designed to prevent its managers from committing violations of legal requirements. As with any risk management approach, the costs of managing compliance risks tend to increase the more an organization commits resources to manage compliance risks.

Objective Setting

The objectives of compliance risk management need to go beyond the simple desire to avoid all compliance violations. Rather, the level of costs related to noncompliance (immediate and reputational losses) and costs of prevention

211

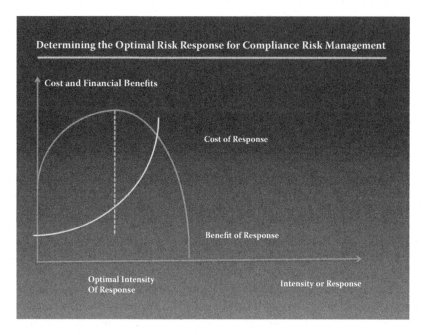

Figure 15.10 Optimal level of compliance risk assurance.

and detection need to be set. In addition, objectives need to address the avoidance of endangerment of the very existence of an organization.

There is an optimal level of compliance risk assurance just as there is for fraud risk management, as set out in Figure 15.10.

The benefits of compliance need to reflect:

- The cost of noncompliance
- The intensity of punishment in civil and criminal proceedings
- The intensity of reputational losses

These form part of these costs of noncompliance. Due to the severity of penalties, the "benefits curve" can be assumed to be more of a steep shape with a clearly defined peak.

What are the factors that influence the required intensity of resources to manage the risk of noncompliance in corruption compliance management?* They include

---

* As will be addressed later, corruption is by far not the only compliance issue that a corporation can face. Given that this book focuses on fraud, examples for compliance risks and their management will be chosen from the field of corruption risk management.

- The size of a corporation
- Its risk potential as determined by its history of noncompliance, its industry, its organizational structure, and the density of the regulatory environment
- The country of operation as differentiated based on studies by Transparency International*
- The complexity and insecurity of a business unit's operation

Essentially, countercorruption mechanisms may not need to be overly intense and expensive in business units with low-risk profiles— for example, in a midsize market entity selling consumer products in Finland—with an efficiently structured organization. On the other hand, countercorruption mechanisms require high levels of intensity when the business unit is in a country with high corruption perception indices and that sells large turn-key operations to buyers closely affiliated with public officials.

Event Identification

First of all, event identification requires a clarification of what compliance means. COSO defines the term compliance plainly and simply as "compliance with laws and regulations."† This is a less narrow definition than some that include internal regulations or even stakeholder perspectives.

Nevertheless, it still is a demanding task to figure out for an individual corporation what to be compliant with and which areas are relevant to its business.

Cartel regulations might mean nothing to a small player, but have huge impacts on large organizations in the technology sector, construction and concrete manufacturing, and elevator manufacturing sectors. These are just a few industries that have faced large fines from cartel commissions in recent years, not to mention cease-and-desist orders and substantial reputational backlash.

Bribery and corruption are relevant compliance issues for most entities, as are issues surrounding gender equality or sexual harassment. Data

---

* Transparency International publishes its survey-based Corruption Perception Index annually. The 2012 survey results can be accessed at http://www.transparency.org/cpi2012/results (accessed July 23, 2013).
† Committee of Sponsoring Organizations of the Treadway Commission (COSO). Enterprise risk management—Integrated framework.

protection and privacy rules are other complex fields of compliance. The level of complexity rises the more an organization expands into international markets even if only by selling its products internationally through web presence.*

The process of event identification should follow the base process for event identification as described previously.

Risk Assessment

The techniques to be used in compliance risk assessments are the same as for other risk management components. Risk assessment for compliance risks does, however, differ in terms of determining likelihoods and financial outcomes.

There is an important differentiation regarding the term "likelihood." The temptation might be to see it as the likelihood that a violation is investigated and results in civil and/or criminal penalties. This perspective would implicitly mean that a corporation would be willing to accept potential violations if the probability of getting caught is low.

While this might reflect reality in some cases, compliance must not be assessed on the basis of the likelihood of getting caught, but rather on the basis of the likelihood that the violation occurs, irrespective of whether the violation indeed becomes pursued in court.

Equally, the assessment of the magnitude of impact must not take into account that a violation might remain undetected and therefore would bear no impact. Instead, the perspective regarding the magnitude of impact should be one of potential impact, thereby being based on the severity of the violation. As with other risk management components, the magnitude needs to include direct as well as reputational losses.

An example of a corruption compliance risk matrix for a globally operating company is in Table 15.7. It has a strong country- and region-specific component and would be much more detailed and specific in real life.

---

* A barrage of regulations. 2012. *Internal Auditor,* http://www.theiia.org/intAuditor/feature-articles/2012/april/a-barrage-of-regulations/ (accessed January 14, 2013).

Table 15.7 Corruption Compliance Risk Matrix

ID	Identified Event	Business Process	Magnitude of Impact (Scale 1–5)	Likelihood (Scale 1–5)
A	Paying public officials in a Caribbean country for favorable decision on tax holidays	Finance	4	4
B	Paying tender administrator in a sub-Saharan African country to design specifications to favor subsidiary	Sales	4	4
C	Paying customs administrators at an Asian country's point of entrance to allow import of banned goods	Sales	4	4
D	Paying public official for preferential treatment in the allocation of land for a sales outlet	Marketing	3	4
E	Paying a public official for rights to increase purchase quota from an oil-producing Middle-Eastern nation	Sales/accounts receivables	4	4
F	Paying customs official in a country with export restrictions to allow passing of embargo products across the border	Shipping	5	3
G	Paying local official in charge of issuing building permits to issue permit in a Western European country	Construction	2	2
H	Paying building inspector for approval of faultily wired building in North America	Construction	3	2

continued

215

Table 15.7 (continued) Corruption Compliance Risk Matrix

ID	Identified Event	Business Process	Magnitude of Impact (Scale 1–5)	Likelihood (Scale 1–5)
I	Paying building inspector for approval of faultily wired building in South America	Construction	5	3
J	Creation of a slush fund in a tax haven country through false billings of consulting fees	Finance	3	4
K	Creation of slush funds through intercompany overbilling for goods in Canada	Finance/ manufacturing	3	4
L	Payment for private school fees in Canada for the child of a public official in a Third World country	Finance/sales	4	4

There is a country focus because attitudes toward bribery and corruption vary among jurisdictions. A widely used assessment prepared by Berlin-based Transparency International* ranks nations based on corruption perception surveys. These surveys are useful in two ways:

1. They help identify jurisdictions where there is a higher risk that business relations are governed by corrupt practices—and thus require heightened vigilance.
2. They may provide useful perspectives with unusual financial flows to determine whether funds might be linked to bribery. Experience shows that countries with weak anticorruption and anti-money-laundering law enforcement are best suited for the creation and disbursement of slush funds.

Last but not least, almost every financial impact assessment arising from bribery is in the high category. The previous example could represent a North American corporation with exposure to the Foreign Corrupt

---

* Transparency International publishes its survey-based Corruption Perception Index annually. The 2012 survey results can be accessed at http://www.transparency.org/cpi2012/results (accessed July 23, 2013).

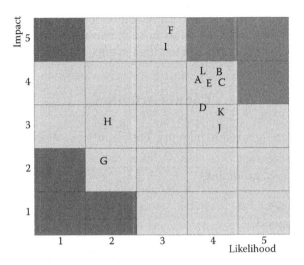

Figure 15.11   Corruption compliance risk matrix.

Practices Act in the United States. A high category is based not on the legislation in the countries where the bribes might be paid, but rather on the extent of penalties and the risk to the going concern resulting from a violation.

Penalties in other countries are often substantially less severe than those in the United States. Organizations solely exposed to such lesser penalties in more lenient nations will find that their assessments for magnitude of impact may be lower. However, countries like the United States and the UK, which impose severe penalties on perpetrators located in less vigilant jurisdictions, work hard to extend their reach with a view on leveling the playing fields. Figure 15.11 illustrates what the risk matrix graphic corresponding to the preceding example would look like.

Risk Response

Risk acceptance is not an option for compliance risk management. Even low-impact/low-likelihood events require some form of a management effort, albeit not as intense as that for increased impact/likelihood scenarios.

Experience shows that risk sharing, too, is an option unavailable for the purpose of compliance risk management; there are no insurance providers willing to underwrite such risks. Risk avoidance is an option not to be discarded. If the assessment for operations in a country is such that economic activity there is practically impossible without bribes, a temporary withdrawal from activities in such countries may be a necessary response. The vast majority of identified events will require risk management through control activities.

Control Activities

Prevention
Control activities geared to help prevent compliance violations include:

- Code of conduct
- Compliance guidelines
- Training
- Help desks
- Due diligence
- Compliance incentives

The **code of conduct** describes the basic values of an organization. It is not limited to compliance issues, but should elaborate on them in general terms. Typically, a compliance portion of a code of conduct should include a clear positioning of the organization to act within the rules of law and should state a zero tolerance policy toward violations of both internal policies and applicable laws and regulations. It should also include principal rules covering what to do when violations are observed, including escalation principles.

Examples for such a component of the code of conduct would be

- Violations of laws or internal compliance guidelines will not be tolerated. Violators will suffer appropriate consequences. Indications of violations will be investigated and confirmed violations will be sanctioned in civil and criminal courts.
- Management at every level is responsible for ensuring that all members of the organization know this code of conduct and will adhere to the compliance guidelines. First line of reporting violations is an individual employee's direct superior. Questions with respect to this code of conduct or compliance guidelines can be directed to the Helpdesk. Indications of potential violations can also be brought to the attention of the compliance hotline.

Compliance guidelines provide more detailed instructions and help members of the organization to take adequate decisions in critical situations. They will describe common violations in order to protect the organization and its members from negligence. Typically, such guidelines prescribe how to interact with public offices, government-owned organizations, business partners, and competitors. They cover such topics as invitations to events and gifts (given and received), avoidance of conflict of interest, and rules on sponsoring and donations.

Training ensures that all members of an organization know the organization's compliance code and guidelines and allows the teaching of more concrete case examples in addition to general principles. Such training can be based on eLearning concepts or in-person training sessions.

Help desks give members of a corporation a means to seek support in specific situations. They can be organized as telephone hotlines or dedicated e-mail addresses such as compliance@...

Due diligence needs to be exercised when an organization develops new sales partners, consultants, suppliers, and joint venture partners. The goal is to ensure that such new relationships are entered into with organizations of integrity that follow principles compatible with those of the evaluating organization.

Compliance incentives in this context refer to positive compliance incentives as well as avoidance of compliance disincentives. Such incentives need to be included in management evaluation processes. The balanced scorecard approach provides flexibility to include compliance incentives in evaluation proceedings and remuneration criteria.

Detection and Response

Detection of compliance violations and response to confirmed violations follow the same approaches and processes as detections and responses to situations of fraud against an organization.

Information and Communication

As stated earlier, information and communication are not stand-alone steps, but will need to be integral to all the steps of the risk management process. Codes of conduct and compliance guidelines are the foremost tools to communicate the importance of the compliance risk management program and the organization's position on compliance.

The individual steps in designing and maintaining the compliance risk management program usually involve different staff and departments. The objectives as well as the level of risk appetite need to be communicated to those charged with risk responses.

When it comes to risk appetite, however, such information and communication should be on a need-to-know basis. Communicating that there is a level of compliance risk appetite might otherwise be misunderstood by some as suggesting that some form of noncompliance can be somewhat tolerated. This would invite such noncompliance to be pursued at elevated intensity, thus altering the precommunication risk profile of such a scheme.

Zero tolerance toward noncompliance and risk appetite are not incompatible, because zero tolerance relates to noncompliance uncovered as part of the risk response level set on the basis of risk appetite.

An important element of information and communication—one that extends beyond the code of conduct and compliance guidelines—is compliance awareness training. It needs to be developed by those in charge of designing prevention concepts and is commonly delivered in seminar and e-learning formats.

Making all members of an organization understand the existence, importance, and quality of a whistle-blower hotline is a form of communication required for the adequate functioning of the hotline process.

Monitoring

Monitoring a compliance risk management process provides:

- Periodic evaluation of compliance controls
- Independent evaluations of the compliance risk management program by internal or external audit functions

Metrics for evaluating the proper functioning of the compliance risk management program are similar to those for the effectiveness of fraud risk management programs. They include the number of allegations of compliance violations received via whistle-blower hotlines or otherwise; the number of resolved and unresolved noncompliance investigations and the ratio between resolved and unresolved case investigations; the level of recurrence of compliance allegations; the extent of financial resources spent on investigations; the number of employees, vendors, and customers who have not signed or otherwise accepted the organization's code of ethics; the extent of participation in ethics training seminars; geographic and industry-specific compliance risks as published in fraud surveys; and results of integrity surveys taken within the organization.

Some of these metrics can be tracked electronically to aid in continuous monitoring and detection activities.

REALITY CHECK—COSO ERM IMPLEMENTATION

Status of ERM Implementation

What are the chances that you are a member of the board of directors or serving in another supervisory role for an organization with a fully implemented enterprise risk management? ERM has become widely recognized as theoretically sound and clearly describing key elements of a robust ERM process.[*] In terms of implementation, however, the size of a corporation seems to impact whether formal ERMs are in place.

A 2001 survey of 130 global multinationals found that 49% had full or partial ERM in place.[†] By 2006, a survey of Fortune 1000 corporations found that 75% were to have a formal ERM function by the end of 2007.[‡] However, a 2010 survey published by COSO provides a different picture. This survey found that only 28% of respondents would refer to the current state of their ERMs as "systematic, robust and repeatable" with regular reporting to their boards of directors.[§]

Close to 60% of respondents described the risk management processes in their organizations as mostly informal and ad hoc.[¶] In addition, 42.4% described the level of functioning ERM processes as "very immature" or "somewhat immature."[**]

Part of the reason for the apparently wide acceptance among large multinational corporations and Fortune 1000 companies is that it helps to meet regulatory requirements implemented in the wake of Enron and other scandals.

Regulators in Canada, the United States, and other Western countries extended the requirement for public companies to maintain systems of internal control by requiring management to certify and the independent auditor to attest to the effectiveness of those systems.[††]

However, the 2010 COSO study evaluated results for the full sample as well as for the subgroup of public companies and found that the results

---

[*] Committee of Sponsoring Organizations of the Treadway Commission. COSO's 2010 Report on ERM, December 2010.
[†] Tillinghast-Towers Perrin. Enterprise risk management: Trends and emerging practices.
[‡] Forrester Research. 2006. Trends 2006: Enterprise risk and compliance.
[§] Committee of Sponsoring Organizations of the Treadway Commission. 2010. COSO's 2010 Report on ERM, December 2010.
[¶] Ibid.
[**] Ibid.
[††] Forrester Research. 2006. Trends 2006: Enterprise risk and compliance.

were largely similar for public companies to the results of the full sample. What this shows is that public companies do not show any more promising results than privately held companies.

Thus, chances are high that individuals tasked with supervisory functions cannot automatically rely on the proper functioning of a risk management system as a guard against fraud and noncompliance.

Risk Appetite and Residual Risk

Even if you are a member of the board of directors or serving in another supervisory role for an organization with a fully implemented enterprise risk management, does this mean that you can let your guard down?

Consider the issue of residual risk. No matter how you design a risk management approach, there will be residual risk. Depending on the risk appetite set as part of the control environment and the objective setting process, the residual risk may be high. No matter whether you were involved in the process of setting your organization's risk appetite or not, risk appetite may well be high enough to allow for material adverse events to occur.

Therefore, even if your organization has a proper risk management process in place, you still need to guard against fraud and noncompliance if you are tasked with a supervisory role.

Inadequate Design of the Risk Management Process

Despite the best of intentions, there are cases where risk management processes fall short because of gaps in their designs or simple errors. Mistakes can happen on any level of the risk management process. Examples for common mistakes are

- Risk appetite set for a subsidiary or business unit might not be in line with the risk appetite set for the organization as a whole.
- Events may not be identified—for example, if an event occurs for the first time. The monitoring process should be in a position to catch such an event and bring corrective action on its way. Unidentified risks would go unassessed and unresponded.
- Risk assessments can be erroneous.
- Risk responses can be inadequate.
- Control activities can be overridden or outmaneuvered by conspiring groups of individuals.

CONCLUSION

There is no doubt that enterprise risk management is a gold standard to conscientious decision making and to managing the risks of fraud and noncompliance. Given its currently limited implementation level and the inherent limitations of ERM, individuals with supervisory roles—especially directors of for-profit as well as non-profit organizations—need to understand warning signs of fraud and noncompliance. The Red Flags laid out in this book should enable these individuals to identify, analyze, and address possible indicators of fraud in a timely manner.

16

The Board of Directors—
First Line of Defense against
Fraud and Corruption

INTRODUCTION

In previous chapters we identified what constitutes a Red Flag in the various activities and documents that an organization might generate in the normal course of business. In this chapter we focus on encouraging members of the board to screen and scrutinize Red Flags and explain why it is important to discover fraud, corruption, or illegal activity within their organizations at an early stage so that serious repercussions can be averted.

RED FLAGS AND DIRECTORS' RESPONSIBILITIES

One of the core obligations of any member of the board is to work toward establishment of a structured compliance management system related to the prevention of fraud. This obligation, as we have shown in detail in previous chapters of this book, goes far beyond simply issuing strict policy statements.

Corporate fraud is usually investigated by law enforcement, regulators, private investigators, and/or forensic accountants long after the frauds have occurred. In our experience, many of these frauds could have been prevented if there had been a more in-depth examination by members of the board of directors or their committee members using the Red Flag screening and scrutinizing system.

So why do board or committee members pay little or no attention to issues that point to potential fraud?

One reason for this lack of action is they may feel that they do not have the skill or knowledge necessary to carry out an effective examination of documents or presenters for potential Red Flags and even less if they should happen to find one. Another reason is because they do not want to "rock the boat" or they may be pressured by other directors to support management no matter what the Red Flag indicators suggest. Or, in a similar vein, the board may be dominated by an aggressive CEO who wants to control all the business at the board and committee meetings.

Whatever the reason may be, members of the board of directors have historically been reluctant to take action against management, even when Red Flags indicating serious fraud involving management have surfaced in the boardroom.

In this chapter we will identify some potentially effective policies and procedures that may be adopted by a board of directors to ensure that they individually have more control in screening and scrutinizing Red Flags. The object here is to identify fraudulent situations that could in time evolve into disaster for the corporation, the shareholders, and possibly the officers or directors themselves.

First, we will examine the Enron and WorldCom cases. In so doing, we will demonstrate that if their respective boards had followed the screening and scrutinizing procedures outlined in this book as Red Flags appeared—and had taken control of management—the outcome for each of the two companies might have been different. In each case the board of directors did nothing and both companies and their stakeholders suffered the consequences.

Case Study—Enron

Enron grew to become America's seventh largest energy company, with offices in over forty countries. *Fortune* magazine named Enron as "America's most innovative company" for six straight years from 1996 to 2001. In December 2001, Enron filed for bankruptcy. It was, at the time, one of the largest Chapter 11 bankruptcies in US history. WorldCom took that record 2 years later.

Kenneth Lay was executive chairman of the board. He and CEO Jeffrey Skilling were aware of and supported the reporting of false profits. They also participated in the failure to disclose losses and debt via an unorthodox accounting method. The outside and supposedly independent accounting firm of Arthur Andersen was also aware of the unlawful activity.

Enron had seventeen board members with fifteen outside or independent* board members. There were two directors—namely, Kenneth Lay and Jeffrey Skilling—who were also officers of the corporation.

The outside board members were respectable, influential, independent men and women that included a former stock market regulator, university professor, former central bank executive, and a member of the House of Lords in the UK. These outside directors have been described as prominent, influential, and financially sophisticated people.

Enron has been accused of keeping significant debt off the regular financial reporting and the board of directors was kept informed of this activity.

In 1999 the board became aware of the potential risks that were involved and agreed to waive the company's ethical code. It also allowed Andrew Fastow, the chief financial officer, to serve as general partner in the partnerships formed to unlawfully absorb the debts that should have been reported on Enron's financial report. This step resulted in Enron falsely reporting its true financial position to the investors and shareholders.

The CEO Jeffrey Skilling and Kenneth Lay were charged with fraud. In 2006, Skilling was found guilty on thirty-five counts of fraud and sentenced to a prison term of 24 years. Kenneth Lay died before his trial could begin. Many other senior managers were indicted for a variety of criminal offenses. The directors settled a lawsuit for the amount of $168 million.

In a report dated July 8, 2002, by the US Senate Subcommittee on Investigations a number of Red Flags that the board missed and that could have prevented Enron's failure were identified:[†]

> Based upon the evidence before it, including over one million pages of subpoenaed documents, interviews of 13 Enron Board members, and the Subcommittee hearing on May 7, 2002, the U.S. Senate

---

* The term "outside director" is used in the United States to indicate a nonexecutive director. In other countries the term "independent director" is used. Both terms mean that the director is not employed by the company in any capacity.

† Report prepared by the Permanent Subcommittee on Investigations of the Committee on Governmental Affairs United States Senate. Congress #13, July 8, 2002.

Permanent Subcommittee on Investigations makes the following findings with respect to the role of the Enron Board of Directors in Enron's collapse and bankruptcy.

(1) Fiduciary Failure. The Enron Board of Directors failed to safeguard Enron shareholders and contributed to the collapse of the seventh largest public company in the United States, by allowing Enron to engage in high risk accounting, inappropriate conflict of interest transactions, extensive undisclosed off-the-books activities, and excessive executive compensation. The Board witnessed numerous indications of questionable practices by Enron management over several years, but chose to ignore them to the detriment of Enron shareholders, employees and business associates.

(2) High Risk Accounting. The Enron Board of Directors knowingly allowed Enron to engage in high risk accounting practices.

(3) Inappropriate Conflicts of Interest. Despite clear conflicts of interest, the Enron Board of Directors approved an unprecedented arrangement allowing Enron's Chief Financial officer to establish and operate the LJM private equity funds which transacted business with Enron and profited at Enron's expense. The Board exercised inadequate oversight of LJM transaction and compensation controls and failed to protect Enron shareholders from unfair dealing.

(4) Extensive Undisclosed Off-The-Books Activity. The Enron Board of Directors knowingly allowed Enron to conduct billions of dollars in off-the-books activity to make its financial condition appear better than it was and failed to ensure adequate public disclosure of material off-the-books liabilities that contributed to Enron's collapse.

(5) Excessive Compensation. The Enron Board of Directors approved excessive compensation for company executives, failed to monitor the cumulative cash drain caused by Enron's 2000 annual bonus and performance unit plans, and failed to monitor or halt abuse by Board Chairman and Chief Executive Officer Kenneth Lay of a company-financed, multimillion dollar, personal credit line.

(6) Lack of Independence. The independence of the Enron Board of Directors was compromised by financial ties between the company and certain Board members.

Case Study—WorldCom

Based in Clinton, Mississippi, WorldCom grew from a small, long-distance telephone public company into a telecommunications giant through the acquisitions of more than sixty companies in 15 years. In 2002 the company admitted to overstating cash flow by booking more than $3.8 billion in operating expense as capital expenditures.

An unorthodox accounting method resulted in the company hiding operating expenses over a 2-year period between 2000 and 2002.

The company founder and CEO was Bernard Ebbers. Over a 2-year period Ebbers secured more than $400 million in personal loans from the company in addition to his annual salary and bonuses that reached over $2 million per year. One specific loan was obtained after a short conversation with the chairman of the compensation committee who was an independent outside director. There were eleven outside directors on the board of WorldCom. However, most of them had become wealthy when WorldCom, represented by Bernard Ebbers, had acquired their corporations.

The chairman of the audit committee and outside director was a dean of a US law school. The auditors, Arthur Andersen, had audited WorldCom on the basis of a low risk assumption despite their internal evaluations showing that WorldCom was considered high risk. They were denied access to important documents—namely, the general ledger at corporate headquarters, where many of the fraudulent entries had been booked.

It appears that the audit committee missed some of the most important questions, such as:

- Did you have unfettered access to all documents and records?
- What is the risk assessment and what impact did this have on your audit procedures?

In July 2002, WorldCom filed for bankruptcy protection with documents showing it was $41 billion in debt. Ebbers and four other senior managers were prosecuted and convicted of numerous counts of fraud. Ebbers was sentenced to a 25-year prison term. In a civil suit that followed, the eleven independent directors settled for over $20 million.

A special investigative committee on WorldCom, in a report on March 31, 2003, found the following:

Adequacy of Board's Oversight of Company[*]

The Board and its Committees did not function in a way that made it likely that they would notice red flags. The outside Directors had little or no involvement in the Company's business other than through attendance at Board meetings.

Nearly all of the Directors were legacies of companies that WorldCom, under Ebbers' leadership, had acquired. They had ceded

---

[*] Report of investigation by the Special Investigative Committee of the board of directors of WorldCom, Inc. March 31, 2003.

> leadership to Ebbers when their companies were acquired, and in some cases viewed their role as diminished.
>
> Ebbers controlled the Board's agenda, its discussions, and its decisions.
>
> He created, and the Board permitted, a corporate environment in which the pressure to meet the numbers was high, the departments that served as controls were weak, and the word of senior management was final and not to be challenged.
>
> The Audit Committee in particular needed an understanding of the Company it oversaw in order to be effective. However, the Audit Committee members do not appear to have had a sufficient understanding of the Company's internal financial workings or its culture, and they devoted strikingly little time to their role, meeting as little as three to five hours per year.
>
> WorldCom was a complicated Company in a fast-evolving industry. It had expanded quickly, through a series of large acquisitions, and there had been virtually no integration of the acquisitions.

WorldCom had accounting-related operations scattered in a variety of locations around the country. These facts raised significant accounting, internal control and systems concerns that required Audit Committee knowledge and attention, and that should also have elicited direct warnings from Andersen.

However, the Audit Committee members apparently did not even understand—though the evidence indicates that Andersen disclosed—the nontraditional audit approach Andersen employed. To gain the knowledge necessary to function effectively as an Audit Committee would have required a very substantial amount of energy, expertise by at least some of its members, and a greater commitment of time.

Neither WorldCom's legal department nor Internal Audit was structured to maximize its effectiveness as a control structure upon which the Board could depend.

The outside Directors had virtually no interaction with Company operational or financial employees other than during the presentations they heard at meetings.

LESSONS FROM ENRON AND WORLDCOM

The Enron and WorldCom examples clearly demonstrate that the board of directors—particularly the independent outside directors—in both of these publicly traded companies allowed management to take control of the board and the committees. They clearly should have recognized their responsibility to shareholders and maintained control over management. They should have taken early action against the fraudulent activity and prevented the bankruptcy that resulted in their respective companies.

Had they screened and then scrutinized the Red Flags when the indicators first appeared, they could have immediately ordered the removal of the officers that were involved. At that point they should have called for a full investigation by either private or public authorities. This was their duty and responsibility as directors of the corporation.

In our experience, many corporate board members feel obligated to management, who provide them with all the amenities of their position:

- Directors are paid for each meeting they attend and receive share options that can be very lucrative if the company increases its share value.
- The independent outside directors often travel long distances to attend those periodic board and committee meetings. All the travel and hotel accommodations are arranged by management.
- They arrive for the meeting and receive the material that will relate to the agenda that is prepared and supplied by management.
- They will again rely on management to guide them through the decision-making process that will be required for a particular board or committee meeting.
- With lunch served in the executive dining room, they will then concern themselves with clearing up the outstanding issues of the day.
- After the meetings, they are often invited to accompany management to sporting or entertainment events, such as golf or theatre, before catching their return flight home.
- Friendships with the senior officers develop over time and this friendship will support a trust relationship. This trust may often influence a director's judgment on important corporate issues that come up in the boardroom.

In this type of environment one can see why it only took a 12-minute presentation by management to convince the audit committee, in the WorldCom case, to approve a $2 billion acquisition or why it only took a few minutes for Bernard Ebbers to have the chairman of the compensation committee approve his $50 million loan.

Management, on the other hand, is focused on receiving quick approvals for various actions that are required from the board and getting the

231

independent directors out of the board room and back to their respective homes as soon as possible.

It does not take long for an enterprising management group to know how to move board decisions in their favor. Lobbying key leaders of independent board members is usually carried out by the CEO in advance of any board meeting. Under the leadership of one or more of the respected independent outside board members, the others will likely follow in supporting key decisions requested by management.

This is why, in hindsight, some of the decisions accepted by a board of directors appears to be willful blindness or perhaps the greed of making personal profits, or both.

Only two cases have been outlined in this chapter. However, most of the reported cases of major fraud in public companies will have the same scenario as described in the Enron and WorldCom cases. This includes companies such as Tyco International, Health South, or Adelphia. All of these companies have experienced similar issues where the board of directors did not look for, or act on, Red Flags that existed long before major financial problems developed.

In the years ahead there will be many more major public companies that we will be able to add to this list. Willful blindness, greed for share option rewards, strong management control, or close personal friendships will likely continue to be the reason directors overlook Red Flags.

Case Example of a Red Flag—The Beginning of a Path to Fraud

An executive chairman of the board and CEO of an international public corporation required immediate funds for a personal investment. Although the executive chairman had considerable personal wealth, he wanted additional funds without liquidating any of his personal assets. The company board consisted of seven board members. There were five independent outside directors, all of whom served as chairpersons on the various committees. The executive chairman approached the chairman of the compensation committee and asked him to consider awarding the executive chairman a multimillion dollar bonus.

This board member was an independent director and personal friend of the executive chairman. The bonus was approved by the committee after a short telephone meeting with the other committee members.

A short, positive report was submitted to the entire board and the issue was placed on the agenda of the next board meeting. Following a brief discussion at the next board meeting, the bonus was approved.

Similar situations occur on a regular basis in corporate boardrooms throughout the world. Although many will never be reported, some will be the beginning of a fraudulent path that will lead the corporation into bankruptcy. This example is clearly a Red Flag that should have been controlled by both the compensation committee and the board of directors.

If this type of activity is allowed, the board immediately surrenders control to senior management. A culture of fraud and corruption will likely emerge among the other officers and employees who will become aware of the unlawful bonus payment. A philosophy of, "if they can do it, we can do it," will more than likely develop within the corporation.

In addition, the executive chairman or CEO will know to what extent he or she can control the board of directors in the future. This combination of power and greed has been an element that has caused the destruction of many profitable business empires.

Case Example—Multinational Construction Company

An international publicly traded construction company had been awarded a major building construction contract by the government of a Third World country. The project involved the construction of a large complex that included roads, parking lots, and a multistory building, with several other smaller buildings.

The CEO of the corporation presented the plans to the entire board of directors. The board of directors consisted of nine independent outside members and two inside directors including the CEO, the vice president in charge of legal services. The board was chaired by an independent, nonexecutive director.

The documents presented to each member of the board included copies of the initial tender documents, the final contract, the bid bond, and the performance bonds, along with the list of subcontractors, equipment requirements, and projected costs and revenue. The contract was awarded following a tender process that included five other bidders.

The CEO made an earlier presentation to the board when the tenders were first published and the board approved moving forward with the bid preparation and submission. The CEO advised the board that although their bid was not the lowest, the government did accept it because of the number of local subcontractors that they were able to include in their tender offer.

The CEO explained that they now had seven subcontractors who had agreed to carry out various parts of this contract. The total cost of the project was $350 million and the company was expected to realize a profit of at least 25% over a 4-year period, the time frame for completion of the contract.

The CEO concluded his presentation by asking if the board members had any questions. A number of board members congratulated the CEO for putting together a team that was able to succeed in the award of the contract. Several questions related to the estimate of profit that was projected.

The region where this country was located has been identified in reports for a number of years as a high-risk location involving public corruption. These reports were prepared by the World Bank and by the Organization for Economic Cooperation and Development (OECD). Not one member of the board asked any questions concerning the issue of bribery or corruption.

The question that follows is, "What should a director do, faced with a Red Flag that points to the suggestion that bribes may have been paid to foreign government officials to obtain a contract?" The directors in this case became willfully blind to the question of corruption and did not ask any questions that might elicit an answer that would reveal evidence of wrongdoing. Some of the directors in this situation may have believed that it was too late to take any action at this stage, since the contract already had been awarded.

If a director had asked the CEO if any bribe was paid to any public official with respect to this contract, the CEO would in all likelihood have responded in the negative. Should that have satisfied the director who asked the question? The short answer is "no."

The Red Flag in this case is clearly that a payment was likely paid to public officials. The question is, "How was it paid?" Was it an agent of the corporation such as an attorney, or was it paid by one of the local subcontractors? If the payment was made by an agent or attorney, how were the funds transferred? Does the company have an "off-book" slush fund to accommodate this type of payment?

If the payment was made by one of the local subcontractors, this would mean that the corporation would, at a later stage, allow that subcontractor to be reimbursed by falsely billing the corporation for an amount equivalent to the amount of the bribe.

Here is a situation where many of the independent directors may have taken the position that bribes are usually paid in these high-risk regions no matter who is awarded the contract. They may have rationalized that with the government in this particular country in control, there is very little danger that the bribe payments will be discovered.

The false invoices will be the only evidence at their head office that there was corruption. The chance of someone discovering that the invoice contained false information was extremely low. So, the directors may have believed that the risk–reward ratio was worth taking the risk.

What the directors, in this case, failed to take into account, however, was that this particular Third World country was in the process of going through a change of government. After taking office, the newly appointed prime minister decided that there would be a full investigation of the corrupt practices involving the previous administration. The bribe payments that were made on this project were discovered and the construction company, the CEO, and the entire board of directors became involved in the criminal investigation that followed.

While the corporation survived this event, the CEO and the directors did not. The CEO was prosecuted with a criminal offense and all the members of the board of directors were removed. While the corporation did avoid bankruptcy, the financial impact that resulted from this event was devastating for the shareholders and investors.

While hindsight is 20-20, there is no doubt that the illegal activity could have been prevented if the appropriate steps had been taken by the independent outside directors as they sat listening to the presentation by the CEO.

CONCLUSION

Members of a board of directors have a fiduciary responsibility to the shareholders and stakeholders of their organization. This responsibility includes the prevention and detection of fraud by the organization itself. To fulfill this duty of care, board members and, in particular, independent board members must develop systems to identify fraud that may be committed by or within their organization.

17

Screening, Scrutinizing, and Investigating Red Flags

INTRODUCTION

When it comes to fraud, even the most well-prepared and -structured organization can become a victim. There is no silver bullet—no single, magical solution—that can safeguard even the most prudent of us from fraud.

However, the prudent measures outlined in this book—collectively called the Red Flag System—can help reduce the risk of fraud and increase the chances that it can be either prevented or detected much earlier.

As we have outlined, the Red Flag System is practical, effective, and empirically tested. It is based on the premise that to prevent fraud successfully or to detect it as quickly as possible after it begins, an organization must have the capacity to identify, analyze, and address possible indicators of fraud, known as "Red Flags," in a timely manner.

Red Flags are like the first wisps of smoke in a forest. Detect them early enough and you can prevent a forest fire. Fail to move decisively and the whole forest may be in danger.

WHEN TO SCREEN FOR RED FLAGS

Members of the board and committee members meet on a regular basis to approve financial statements, budgets, and major contracts or projects. Prior to each meeting, each director is provided with copies of all relevant documents prepared by management. During the meetings, management presenters introduce the documents and provide the necessary background information. Each meeting provides opportunities to screen for Red Flags.

These presentations may also involve an update on major ongoing operational projects in regions of the world that are at high risk for fraud and corruption. These are opportunities for directors to examine details that will ensure that the procurement process provides senior management with enough information to be able to screen for Red Flags.

The important question here is how a director who meets occasionally at corporate headquarters for board meetings can look for Red Flags that are indications of fraud and corruption in the company's procurement system.

The Red Flag that a director might look for is not necessarily the same type of Red Flag that a company auditor should identify. The auditors have access to all the files and invoices that make up a particular procurement contract. They may examine the files and invoices in detail. Some of these files and records are physically situated in foreign jurisdictions and may be in the language of the country where the project is located.

The director may, however, ask the CFO or the internal auditors to explain a particular concerning feature of a procurement process. This may then be followed up by a request for additional information that may include the actual documents. The Red Flag for the director may often be the inconsistencies that are presented. This process by the director may occur over a period of several meetings.

The director also has the opportunity to ask for additional information and documentation prior to the next meeting. So the process of screening for Red Flags may occur over a period of time. Any misleading or false information that is uncovered by the director is clearly a Red Flag that should be pursued.

Officers and employees who are involved in fraud and collusion will not be able to withstand scrutiny over a period of time. If senior managers come to the defense of any officer or employee who is involved in making misleading statements, this would be another Red Flag indicating that fraud or corruption may be institutionalized and perhaps more widespread within the culture of the company.

Committee members often receive financial reports from the CFO and internal and outside auditors. These reports are often submitted in person to the committee or, in some cases, the entire board of directors.

Screening for Red Flags—The Budget

The first screening for Red Flags may occur at the budget planning stage. The budget documents are usually first presented to the audit committee. These documents will likely set out the major contracts and projects for the next financial year. The budget is often presented by the chief financial officer and supported by members of the staff in the financial and relevant operational departments.

The first examination of the proposed budget by an audit committee is conducted at a forum in which directors

- Ask questions of the budget presenters
- Examine presenters who have knowledge of or responsibility for preparing the budget and overseeing the resulting procurement

The process in an audit committee's budgetary meeting is generally the same whether the organization is a private or public corporation, or whether it is an agency of government or a private or public institution.

Committee members are provided with relevant documents and submissions relating to the budget. They are expected to review that material before the meeting and be prepared to examine the presenters. The officials and other presenters are generally aware of all the details of the budget documents and can anticipate the general questions that will be asked by the committee members.

Screening for Red Flags—Financial Reports and Project Reports

The second Red Flag screening opportunity may occur with presentation of the financial/audit or project reports. The financial/audit reports are presented following an audit by the external auditors and project reports may be presented by the CFO and the operational officers of the corporation.

The first presentation of the financial reports will likely be made to the audit committee. The financial and project reports may include large procurement contracts that have been awarded or are in the process of being awarded. The audit committee is usually focused on two major issues:

- Determine if the proposed goods or services in the budget will meet the objective
- Confirm that related costs make sense and that the anticipated revenues justify the expenditure

Project reports may be presented to the governance or oversight committee responsible for the organization's overall management.

In every organization the contracting process begins with setting out the objectives of the project. This is followed by the planning process and then the preparation of the project's budget. The budget document will usually include a breakdown of anticipated revenues and expenditures. Some of the expenditures will itemize the list of all goods and services to be purchased.

Board and committee members may find that reviewing a proposed project replete with subsets of transactions and phases may be extremely complex. The documents themselves may have been prepared by teams of attorneys, engineers, and accountants who rely too heavily on their respective professions' jargon. On occasion the technical description of a project that is used in the documents may go beyond the individual directors' expertise and experience. The result is that the financial statement, budget, or contract documents may be not only difficult to understand but also extremely difficult to challenge.

Many committee members may feel that they are at a disadvantage when management appears before them presenting such complex issues. When a board or committee member allows his or her eyes to glaze over from long and boring complex presentations, he or she may have no other option but to accept the recommendation of management to approve the presenter's proposal.

It is at precisely this point, however, when the member believes that it is easier to go along with management, that a cross-examination of the presenter should be undertaken. So, without being overwhelmed with the entire complexity of the presentation, the director should select one issue that we have previously identified as a high-risk issue and begin a passive cross-examination of the presenter.

A case in point is the behavior of some directors of a major conglomerate that has been the subject of major fraud allegations. At the fraud trial of several senior executives, one director testified about the documents indicating that some noncompetition payments were perhaps improperly going to the senior executives and not to the company. This director said that he did not read the documents thoroughly because he and other directors relied on management to point out salient issues.

HOW TO ASK QUESTIONS IN THE RIGHT MANNER

When directors ask questions related to possible Red Flags, they should follow the best practices of a good law enforcement interview. A good interview is not a confrontation or a cross-examination. It is a fair and impartial fact-finding exercise. These are vital elements to maintain a positive environment at the board level and in relations with management.

The following are characteristics of good interviewing techniques relevant to the Red Flag process at the board level:

- All important questions central to the issue are asked and the answers recorded.
- Everyone is treated fairly and impartially.
- Those answering questions are not disrupted with unnecessary questions.
- Whoever has knowledge of the issue is allowed the opportunity to tell his or her side of the story fully and to explain all apparent inconsistencies.
- Anyone who appears to be the subject of negative inferences is allowed to respond and address all allegations.

It is important to set the appropriate professional tone right from the start of the interview. Be courteous, fair, and impartial in dealing with everyone at the meeting. Do not appear to be a threat. Do not appear to have reached conclusions and to be merely looking for information to confirm them. Do not attempt to impress everyone with your knowledge, intelligence, or experience. Make everyone feel comfortable.

The Association of Certified Fraud Examiners advises:

> Professionalism in the interview often involves a state of mind and a commitment to excellence. The interviewer should be on time, be professionally attired, and be fair in all dealings with the respondent. It is absolutely vital that the interviewer not appear to be a threat. If people perceive that they are the target of an inquiry, they will be less likely to cooperate.[*]

Communication theorists have long known that some types of behavior promote good communication and others inhibit it. The following types of behavior will improve your chances of having a productive and positive dialogue:

- Be courteous and develop a rapport with everyone. Do not be authoritarian or act in a superior manner. Give everyone reason to trust you and to open up to you.
- Let whoever is responding to your questions complete their thoughts. Do not interrupt.

---

[*] Association of Certified Fraud Examiners. *Fraud examiners manual*, p. 3.202.

- If someone is rambling or has trouble focusing on the issues at hand, maintain the focus of the dialogue in a respectful manner.
- Be impartial. Be sympathetic and understanding. Do not be judgmental. Do not give the impression that you will disapprove if someone makes an admission of an improper act.
- Use an open and relaxed posture. Nod in agreement. Make eye contact. Occasionally say, "OK," "uh huh," or some other affirmative comment.
- Individuals who are genuinely trying to cooperate sometimes make what appear to be inadvertent errors in terms of chronology, distance, and description. Be supportive in such cases and ask these people to remember to the best of their ability. Do not ridicule. By being helpful, you will be able to better determine whether the errors are indeed inadvertent or an attempt at deceit.

Preparation is "the most important fact" in conducting a positive and fruitful dialogue regarding Red Flags.[*] Appropriate preparation includes but is not limited to:

- Thoroughly reviewing the available documents
- Identifying the general objectives of the discussion
- Identifying apparent inconsistencies in prior documents and discussions
- Setting out questions to be asked and the order in which they are to be asked

It is important that care be taken in the way questions are asked:

- Ask clear, simple questions.
- Ask one question at a time.
- Do not ask compound questions—that is, two or more questions strung together. If asked more than one question at the same time, not all the questions may be answered or the respondent may simply get confused.
- Try to create a logical sequence to your questions. Sometimes it is easiest simply to follow the chronology of transactions or projects. Jumping around the chronology may be confusing to everyone.

---

[*] David Vessel, J. D. 1998. Conducting successful interrogations. *FBI Law Enforcement Bulletin* 67:1–6.

- Sometimes, however, stepping away from the chronology can be a useful interviewing technique. Deceitful individuals may have trouble maintaining their deceit if they are asked questions out of chronological sequence.
- Do not telegraph the answer to a question. Let the individual answer the question in his or her own words and on the basis of his or her recollection and knowledge.
- If answers are confusing, make sure the individual has an opportunity to clarify his or her response.
- Do not ask leading questions.

There are generally two types of questions:

- Open-ended questions
- Closed questions

Open-ended questions have no prespecified answers and encourage the interview subject to provide a broad response. Examples are "Tell me what happened..." "Explain to me...," "What happened when...," etc. Open-ended questions promote the gathering of complete information and allow the interviewer to assess the interview subject's normal behavior.

Closed questions are intended to elicit a more narrowly defined response. Examples are "When did this happen?" "What time was it?" "Who was there?" etc. Closed questions are intended to elicit specific details and limit the interview subject's response. Their purpose is not to elicit general information, but to obtain specific details or corroborate information from other witnesses. Closed questions also help the interviewer to detect possible efforts to deceive.

Good interviews contain an appropriate mix of open-ended and closed questions. Research has found that each has certain kinds of benefits. Research revealed that the use of open-ended questions generated more complete information, but potentially less accurate information, than the use of more direct closed questions.[*]

The FBI has a useful model for logically structuring an interview and appropriately balancing open-ended and closed questions. This is known as the "funnel approach" and suggests beginning with open-ended

---

[*] Vincent A. Sandoval. 2003. Strategies to avoid interview contamination. *FBI Law Enforcement Bulletin* 72 (10): 1–12.

questions and then asking more and more precise, closed questions. The FBI's *Law Enforcement Bulletin* said:

> Using this analogy and employing the categorization of questions as either closed or open-ended, interviewers should begin the information-gathering phase with broad open-ended inquiries designed to obtain as much information as possible and culminate the process with very direct and specific closed questions.*

PRUDENT STRATEGY

Board and committee members may not receive all the information necessary to identify a Red Flag at only one meeting. It is therefore important carefully to record in the minutes of each meeting every reply to questions about areas of concern. By recording every response, a pattern of conduct may become evident, helping to demonstrate that false or misleading information may have been supplied. The inconsistencies of verbal presentations on the part of management may in themselves give rise to the identification of Red Flags.

While meetings provide a vital opportunity to detect Red Flags, it is equally important to closely examine all documents that have been presented for approval. These documents may contain information that outlines the high-risk or suspicious item. If such an item is identified, the members have identified a Red Flag. At this stage the presenter should be carefully questioned about the potential Red Flag item. In a nonaccusatory tone, it is prudent simply to obtain as much information as possible about the item and carefully record the answers. Later, the committee can discuss how to carry out an effective investigation into the issue.

Frauds in public corporations like Enron and WorldCom, for example, were detected too late by whistle-blowers and outsiders or by accident. They were not reported by directors or audit committee members, despite the large number of Red Flags.

Indeed, many insiders at Enron and WorldCom were suspicious of certain transactions and activities, but were reluctant to blow the whistle because they feared losing their jobs. Eventually, the head of internal audit at WorldCom, Cynthia Cooper, overstepped her boundaries and investigated apparent Red Flags against explicit orders by WorldCom's CEO at night and using unauthorized backdoor access to WorldCom's general ledger.

---

* Ibid.

SCREENING COMPLAINTS FOR RED FLAGS

Many corporations have developed and support whistle-blowing programs. Some do so in name and policy only, with little attention given to ensuring that those employees who submit complaints or information are fully protected or that the information they provide reaches the board level. An effective complaint program will provide an early warning in the Red Flag screening process.

A second and important source of information is often found in the public media and the Internet when disgruntled shareholders or market analysts report negatively on corporate activities.

Developing effective policy that will allow board and committee members to examine and screen all complaints against the organization is a very important extension to the Red Flag screening program.

Some of the complaints against the corporation, especially those that are published by aggressive short sellers, may become the subject of potential lawsuits by the organization. In spite of the potential legal action, it is important for the directors to screen the facts of the case for potential Red Flags that may indicate illegal activity on the part of management or employees.

To ensure that such a program will be effective, it may be useful to establish a formal permanent committee of the board to receive and analyze all complaints concerning the organization. The committee would, like the audit committee, comprise independent outside directors entirely.

This committee would be responsible to screen the complaints for Red Flags and then respond with the appropriate action. In organizations that are structured with an internal audit unit reporting directly to the board of directors, that unit could be tasked with the management of this program.

SCRUTINIZING RED FLAGS

What should a director do if a Red Flag is detected? As we have indicated, a Red Flag does not by itself mean that fraud has occurred. It does, however, suggest that there is a need to carry out further enquiries.

The next step is scrutinizing the Red Flag. What is involved in the process of scrutinizing a Red Flag? An investigation by the board of the circumstances surrounding the Red Flag indicator is the next step in the fraud detection process.

Up to this point we have focused on how to screen corporate records and transactions for irregularities. This process has been described as a search for Red Flags. Finding a Red Flag is simply the first step in what can become a long and sometimes difficult task to scrutinize the information and then, if justified, to investigate the matter and finally to implement an appropriate solution or action.

In most companies, a board member has only a small window of opportunity to find the Red Flag and then to investigate to determine if improper or illegal activity has occurred. Most of the information given to board members in preparation for a board or committee meeting is provided exclusively by management and employees of the corporation and, on occasion, by the outside auditors. Often they are the same officers or employees that may be involved in the suspicious Red Flag activity.

How does the independent outside director sift through the material provided by management to further identify the suspicious activity when Red Flags have been discovered? The role of a director is much like that of a "gatekeeper" and, as a gatekeeper, he or she will not open any gate to management without being satisfied that the decision or approval before the board is in the best interests of the company, the shareholders, and the investors.

This means that directors must continue to ask penetrating questions until they are completely satisfied before a decision to support any issue is granted. The director may ask for additional documentation and information and also seek advice from independent experts.

There may be opposition from other directors who historically have always supported management, but as questions are put forward and answers received, other directors may follow and understand that a Red Flag must be scrutinized to determine if improper or illegal activity has occurred.

ROLE OF INTERNAL AUDITORS

In the United States, internal audit units in publicly traded companies are required to report functionally to the board of directors. The oversight responsibility for internal audit is usually assigned to the audit committee or the governance committee.

Many companies, however, require that the internal auditor report to a senior corporate officer, such as the CFO, for administrative control. In order to ensure that complete independence and objectivity is achieved, it is important that all personnel appointments, along with the control of this office, are retained directly by the board. The board is then able to carry out an effective risk management program and focus on the high-risk issues that surface from time to time.

All reports from internal audit should be submitted directly to the board or audit committee rather than to management. Once a report is submitted, it may then be disseminated to management and onward within the organization.

In addition, the board or audit committee members can assign specific tasks to internal auditors to assist in screening or scrutinizing Red Flags. They may also assign specific tasks or programs to detect fraud within the organization. One such program is the Fraud Diagnostic Test developed by the Association of Certified Fraud Examiners.

INCENTIVES TO INVESTIGATE PROPERLY

Even the best run companies can run afoul of fraudulent schemes. Many companies with strong antifraud policies have found that an aggressive company officer or employee has in fact set up and participated in the payment of bribes to foreign government officials in order to secure contracts. However, if appropriate policy and procedure had been in place at the board level, the directors are more likely to have had the incentive to investigate any Red Flags that indicated fraudulent behavior.

The corporation should have a policy relating to independent board members, which should include:

- Periodic meetings without inside directors or management present; during these meetings, boardroom policy and procedures should be developed and implemented at the full board meeting
- Continued educational and training programs for independent directors that will focus on screening and scrutinizing Red Flags along with other fraud prevention programs
- An independent outside director selected as the nonexecutive chair of the board of directors and all committees

To maximize the ability to prevent fraud, corruption, and mismanagement and to screen and scrutinize Red Flags, a board should implement the following policies and procedures:

- Ensure that any director participating or involved in the identification of a Red Flag involving a suspicious transaction will be supported by the entire board of directors.
- Allow the director time during board or committee meetings to introduce and complete any Red Flag screening of documents or the examination of presenters.
- If a Red Flag is indicated during this process, allow the director to carry out further screening, which may include the production of corporate documents or the examination of management or employees.
- If a Red Flag indicates fraud, corruption, or other illegal activities on the part of any member of the organization, a full preliminary inquiry by the board or committee should be implemented.
- Any director may call for a preliminary inquiry, on a point of order, during any meeting of the board or committee to examine or further screen a Red Flag.
- When a Red Flag indicates fraud, corruption, or other illegal activity by anyone in management of the organization, a special committee of the board would be established to inquire into the allegation.
- This special committee inquiry may also be commenced on a point of order made by any director.
- The special committee should include the director or directors who raised the initial Red Flag(s).
- The special committee should also include any expert that is deemed necessary to advise the committee or assist them with the inquiry.
- The special committee must not include an officer or employee of the organization, except for the internal auditors of the organization who report directly to the board or audit committee.
- The special committee must be allowed to call any officer or employee of the organization to provide information and deliver any corporate records that are deemed necessary by any committee member.
- If a Red Flag that is scrutinized by the committee is found to be an indication that mismanagement or fraud has occurred, a report to the full board must be made.

On receiving a report from this special committee indicating that further investigation is required, the following must take place:

- Continue the appointment of the special committee to structure and supervise any action that was recommended by the committee, including any private or public investigation.
- Appoint any additional experts as may be required to assist the committee, such as lawyers, internal auditors, private investigators, or forensic accountants.
- The committee will keep the board informed of all investigative developments.
- The committee will continue to oversee all legal action that may be undertaken as a result of the investigation.

The duties of this special committee could include:

- Recommendation to the board for the dismissal of senior officials and employees who may have been found to be involved in misconduct during the course of the inquiry
- Recommendation to the board to launch civil or criminal action
- Continuing to monitor all civil, criminal, and internal investigations that are part of the initial inquiry

The implementation of this type of policy would ensure that early damage control by the board is undertaken when a Red Flag is initially identified. There is little doubt that such types of policies and procedures could have prevented the downfall of many of the organizations that have been devastated by fraud, corruption, and other illegal activity by officers and employees.

CONCLUSION

Directors and committee members in public entities must have the opportunity, ability, commitment, and full support to carry out their fiduciary duty and legal responsibilities as representatives of the shareholders and investors. A major part of that duty and responsibility is to control material fraudulent conduct within their entity.

To summarize, the main points outlined in this chapter are to

- Develop a strong corporate position from the board of director's level that fraud, corruption, and other illegal activity will not be condoned within the organization.

- Provide continuing education programs for independent outside board members. Such training programs should include training on how to screen and scrutinize Red Flags of fraud.
- Implement a fraud diagnostic assessment and prevention program within the organization, supervised by internal audit.
- Support a whistle-blowing program within the organization and ensure that whistle-blower complaints reach designated members of the board for review and investigation.
- Develop a program at the board level to review and analyze all public complaints against the organization that indicate fraud, corruption, or other illegal activity allegedly committed by someone within the organization.
- Implement an organizational structure that ensures that internal audit is not controlled by management and reports directly to the board or the audit committee.
- Have periodic meetings of the independent directors to focus on fraud prevention and detection, ensuring that individual directors are given opportunity and support to screen for Red Flags.
- Develop a Red Flag check-off list for all high-risk corporate involvement.
- Develop specific board policies and procedures that permit a member of the board or committee to request a special committee of the board, on a point of order, to screen and scrutinize a Red Flag presented by that board or committee member.

We have indicated throughout this book that failure to take action can, on many occasions, not only end up in a loss to the company, but also may leave the individual directors open to personal liability. While most corporations have liability insurance to protect directors against any civil action, it will not necessarily cover them for negligence, gross negligence, or criminal behavior related to the performance of their duties.

In particular, the focus has been on directors taking an aggressive stand against any wrongdoing by or within the corporation. To ensure that directors are fulfilling their fiduciary duty to the company, shareholders, and employees, they must always be vigilant when there are indications of fraud and corruption.

Indecision or "keeping your head down," as they say, during crucial decisions in the boardroom may still bring an accusation of wrongdoing. Willful blindness is a term that is used when people in authority who have specific responsibility to act intentionally fail to act. Willful blindness may very well result in a finding of negligence or even gross negligence. Directors who fail to act when a Red Flag of criminality is factually established may be seen as being implicated in the crime.

Being a coconspirator or a party after the fact to a criminal act can have serious consequences for the individual director, particularly in the global marketplace, where laws of one jurisdiction can be enforced in another country. Consequently, an agent of the company that commits a criminal act in a country where a multinational corporation has its field operation could have criminal consequences for a director at the head office, if appropriate action is not taken by the board in connection with that activity.

This is becoming a more distinct problem as international conventions and agreements are introduced to enforce criminality on a global basis between member countries.

APPENDIX A: SUMMARY OF RED FLAGS

This appendix is a quick reference to all the Red Flags that are outlined in this book. They are listed under their respective headings.

FINANCIAL STATEMENT FRAUD RED FLAGS

- Overstating assets or revenues
- Understating liabilities or expenses
- Deliberately omitting or misrepresenting material information used to prepare financial statements
- Intentionally circumventing the proper application of accounting principles when recording material events, transactions, and/or accounts
- Understating the bad debt allowance for receivables
- Overstating the value of inventory, property, plant, and equipment and other tangible assets
- Recording fictitious assets

Overstatements generally occur in the following business scenarios:

- In preparation for major divestiture activities
- In preparation of joint venture arrangements as a defense mechanism to deter hostile takeovers
- To improve credit rating and to obtain favorable financing conditions
- To demonstrate compliance with financing/loan agreements
- To postpone insolvency proceedings
- To increase bonus entitlements for management
- To stave off situational pressures created by unrealistic budgets or sudden changes in the market

Understatements generally occur in the following business scenarios:

- To reduce an organization's tax burden
- In buyouts of minority shareholders

- As clean-up strategies upon change of senior management, in what is often called "Big Bath Accounting"
- To make it easier to get financial assistance in government contracts, since they typically make funds more easily available to entities with lower financial capabilities

The methods used to perpetrate financial statement fraud can be classified into three categories:

- Manipulation of net assets—that is, of assets less liabilities
- Manipulation of earnings
- False or inadequate disclosure

Manipulation of net assets—total of all the assets less the liabilities owed to outsiders—can occur in any balance sheet items, but especially with regard to:

- **Fixed assets,** defined as assets such as land, buildings, and machines that are continually used in the business
- **Inventories** comprising raw materials, work in progress, and finished products ready for sale
- Accounts receivables, which are debts owed by customers
- Cash at banks
- Liabilities and accrued liabilities—liabilities recorded in an organization's financial records before they are paid or even invoiced by the vendor

The value of inventories can be misrepresented by:

- Manipulating the physical inventory counts
- Overstating or understating the cost applied to determine the value of counted inventories

Sophisticated methods include:

- Counting of inventory on consignment as being actually owned by the entity
- Borrowing the inventories of coconspirators
- Including so-called "bill and hold" items, which were already booked in the financial records as having been sold, as inventory

Sophisticated methods include manipulating:

- The percentage of completion documentation in large manufacturing and construction projects

- The split of long-term construction projects into individual project components when applying the completed contract method of valuation, which can also lead to fraudulent recording of both the sale of a project and its inclusion as work in progress

Intentional failure to write off or reduce accounts receivables may involve:

- Manipulating documentation about the credit worthiness of customers
- Dividing a large receivable with one customer into numerous smaller receivables with several customers
- Manipulating the aging of receivables
- Using a circular flow of funds to make the receivable appear paid
- Factoring receivables—that is, raising cash by selling its accounts receivables at a discount—to nonconsolidated entities similar to the "asset light strategy" for fixed assets
- The nondisclosure or understatement of the amount of future lease commitments and guarantees for third party liabilities
- Risks resulting from off-balance sheet items such as trading in derivatives

Omissions of negative developments such as:

- The loss of key customers
- The cancellations of joint venture arrangements
- The loss of key suppliers
- Setbacks in technological developments, which render the organization's manufacturing processes inferior to its competitors or make substantial investments necessary in the near future

Dominant behavior often coincides with a lack of respect for:

- Oversight institutions
- Regulatory authorities
- Laws and regulations in effect in countries other than the company's home country

Red Flags pertaining to organization-specific conditions include:

- Dependence on small numbers of products, suppliers, customers, or business transactions (bulk risks)
- Risk of hostile takeovers
- Rapid business expansion

- Liquidity shortage due to rapid expansion
- Rapid increase of corporate acquisitions
- Conflict between shareholders or groups of shareholders with CEO or members of senior management having strong relations to one group of shareholders

Industry-specific Red Flags include:

- Operating in highly competitive markets
- Operating in industrial sectors with short product life cycles, often due to susceptibility to technological changes
- Profitability inconsistent with industry sector (i.e., profitability substantially above or below industry standard)
- Operating in markets with a high degree of saturation and shrinking margins
- Increasing number of bankruptcies within the industry sector

ORGANIZATIONAL RED FLAGS

- Organizational Red Flags are warning signs resulting from deficiencies of governance structures and internal controls over the financial process.
- Financial Red Flags result from financial ratio analysis or the observation of phenomena that have been found to be correlated to financial fraud schemes.

Red Flags on financial statement fraud include:

- Recurring negative cash flows from operations while reporting positive earnings or even earnings growth
- Unusual growth in the number of days sales in accounts receivables
- Unusual surge in sales by a minority of units within the organization or surge in sales by corporate headquarters
- Unusual growth and profitability, especially compared to that of other companies in the same industry
- Unusual increase in gross margin or gross margins in excess of industry peers
- Unusual decline in the number of days purchases in accounts payables
- Significant declines in customer demand and increasing business failures in the industry

- Assets based on significant estimates that involve subjective judgments or uncertainties that are difficult to corroborate
- Declining allowances for bad debts, excess, or obsolete inventories
- Unusual change in the relationship between fixed assets and depreciation
- Increases in fixed assets, while the industry is reducing its capital intensity

TRANSACTIONAL RED FLAGS

Transactional Red Flags relate to anomalies in certain types of transactions that can indicate the use of structures to perpetrate financial statement fraud schemes:

- Significant levels of transactions with entities in tax haven countries
- Subsidiaries in tax haven jurisdictions
- Significant levels of transactions with organizations not subject to audit requirements
- Significant sales volume with entities whose substance and ownership are not known
- Existence of legal entities without perceived relationship to core business activities
- Accumulation of significant transactions close to period end
- Existence of significant numbers of transactions whose reasons and structures are difficult to comprehend or justify

Weaknesses in internal control systems are strongly correlated with the occurrence of financial statements frauds. Red Flags for weak internal controls often involve their lack of integration in the organization or their performance. External and internal auditors are crucial to the success of an organization because they have the highest level of insight over internal controls. Such Red Flags include:

- Internal audit staff not reporting to the board of directors or its audit committee
- Any indications that management is trying to control or inhibit communications from internal audit staff to the board of directors
- A reduction of or increased turnover in internal audit staff
- Internal audit not meeting the audit schedule or not adequately covering significant risk areas

- A significant decrease in the audit budget
- Unexplained or unexpected changes in external auditor or significant changes in the audit program
- Internal or external auditors relying heavily on the other's conclusions
- Audit reports not addressing identified internal control weaknesses
- Significant deficiencies in internal controls noted in audit reports that have not been corrected
- A qualified, adverse, or disclaimer opinion from an external auditor
- The inability of management to provide timely and accurate financial, operational, and regulatory reports
- Dominance of top management by one individual or a small group of individuals, which leads to blocking of controls by other members of senior management
- Weaknesses in control activities
- Management's attempts to satisfy unrealistic expectations of stakeholders
- Profitability of company inconsistent with industry standard
- Large number of complex transactions
- Aggressive approach to financial statements reporting by management
- Management lying to external auditors
- Industry conditions that are negative
- Rapid growth
- Irregularities in the accounting system
- Significant accounts whose balances were based on estimates
- Increasing number of bankruptcies within the industry sector
- Extraordinary dependence on contractual obligations
- Cash flow shortages
- Operating result inconsistent with industry development
- Rapidly changing industry
- Individual transactions with significant impact on annual earnings
- Recurring differences between management and auditors over the application of accounting principles and auditing standards
- Certain accounts requiring complex calculations
- Conflicts of interest between management and corporation
- Procurement contracts

Red Flags indicating collusive bidding will include the following:

- Bid suppression
- Bid rotation agreement among bidders

- Complementary bidding
- Subcontracting agreements prior to bidding

RED FLAGS ON CONTRACT FRAUD

- One or more of the unsuccessful bidders become subcontractors after the contract is awarded.
- Contractors who would normally bid alone become a subcontractor or a joint venture partner.
- Bid prices are reduced when a new contractor becomes involved in the bidding process.
- Bid prices are separated by an equal percentage difference.
- Losing bidders cannot be located, have no telephone or e-mail contact information, and address information is vague or misleading. All this indicates that a fictitious company may have submitted a complementary bid.
- Winning bidder rents equipment from the high or losing bidders.
- There is public or private information that an industry, or sector, is controlled by organized crime.
- There are forged bid and performance bonds.
- False financial statements are required to prove capability to perform the contract.

RED FLAGS INDICATING CORRUPTION AND BRIBERY IN THE COLLUSIVE BIDDING PROCESS

- Advertising for tenders is done on a restricted basis. Ads are placed in limited locations to which only some contractors have access.
- There is a short time period between tender call and bid closing date, thus allowing only favored contractors to bid, who have been provided with the contract specifications at an earlier date.
- Invitation to bid is only sent to certain contractors, and other qualified contractors are not invited.
- Bids are opened in private or opened early before the bid closing date, indicating that bid prices may have been released to the favored bidder.

- The lowest and potentially the successful bid contains information that closely resembles confidential information on price and favored methods of performing the project work.
- Tailored specifications favor only one bidder.

RED FLAGS ON RESTRICTIVE SPECIFICATIONS

- Specifications call for bid bonds or performance bonds that only one company can issue to all bidders.
- Requirements in the specifications will direct bidders to one location to release bid information with the same results as the bid bond issue.
- Requirements are that only one supplier/manufacturer may supply items or goods required to perform the contract. Each bidder will be required to seek pricing from that one supplier.
- A requirement is for excessive amounts of bid and performance bonds, for the sole purpose of limiting the number of contractors that would be able to acquire the bonds.
- There is a requirement for excessive net worth of contractors relating to contract performance capability.
- Change orders are implemented after the tender has been awarded.

RED FLAGS ON CONFLICT OF INTEREST AND CORPORATE OWNERSHIP

- Employee or manager is related to the owner of a favored bidder.
- Employee or manager has a secret financial interest in the company that is a favored bidder.
- Employee or manager secretly owns company that is a favored bidder.
- Employees have been offered future employment with successful bidder.
- Employee is a member of same club, group, or church as favored bidder is.
- Employee is intimidated or pressured into providing confidential information.

RED FLAGS ON CONTRACT SPLITTING

- Numerous contracts for smaller amounts are issued for the same project, which was budgeted as one project.
- Questionable relationships exist between employees and favorite contractors and suppliers.
- Contracts that were previously bundled into one contract are split into several smaller ones.
- Goods that were ordered in certain quantity are split into smaller quantities and from different suppliers.

RED FLAGS ON CONTRACT BUNDLING

- Employees have control over the collusive bidding process, indicating a conflicted relationship with contractors involved in the bidding system.
- The goods or services that are involved in the one contract are not related.
- Smaller contractors, who would normally bid, are unable to do so because of the larger bundled contract.

Collusive contracting schemes include:

- Organized crime's control of an industrial sector or territory
- Comingling contracts
- Duplicate contract payments
- Defective pricing
- False invoices

Red Flags relating to false invoices include:

- Time and date on the invoice are not commensurate with services rendered and goods delivered.
- The frequency of invoices is questionable—too many or too few.
- Locations described on the invoice—such as delivery addresses or receiving information—are not correct.
- Amount on invoices is anomalous—too high, too low, too consistent, too alike, too different.
- The name of supplier or contractor on the invoice raises questions—for example, a vague corporate name.

- Address of supplier or contractor is not shown on the invoice, fictitious, a mailbox, a virtual office, and/or the office address is that of the home of an employee or relative.
- Telephone numbers are not shown on invoice or appear to be a cell phone number.
- The website may be generic looking and not consistent with suppliers qualified to deliver goods and services, or there is an absence of a website.
- Yahoo, Gmail, or other similar e-mail addresses are used, as opposed to a corporate address.

CONTRACT FRAUD RED FLAGS

- False representations
- Front-end loading or advance payment fraud
- Information theft
- Inflated local purchase order or split purchases
- Phantom contractor
- Product substitution
- Progress payment fraud
- Purchases for personal use
- Time limitations and restricted advertising
- Unnecessary purchases
- Bids solicited for goods or services that are not actually required or that are a duplication of another contract

BRIBERY AND CORRUPTION RED FLAGS

- Payments to offshore corporations
- Sale of equipment at book value
- Consultancy services from nonestablished consulting providers
- Intercompany exchange of goods using intermediaries
- Equipment always sold at or near the actual book value

RED FLAGS ON THE USE OF LAWYERS/ AGENTS FOR CORRUPT PAYMENTS

- More than one lawyer in a foreign country transaction
- Legal fees in the absence of legal services

- Unusually high fees for legal services
- No recognizable service provided by foreign agent or consultant and no record of service delivery
- Unusually high fees paid for the services rendered
- Winning bids, where products are not invoiced directly to the principal purchaser on record for the tender
- Marked fluctuation in marketing expenses
- Increases in commission expenses when the use of agents is first introduced
- Advances to subcontractors or joint venture partners in the absence of contracts, but within short time of a winning bid
- Permitting nongroup importers to bid for contracts while such permission is contrary to corporate policies in other markets

MARKET MANIPULATION AND START-UP CORPORATIONS—RED FLAGS

- Promoters of start-up company using friends instead of seasoned professionals to guide the corporation through the early stages of development
- Promoter failing to carry out extensive and comprehensive due diligence on planned takeover of new company
- Fellow company insiders involved in excessive trading of company shares on the public market
- High trading volumes of shares before confidential information is released to the public; share price increasing before forthcoming positive information is released
- Short selling and share price drop before negative information is released to public
- Significant share price fluctuations on the public market without reason

PYRAMID SCHEMES—RED FLAGS

- Corporations report more revenue from the recruitment of agents and distributors than from the sale of their product.
- Commissions are paid to recruit agents or distributors.
- Disproportionately large commissions are paid for marketing investments.

- Interest rates on investments are higher than the average for the same level of risk; in particular, interest rates on "safe deposits" exceed market rates for equivalent certificates of deposits with insured banks.
- Investment plans are secret.
- There are rapid growth programs.
- Promoters fail to meet obligations and ask for unreasonable delays.
- There is a lack of disclosure of specific assets held by a company even for investments in publicly traded securities.
- The promoter's business plan relates to new high-tech or unregulated markets.
- There are many interlocking and/or affiliated corporate entities.
- Small public accounting firms that are unable to service a large operation with complex legal structure are engaged.
- There is a small group of tightly bonded senior managers, consisting predominantly of family members and friends.
- There is a lack of proven expertise and track record of senior managers.
- Principal senior managers have a lavish lifestyle.
- Media releases and reports publish all or some of the aforementioned inconsistencies.

APPENDIX B: GLOSSARY

A

Accounts receivable: Money owed to a business entity by a client and recorded as an asset on the balance sheet.

Adelphia: Adelphia Communications Corporation was a public company listed on the NASDAQ exchange. It was incorporated in Pennsylvania in 1952. The company was one of the largest cable companies in North America. It went into Chapter 11 bankruptcy following the prosecution of five of its senior officers for securities fraud. Its founder and others were convicted.

Association of Certified Fraud Examiners: A worldwide professional association that governs its members who have the designation of certified fraud examiners (CFEs). The association provides anti-fraud training and courses for potential members to qualify in order to become a certified fraud examiner. The organization also prepares and distributes material and information on fraud and related topics.

Audit committee: A committee comprising members of a board of directors and delegated to have oversight of the corporation's financial matters, including audits and audit reports.

Auditor General of Canada: The auditor general is appointed by the House of Commons of the Parliament of Canada. In turn, the auditor general manages an office that engages professional personnel to conduct audits of the federal government and its departments and agencies. The auditor general prepares reports of the audit findings and submits them to the House of Commons. The reports become a public document and assist in maintaining government accountability.

B

Bank secrecy: All banks exercise client or depositor confidentiality; however, certain jurisdictions impose secrecy, through criminal legislation, on banks within their jurisdiction. Any release of information on depositors by bank officials or employees is punishable as a criminal offense.

Balance sheet: Balance sheets present the organization's financial health at a single moment in time as measured by its assets, which include cash, inventories, and amounts owed by customers, and its liabilities, which include loans and debts owed to trade creditors.

Board of directors: Directors that have been appointed by the shareholders of a corporation at the annual meeting. The board has the authority to manage the corporation by appointing officers and providing operational oversight.

Bribery: The illegal payment of any benefit to public officials by persons or corporations who have official business with that public official. The term is also used when secret commissions are paid to private officials with the knowledge of their employers.

Budget: A financial plan for a precise period of time outlining a forecast of revenues and expenses. The budget document will provide an actual measurement of the business operations against the forecast.

C

Capital appreciation: The actual increase in value of any asset.

Capital investment: Funds invested in a business enterprise for the purpose of furthering its objectives.

Cash flow statement: Summarizes an organization's sources of cash and how it has used that cash during a particular time period.

Charitable organization: A nonprofit organization that usually collects donations from the public and is registered with the tax authorities to issue taxable receipts for the donations. The organization provides all profits from its activities for a specific public benefit.

Chain letters: Messages that one person, called the promoter, sends to a number of other people soliciting that something of value be sent to the promoter and a request that each recipient of such a letter send a similar letter to a number of other people. The promoter's name is placed first on the list and the recipient places his name second on the list in this first level. As a second level begins, the promoter's name is removed and the first recipient's name is on top. This process continues as the subsequent levels are established. The letter promises significant benefits to the participants. Chain letters are illegal in most jurisdictions because the process is basically a scheme to defraud. Mathematically, there are not enough people to fulfill the promise that the chain letter outlines. These illegal schemes are also referred to as Ponzi schemes.

Chief executive officer: A CEO is appointed by the board of directors and is the highest ranking officer in a corporation. In some corporations this position is also called a president, although some companies have a CEO and a president. In this case the president is subservient to the CEO. The CEO reports directly to the board of directors.

Chief financial officer: A CFO is the most senior financial officer in a corporation and is appointed by the board of directors. He reports directly to the CEO and is responsible for all financial matters of a corporation.

Civil action: A lawsuit commenced by a plaintiff against a defendant in a civil court. This procedure is a private dispute between two or more parties.

Collateral debt obligations: A CDO is a promise to pay cash flows to investors in a prescribed sequence, based on how much cash flow the CDO collects from the pool of bonds or other assets it owns. If cash collected by the CDO is insufficient to pay all of its investors, those in the lower layers (tranches) suffer losses first.

Collateral mortgage obligation: Legally, a CMO is a debt security issued by a special purpose entity abstraction and is not a debt owed by the institution creating and operating the entity. The entity is the legal owner of a set of mortgages, called a *pool*. Investors in a CMO buy bonds issued by the entity, and they receive payments from the income generated by the mortgages according to a defined set of rules.

Commodity trading: Buying and selling primary products in the commodity markets. Commodity markets are situated in various cities in the world much like a stock exchange. They provide traders the opportunity to buy, sell, and hedge products that include agricultural, mineral, and energy products. Grain, gold, and oil are primary products that can be traded in this market. The products will include those that are currently in existence or that may be produced in the future.

Company: An association of individuals and legal entities (corporations) focused on a specific goal or objective. It can be incorporated as a legal entity or it can be an agreement between various parties. The word "company" is often used in place of the word "corporation."

Compensation committee: A committee appointed by a board of directors of a corporation specifically to make recommendations with respect to the salary and benefits of all officers and employees of a corporation. The committee reports directly to the board of directors and the board as a whole will provide the instructions and direction to the CEO.

Compliance risk management: The strategies to manage risk typically include transferring the risk to another party, avoiding the risk, reducing the negative effect or probability of the risk, or even accepting some or all of the potential or actual consequences of a particular risk.

Conspiracy: A civil conspiracy is an agreement between two or more persons to deceive, mislead, or defraud others of their legal rights, or to gain an unfair advantage. A criminal conspiracy is an agreement between two or more persons to carry out some specific act that is designated a crime under the criminal laws of a jurisdiction.

Conspirator: A person who enters into a civil or criminal conspiracy with one or more other persons.

Contract: An agreement between two or more persons, which is enforceable under the laws of the jurisdiction where it is made. The contract may also stipulate the jurisdiction where it can be enforced. For a contract to be legal it must, among other things, be entered into freely by all the parties. It must have specific terms that are identifiable and there must be some form of consideration involved.

Corporate espionage: Corporate espionage or corporate spying involves one corporation obtaining trade secrets or confidential information from another person, corporation, or government without permission. The methods used are usually clandestine in nature, using agents, extortion, or cybercrime to penetrate the security of the other entity. This activity is illegal and if discovered is clearly punishable under the criminal law.

Corporate shares: Shares issued by a corporation to its shareholders to signify ownership in the corporation. There are different classes of shares that can be issued to indicate different forms of authority to control or participate financially in the corporation. Shares of a public corporation are usually traded on the stock exchange and can be purchased and sold without restrictions. Shares of a private corporation are not traded publicly in the marketplace, but may be sold privately to other specific persons.

Corporation: An entity that is incorporated under a specific law of a specific jurisdiction. It is considered to be a legal person and have most of the rights of an individual person under the law. There are many different forms of corporations, which are incorporated for different purposes. Corporations are controlled by stakeholders that are shareholders in a for-profit corporation or they can be members as in a nonprofit corporation. The corporation is governed by a board of directors appointed by the members or shareholders. The board of directors, in turn, appoints officers and employees to manage and operate the corporation.

Corrupt benefit: Any benefit that is given to a person for an unlawful or illegal purpose.

Corruption: Corruption includes any unlawful activity including bribery, secret commission, and other undisclosed benefits that are provided to any public or private official or any employee acting in an official capacity for his or her own personal gain.

Criminal charge: A criminal charge includes any information, complaint, or indictment that is prepared and entered in a criminal court proceeding accusing any person of having committed a criminal act.

Criminal conspiracy: An agreement between two or more persons to carry out some specific act that is designated a crime under the criminal laws of a jurisdiction.

Criminal offense: A violation of the criminal law.

Culture of fraud: When dishonesty and corrupt behavior become the work style at the senior officer level within an organization, there is a tendency for lower level employees to develop a similar unethical attitude. This results in a culture within the organization where fraud and corrupt behavior are accepted.

D

Director: An individual who is appointed by the stakeholders of a corporation to become a member of the board of directors. The board, in turn, has the authority to appoint the management of the organization and oversee their activities.

Dividends: A distribution of profits by a corporation to its shareholders.

E

Employee: An individual who has been engaged by the officers of a corporation under the authority of the board of directors.

Enron: Enron was a publicly traded US energy corporation with headquarters in Houston, Texas. The company was a major producer of electricity and natural gas. It also controlled many subsidiary corporations that owned pulp and paper mills and communication networks. Prior to bankruptcy in 2001, Enron employed more than 20,000 people and was listed on the New York Stock Exchange. The company reported revenues of over $100 billion in 2000. Accounting fraud caused the company to spiral into bankruptcy on December 2, 2001. The aftermath of this massive fraud resulted in new legislation being enacted in the United States that altered many of the existing accounting practices and required public companies to change their system of governance. The law became known as the Sarbanes–Oxley Act.

Enterprise risk management: ERM is a system used by organizations to manage risks that relate to their business by identifying events that may impact negatively on their business objectives. Developing a monitoring system and a response strategy will allow the organization to respond in a proactive manner to minimize the impact of the risk.

Executive chairman: A chairman of the board of directors who is also the chief executive officer of the corporation.

Executive committee: A committee comprising members of the board of directors. The committee usually includes the CEO and CFO if the board is chaired by a nonexecutive chairman. This committee, which reports to the board of directors, is charged with the more detailed management issues related to the operation of the corporation.

External auditors: Accountants that are appointed to carry out independent audits of the corporation's financial books and records. They are engaged as independent contractors and are not employees or officers of the corporation. In a public corporation the independent auditors report directly to the audit committee.

F

Facilitation payments: A type of bribe. A common example is when a government official is given money or goods to perform (or speed up the performance of) an existing duty. Facilitation payments were illegal before the Bribery Act came into force and they are illegal under the Bribery Act, regardless of their size or frequency.*

False pretense: A representation of a matter of fact either present or past, made by words or otherwise, that is known by the person who makes it to be false and that is made with a fraudulent intent to induce the person to whom it is made to act on it. Exaggerated commendation or depreciation of the quality of anything is not a false pretense unless it is carried to such an extent that it amounts to a fraudulent misrepresentation of fact.†

Fictitious goods: Goods that are recorded in the books and records, but which are not, in fact, physically in the inventory.

Fiduciary duty: The highest standard of care as a legal requirement. A fiduciary duty requires that an individual must not personally profit from the position occupied without consent and must not place personal interest before the interest of the person who is owed that duty.

Financial Action Task Force (FATF): An intergovernmental body established in 1989 by the ministers of its member jurisdictions. The objectives of the FATF are to set standards and promote effective implementation of legal, regulatory, and operational measures for combating money laundering, terrorist financing, and other related threats to the integrity of the international financial system. The FATF is therefore a "policy-making body" that works to generate the necessary political will to bring about national legislative and regulatory reforms in these areas.

Financial auditing: An accounting process used in business. Independent auditors are used to examine the financial transactions and statements. The purpose of the audit is to present an accurate account of a company's financial business transactions. The practice is used to ensure that the company is presenting an accurate financial picture to the shareholders and the public.

Financial statements: Business reports consisting of the following: a balance sheet, which is a statement of the financial position for a given period of time; an income statement, which outlines the revenues less the expenses, for a certain point in time; a statement of retained earnings; a statement of cash flows that summarizes

---

* United Kingdom statute—The Bribery Act 2010.
† Section 361, Criminal Code of Canada, Revised Statutes of Canada, C-34.

the sources and use of cash and outlines if there is enough cash to carry out the routine business operations.

Fixed assets: A term used in accounting to identify those assets that are not easily converted to cash, but nevertheless have value to be recorded in the financial statements.

Foreign Corrupt Practices Act: A US federal statute enacted in 1977 (15 U.S.C.–78dd-1). The statute applies to persons who have a connection to the United States and who engage in corrupt practices in foreign jurisdictions. The act also applies to US companies and foreign corporations that trade securities in the United States.

Forensic accountants: Professional accountants who specialize in investigating and identifying improper or unlawful activity through the examination of the financial records of an organization. In addition they also examine all the individuals who may be connected to that unlawful or improper activity. They preserve the relevant information of such activity and present their findings as evidence in a court of law. They also are usually qualified to give opinion evidence to a court concerning their findings.

Forgery: A criminal offense in most jurisdictions that prohibits anyone from making a false document, knowing that it is false, with intent that it should be used or acted upon as genuine, to the prejudice of anyone. It is also an offense to make a false document with the intent to induce someone to believe that it is genuine in order to have any person do something or refrain from doing something. It is usually also an offense to use a document knowing that it has been forged.

Foundation: A legal entity that has been created typically to provide or donate funds to someone or some organization for a specific purpose. That purpose may be to donate funds from charitable purposes to other nonprofit organizations. This type of entity can also be structured to provide financial endowments to an individual family or members of a family.

Fraud auditing: An examination of financial records and employees specifically to detect fraud or any other related activity.

Fraud risk management: The integration of antifraud initiatives into the overall risk management programs of a corporation. This type of program would identify and assess fraud risks from any source. This would identify if there was a culture of fraud within the organization and promote fraud awareness and an antifraud culture. It would also develop a system of internal controls to identify the risks of fraud. The program would in addition identify how to identify and respond to fraud and related activity.

Fraud scheme: Any plan or conspiracy to commit a fraudulent act.

G

Gatekeeper: A term used to signify that a person has the power to authorize unilaterally some plan, activity, or action to proceed.

Ghost employees: Purported employees, whose names are on an organization's payroll, but not in fact employed by that organization.

H

Hedge fund: Private investment funds that are managed under the control of regulatory requirements in each country. Funds are invested in a wide range of markets and investments. In the United States, hedge funds are regulated to certain classes of accredited investors. Some are open ended, which permits investors to withdraw their investment. The funds are valued by their net asset value, which is then calculated into a value for each share.

House of Lords: The upper chamber of Parliament in the United Kingdom. Members of this legislative body are either appointed by the Queen (known as temporal lords) or become members by virtue of their position as bishops in the Church of England (known as spiritual lords). The number that can be appointed to this body is not fixed and there are currently over eight hundred members. Some members of this chamber inherited their position and are called hereditary lords. This practice was abolished in 2012.

I

Illicit drugs: Psychoactive compounds that have been placed on a restricted or prohibited list that regulates the production, manufacturing, distribution, and possession of those substances. Violations are punishable as a criminal offense. The laws regulating these compounds are enacted in each jurisdiction through guidance and direction from international conventions. For example, the United Nations Single Convention on Narcotic Drugs, 1961,* and the Convention on Psychotropic Substances, 1971,† require all member countries of the world to enact criminal laws to prohibit or regulate the production, manufacture, distribution, and, in some cases, possession of the compounds listed.

Income statement: Summarizes an organization's revenues and expenses during a particular time period as a way of measuring its financial performance.

Inflated invoices: Invoices that have been forged to illegally increase the prices of the goods or services that are listed on the invoice and that have been provided or delivered.

Internal auditors: Employees of a corporation who usually report to the Audit Committee of a corporation and have the responsibility to carry out operational audits of the various departments and branches of the corporation.

International postal reply coupons (IRCs): A coupon that can be purchased from postal authorities in one country and exchanged for postage stamps in another country. This system was developed to allow a person in one country to send an IRC to a person in another country so that person could reply by letter with postage paid to the sender. IRCs were authorized by the Universal Postal Union to accommodate member countries in making postage stamps available at a local rate. Charles Ponzi started a business that involved the purchase and sale of IRCs. Ponzi discovered that if he purchased IRCs in various foreign countries like Italy, he could then convert them in the United States for a much higher value. Through this conversion process he could make huge profits. This business venture was so profitable that he made over 400% on his initial investments.

Interpol (General Assembly): The International Criminal Police Organization (ICPO) is also known as Interpol. There have been a number of international police organizations, starting with the International Criminal Police Congress, which was established in Monaco in 1914. This was followed in 1923 with the establishment of the International Criminal Police Commission in Vienna,

---

* https://www.incb.org/documents/Narcotic-Drugs/1961-Convention/convention_1961_en.pdf (accessed July 23, 2013).
† Ibid.

Austria. The organization was taken over by Nazi Germany in 1938. In 1945, after the end of WWII, the organization was revived with the establishment of the present ICPO structure. It was based in Saint Cloud, France, and remained there until 1989, when it was moved to its present location in Lyon, France. Currently, over 160 countries are members of this organization. Interpol maintains a central data bank that is available to all member agencies. The basic concept of this organization is to allow domestic police agencies in each member country to obtain information quickly in other countries through the facilities of Interpol without going to the diplomatic or political level within the respective countries. This allows more rapid movement of information. Interpol does not have any active police investigators. The organization merely provides assistance to link domestic police to their counterparts in other countries.

Investment scam: A scheme designed to obtain investment funds through deceit and other fraudulent means.

K

Kickback: A term used to describe the payment of a bribe or secret commission to someone who will in return award a contractual benefit to the person who pays the bribe. The amount of the bribe is sometimes added to the contractual benefit, thereby "kicking back" the amount of funds that were added.

L

Larceny: A criminal offense under common law and a statutory offense in the United States and Australia that has been abolished in the United Kingdom and Canada. The crime involves the acquisition of personal property from another person. The offense includes the taking of property with the intent of depriving that person of its possession and use. It also includes the custody of that property or exercising physical control over that property.

Law enforcement: A term used to identify all agencies of government who are authorized to enforce the laws in a specific jurisdiction. The term includes police and all agencies that have investigative powers and authority.

Lawsuit: A private civil action that has been commenced by a plaintiff against a defendant in a court of law.

M

Mail fraud: Fraud that has been carried out, in part, with the use of the postal service. Mail fraud is a federal crime in the United States and it usually is used by authorities when the fraud extended beyond the boundaries of one state through the use of the mail.

Market value: The value set by a specific market or the value of property that has been determined from a previous arms-length purchase and sale.

Money laundering: An illegal act of moving funds from one source to another by disguising the process through the use of various schemes including the use of fictitious names and entities. It is used to conceal that the source of the funds originates from unlawful activity.

Multinational corporation: A corporation that is incorporated in one country and carries out its business operations in other countries. These operations in other countries may be carried out through subsidiary companies or partnerships.

N

Net stock value: The market value of shares after deducting expenses and liabilities.

New York Stock Exchange: The NYSE is a stock exchange located in New York City, in the United States. The exchange provides a location where buyers and sellers can trade shares in corporations that are registered for public trading. The exchange dates back to 1792 when a group of stockbrokers agreed to trade in stocks at a location on Wall Street. In 1817 this organization drafted a constitution and was renamed the New York Stock & Exchange Board. It later became the New York Stock Exchange, but it is still referred to as the "Board."

Nominating committee: A committee that has been established under the authority of a general annual shareholders meeting to select and nominate individuals to serve on a board of directors of a corporation or an organization for the next year.

Nonprofit corporation: A nonprofit corporation, sometimes referred to as a not-for-profit corporation, is one that has been incorporated under the laws of a jurisdiction to operate under the control of stakeholders. The corporation may earn income but the profits may not be distributed to the stakeholders. This type of corporation is often created to operate community activities, sports facilities like golf courses, and charitable organizations where the profits are used to improve their facilities or are donated for charitable purposes.

Nortel: Known as Nortel Networks Corporation, previously called Northern Telecom Limited. It was founded in Montreal, Canada, in 1895 and later moved its headquarters to Mississauga, Ontario. The company was controlled by Bell Canada and manufactured communication equipment. It became a world leader in the production of high-tech communications systems including fiber optics. The company went into receivership and is in bankruptcy protection as it sells off most of its business units and technology.

O

Occupational fraud: Occupational fraud means to providing false information to people seeking employment or providing a false hope of higher earnings. The schemes are designed to lure victims with promises of high wages, flexible hours, and lack of skills required to perform the work described.

Officer: An official of an organization occupying a position that is authorized by the board of directors. The person has specific authority to act on behalf of the organization and is usually part of the management of the entity.

Offshore bank: The expression "offshore bank" usually means a bank that is situated in a jurisdiction that has laws making it a criminal offense to release any unauthorized information concerning the identity of clients and any information concerning their deposits or business with the bank.

Offshore corporation: A corporation that has been incorporated in a jurisdiction that prohibits the release of any information concerning the corporation, its shareholders, and officers.

Organized crime: A group of individuals that have agreed with each other to commit certain criminal acts for the sole purpose of making profit over a period of time.

Outside audit: The auditing of the financial records of an organization by auditors who are not employees of that organization. The audit is performed by accountants employed by a firm that is independent from the organization.

P

Physical inventory count: The procedure of physically counting the entire inventory of a business entity in order to calculate the actual value of the inventory for accounting purposes and to ensure that a restocking process is implemented.

Ponzi scheme: An investment fraud that involves the payment of purported returns to existing investors from funds contributed by new investors. Ponzi scheme organizers often solicit new investors by promising to invest funds in opportunities claimed to generate high returns with little or no risk. In many Ponzi schemes, the fraudsters focus on attracting new money to make promised payments to earlier stage investors and to use for personal expenses, instead of engaging in any legitimate investment activity.[*]

Private corporation: A corporation that has been incorporated under laws of a jurisdiction that provides that the shares may not be traded on the public market.

Private investigators: Investigators that are usually licensed to provide investigative services to private individuals or corporations. They are independent contractors that provide their service for a fee.

Proceeds of crime: Any benefits or profits, including anything of value, acquired from criminal activity. Some property can be obtained directly; this can include goods that have been obtained by theft or money that has been obtained from the sale of stolen goods. It also includes property that was obtained by converting the direct

---

[*] US Securities and Exchange Commission.

proceeds. Therefore, the automobile purchased with money obtained by the sale of illicit drugs would be the proceeds of the drug crime.

Procurement contract: Any contract entered into by two or more parties that provides for the delivery of goods or services.

Procurement fraud: Any fraud that is committed in connection with a procurement contract.

Promoters: Individuals or organizations that actively encourage others to participate in a business activity, investment, or scheme. Promoters begin pyramid schemes and entice others to join a particular venture.

Public agency: A branch or entity created by a government to manage or regulate some public activity.

Public corporation: A corporation that has been incorporated under the laws of a jurisdiction that authorizes the corporation to issue shares that may be sold to the general public. The shares may be subsequently traded in the public marketplace or stock exchange.

Public investigation: An investigation conducted by any agency of government. This includes a police investigation or any investigation that is carried out by an agency that has been authorized to do so by statute.

Public officer: A senior employee of a government.

Public official: An individual who has been appointed or elected to a particular position of government in accordance with the laws of a jurisdiction.

Pyramid scheme: A scheme devised basically to take funds from many people to benefit a few at the top of the so-called pyramid. The modern business pyramid schemes are usually bundled up in some type of investment scam that produces millions of dollars through the sale of investment certificates, territory, or products. Only the promoters really benefit from this type of scheme.

R

Red Flag System: A system of identifying something abnormal indicating a problem.

Regulators: Agencies created by a government to control trading markets.

Retained earnings statement: Retained earnings are profits of an organization that have not been distributed to shareholders. The retained earnings statement summarizes the earnings for a specific period of time.

Risk management: A system used by organizations to manage risks that relate to their business by identifying events that may impact negatively on their business objectives. Developing a monitoring system and a response strategy will allow the organization to respond in a proactive manner to minimize the impact of the risk.

Round tripping: A term used to describe a strategy used by organizations that sell an asset to another organization with a contract that the asset will be bought back at some stated time in the future.

S

Scams: A term used to indicate an unlawful fraudulent scheme.

Screening for Red Flags: A process of systematically looking for indicators that may suggest that some questionable activity has taken place.

Scrutinizing Red Flags: A process of examining Red Flags that have been identified to establish if improper activity has actually occurred.

Secret commissions: A corrupt payment to a nonpublic official for some action within the scope of his employment without the permission of his employer. It is a bribe in commercial transactions, and an offense under the criminal law in most jurisdictions in industrialized countries. Some English-speaking jurisdictions have used the term "bribery" for corrupt payments to both public and nonpublic officials. For the most part, the concept of corrupt payments to nonpublic officials is similar whether the term used is bribery or secret commission.

Secret off-book funds: Funds that are not shown in the financial records of an organization. The funds are generally placed in this state to permit the organization to use them for some unlawful purpose without being detected by anyone conducting an audit of the financial records.

Secret offshore bank accounts: Accounts that contain deposits in offshore banks. The purpose of these types of accounts is to ensure confidentiality through the strict nondisclosure laws in the jurisdiction where the bank is situated.

Securities and Exchange Commission: The US Securities and Exchange Commission is an agency of the federal government. Its prime responsibility is to enforce US securities laws. It also is responsible for regulating the securities industry.

Securities fraud: A fraud connected to the trading of securities. This term covers a number of specific criminal offenses directed at specific activity in the process of buying and selling securities. These offenses include distributing false information to affect the price of a particular stock and manipulating the price of a particular stock by selling or buying stock at an artificially high or low price (also known as "insider trading").

Security Exchange Company: A corporation incorporated in Massachusetts by Charles Ponzi in 1919. The company was used to perpetrate his infamous illegal pyramid scheme.

Short selling: Selling stock that the seller does not own or possess. Under most regulations, the seller must cover his short position within a certain period of time by buying the equivalent amount of stock on the market to cover the short position. Selling short is the opposite of going long, which is selling stock that is owned by the seller. Short sellers make money if the stock goes down in price. This is an advanced trading strategy with many unique risks and pitfalls. Novice investors are advised to avoid short sales.

Solicitor–client privilege: A right of a client of an attorney that any disclosure or communication made to the attorney will remain confidential. This right is enforced by the courts. The privilege of nondisclosure belongs to the client.

Special-purpose entities: An entity created under a special statute of a jurisdiction for the purpose of some special activity.

Stakeholder: This term is used to describe individuals who have the governing rights in a nonprofit corporation. They usually have the right to appoint a board of directors who will govern the organization's business.

T

Tax haven countries: Countries that have laws preventing the disclosure of any information concerning the existence of a corporation, trust, bank account, or other financial information that would create a tax liability in another country.

Theft: Fraudulently taking or converting another person's property without any right. This would include depriving a person of the right to use or possess the property.

Theft by conversion: A criminal offense that occurs when possession of property is voluntarily turned over to another person on a temporary basis and that person then fraudulently converts that property to his or her own use permanently.

Third party: A person who is not directly involved in an interaction or relationship.

Trade secrets: Includes information that an organization has protected and kept secret to ensure that it can achieve some economic advantage. It can consist of a formula, a patent, or a design that may be used to produce a product.

Transparency International: A nongovernmental organization with head offices in Berlin, Germany. The organization maintains over one hundred chapters throughout the world and monitors and publicizes public corruption. It publishes an annual publication entitled *Corruption and Perceptions Index*, which identifies comparative corruption issues around the world. This publication ranks countries around the world on the prevalence of corruption. The research for this publication is based on a survey of business people.

Trust: A formal document that names a local company, bank, or person as a trustee to act as the legal owner of the named property. The trustee carries out the duties and authority outlined in the trust document and holds that property in accordance with the terms specified for the real or beneficial owner.

Tyco: Tyco International Ltd. is a publicly traded company incorporated in Switzerland with a subsidiary company and operational headquarters in New Jersey, in the United States. The US corporation is known as Tyco International (US) Inc. The company became involved in a major business fraud in 2002. The former chairman and CEO, Dennis Kozlowski, was convicted in 2005 for crimes related to the receipt of over $81 million in Tyco corporate bonuses.

U

United Nations convention: A convention that has been adopted by the General Assembly of the United Nations. The adopted convention is then signed by individual member countries who will attempt, through their own governmental systems, to ratify the convention. The convention will require all member countries that ratify the convention to adopt domestic laws to deal with the issues raised in the convention. A convention is usually developed by one of the organizations of the UN by assembling experts from member countries who are interested in developing the document. The proposed convention is then presented to the General Assembly of the United Nations, where the member countries adopt the convention. The General Assembly is composed of representatives from 160 member countries.

W

Whistleblower: A person who has confidential information indicating impropriety and who provides that information to the public or someone in authority.

Willful blindness: A term used in law when a person attempts to avoid civil or criminal liability for wrongful acts by intentionally avoiding identification as being aware of the facts that would create such liability.

Wire fraud: A federal criminal offense in the United States that covers any fraudulent scheme designed to deprive another person of property or honest services intentionally through the use of any wire communication system.

WorldCom: A public corporation with headquarters in Mississippi. The company began as Long Distance Discount Service Inc., in 1983. In 1985 Bernard Ebbers became its CEO. The company became a publicly traded corporation in 1989 when it merged with Advantage Companies Inc. The corporate name was changed to LDDS WorldCom in 1995. In early 2000 the company became involved in accounting-related fraud that resulted in a situation where the total assets of the company were inflated by more than $11 billion by the year 2003. In addition, Bernard Ebbers convinced the board of directors of the company to allow him to borrow or cover his margin calls in the amount of $400 million. The accounting irregularities, the Ebbers loans, and a significant decline in business caused WorldCom to file for bankruptcy in 2003.

INDEX

M

Madoff, Bernard L., 9, 138–139
mail fraud, 16, 103, 138, 139, 276
management, 25–26
management discussion and analysis
   (MD&A) reports
  financial statements, 41
  internal control, financial
   reporting, 167
  perpetration of fraud, 50–51
"Managing the Business Risk of
   Fraud," 172
manipulation and manipulation
   schemes
  accounts receivable, 47
  accrued liabilities, 48
  bid rigging, 72–79
  bribery, 74–75
  "cash in the bank," 47
  collusive bidding, 72–79
  corruption, 74–75
  expenses, 50
  fixed assets, 43–46
  inventory, 46
  liabilities, 48
  management discussion and
   analysis reports, 50–51
  market manipulation, 128–134
  net assets, 43
  notes to statements, 50
  sales, 49–50
marine construction contracts, 65
market manipulation, 127–134, 263
market value, 276, *see also* Shares, loss
   of value
Markopolos, Harry, 139
McNulty, Paul, 4
MD&A, *see* Management discussion
   and analysis (MD&A) reports
mens rea, 18
metrics, monitoring, 210
monetary penalties, 97–99

money laundering
  antibribery laws, 99–100
  defined, 276
  fictitious records, 125
  fraud and, 123
  insider beneficial relationships,
   undisclosed, 125
  Koop fraud, 117–118
  laws development, 118–120
  offshore corporations, trusts, and
   bank accounts, 124–125
  overview, 121–123, 125
  undisclosed corporations, trusts,
   and bank accounts, 124–125
monitoring
  compliance risk management, 220
  enterprise risk management, 195
  fraud risk response, 210
mortgage fraud, 10, 191
motivation, 24, 42
multinational construction company,
   233–235
multinational corporation, 276

N

NASA, 189
negative development omissions, 255
net assets
  manipulation, Red Flags, 254
  perpetration of fraud, 43
net stock value, 276
New York Stock Exchange (NYSE),
   276
nominating committee, 277
noncompetitive contracts, 65–66
noncompliance, 4, *see also* Compliance
nonconsulting contracts, 65
nondisclosure, liabilities and accrued
   liabilities, 51
nonprofit organizations, 1, 25–26, 277
nonpublic officials, 100–102

Printed in the United States
by Baker & Taylor Publisher Services